Hands-On Mathematics for Deep Learning

Build a solid mathematical foundation for training efficient deep neural networks

Jay Dawani

BIRMINGHAM - MUMBAI

Hands-On Mathematics for Deep Learning

Commissioning Editor: Sunith Shetty
Acquisition Editor: Ali Abidi
Content Development Editor: Athikho Sapuni Rishana
Senior Editor: Roshan Kumar
Technical Editor: Manikandan Kurup
Copy Editor: Safis Editing
Project Coordinator: Aishwarya Mohan
Proofreader: Safis Editing
Indexer: Priyanka Dhadke
Production Designer: Alishon Mendonsa

First published: June 2020

Production reference: 1120620

Published by Packt Publishing Ltd.
Livery Place
35 Livery Street
Birmingham
B3 2PB, UK.

ISBN 978-1-83864-729-2

www.packt.com

About the author

Jay Dawani is a former professional swimmer turned mathematician and computer scientist. He is also a Forbes 30 Under 30 fellow. At present, he is the director of Artificial Intelligence at Geometric Energy Corporation (NATO CAGE) and the CEO of Lemurian Labs—a start-up he founded that is developing the next generation of autonomy, intelligent process automation, and driver intelligence. Previously, he has also been the technology and R&D advisor to Spacebit Capital. He has spent the last 3 years researching at the frontiers of AI with a focus on reinforcement learning, open-ended learning, deep learning, quantum machine learning, human-machine interaction, multi-agent and complex systems, and artificial general intelligence.

About the reviewers

Siddha Ganju, an AI researcher who Forbes featured in their 30 Under 30 list, is a self-driving architect at Nvidia. As an AI advisor to NASA FDL, she helped build an automated meteor detection pipeline for the CAMS project at NASA, which ended up discovering a comet. Previously at Deep Vision, she has developed deep learning models for resource constraint edge devices. Her work ranges from visual question answering to GANs to gathering insights from CERN's petabyte-scale data and has been published at top-tier conferences, including CVPR and NeurIPS. As an advocate for diversity and inclusion in tech, she spends time motivating and mentoring the younger generation. She is also the author of *Practical Deep Learning for Cloud, Mobile, and Edge*.

Sal Vivona has transitioned from physics to machine learning after completing his Master's Degree at the University of Toronto's Department of Computer Science with a focus on Machine Learning and Computer Vision. In addition to reinforcement learning, he also had the privilege to work extensively across a variety of machine learning subfields, such as graph machine learning, natural language processing, and meta-learning. Sal is also experienced in publishing at top-tier machine learning conferences and has worked alongside the best minds within Vector Institute, a think tank that was in part founded by Geoffrey Hinton. He is currently positioned as one of the leading machine learning research engineers at a Silicon Valley Health AI company doc.ai.

Seyed Sajjadi is an AI researcher with 10+ years of experience working in academia, government, and industry. At NASA JPL, his work revolved around Europa Clipper, mobility and robotic systems, and maritime multi-agent autonomy. He consulted Boeing at Hughes Research Laboratory on autonomous systems and led teams to build the next generation of robotic search and AI rescue systems for the USAF. As a data scientist at EA, he architected and deployed large scale ML pipelines to model and predict player behaviors. At Caltech, he designed and applied DL methods to quantify biological 3D image data. He is part of the Cognitive Architecture group at the University of Southern California where he actively contributes to the R&D of virtual humans.

Packt is searching for authors like you

If you're interested in becoming an author for Packt, please visit authors.packtpub.com and apply today. We have worked with thousands of developers and tech professionals, just like you, to help them share their insight with the global tech community. You can make a general application, apply for a specific hot topic that we are recruiting an author for, or submit your own idea.

Table of Contents

Preface   1

Section 1: Essential Mathematics for Deep Learning

Chapter 1: Linear Algebra   9
  Comparing scalars and vectors   10
  Linear equations   12
    Solving linear equations in n-dimensions   16
    Solving linear equations using elimination   17
  Matrix operations   22
    Adding matrices   22
    Multiplying matrices   22
    Inverse matrices   25
    Matrix transpose   26
    Permutations   27
  Vector spaces and subspaces   28
    Spaces   28
    Subspaces   29
  Linear maps   30
    Image and kernel   31
    Metric space and normed space   31
    Inner product space   33
  Matrix decompositions   34
    Determinant   34
    Eigenvalues and eigenvectors   38
    Trace   39
    Orthogonal matrices   40
    Diagonalization and symmetric matrices   41
    Singular value decomposition   42
    Cholesky decomposition   42
  Summary   44

Chapter 2: Vector Calculus   45
  Single variable calculus   45
    Derivatives   46
      Sum rule   49
      Power rule   49
      Trigonometric functions   50
      First and second derivatives   51
      Product rule   52
      Quotient rule   53

Chain rule	54
Antiderivative	54
Integrals	56
The fundamental theorem of calculus	61
Substitution rule	62
Areas between curves	64
Integration by parts	65
Multivariable calculus	66
Partial derivatives	67
Chain rule	68
Integrals	69
Vector calculus	75
Derivatives	76
Vector fields	80
Inverse functions	81
Summary	81
Chapter 3: Probability and Statistics	83
Understanding the concepts in probability	83
Classical probability	83
Sampling with or without replacement	85
Multinomial coefficient	86
Stirling's formula	87
Independence	89
Discrete distributions	90
Conditional probability	91
Random variables	93
Variance	95
Multiple random variables	97
Continuous random variables	98
Joint distributions	102
More probability distributions	103
Normal distribution	103
Multivariate normal distribution	104
Bivariate normal distribution	105
Gamma distribution	106
Essential concepts in statistics	106
Estimation	106
Mean squared error	107
Sufficiency	107
Likelihood	109
Confidence intervals	109
Bayesian estimation	110
Hypothesis testing	112
Simple hypotheses	112
Composite hypothesis	114
The multivariate normal theory	114
Linear models	116

Hypothesis testing 118
Summary 119

Chapter 4: Optimization 121
  Understanding optimization and it's different types 122
    Constrained optimization 123
    Unconstrained optimization 124
    Convex optimization 125
    Convex sets 125
    Affine sets 126
    Convex functions 127
    Optimization problems 128
    Non-convex optimization 128
  Exploring the various optimization methods 129
    Least squares 129
    Lagrange multipliers 129
    Newton's method 131
    The secant method 132
    The quasi-Newton method 133
    Game theory 133
    Descent methods 136
      Gradient descent 136
      Stochastic gradient descent 138
      Loss functions 139
      Gradient descent with momentum 139
      The Nesterov's accelerated gradient 140
      Adaptive gradient descent 140
      Simulated annealing 141
      Natural evolution 142
  Exploring population methods 142
    Genetic algorithms 143
    Particle swarm optimization 144
  Summary 144

Chapter 5: Graph Theory 145
  Understanding the basic concepts and terminology 146
  Adjacency matrix 149
  Types of graphs 151
    Weighted graphs 151
    Directed graphs 152
    Directed acyclic graphs 153
    Multilayer and dynamic graphs 154
    Tree graphs 156
  Graph Laplacian 157
  Summary 157

Section 2: Essential Neural Networks

Chapter 6: Linear Neural Networks   161
Linear regression   161
Polynomial regression   164
Logistic regression   166
Summary   167

Chapter 7: Feedforward Neural Networks   169
Understanding biological neural networks   170
Comparing the perceptron and the McCulloch-Pitts neuron   171
  The MP neuron   172
  Perceptron   172
  Pros and cons of the MP neuron and perceptron   174
MLPs   175
  Layers   178
  Activation functions   185
    Sigmoid   185
    Hyperbolic tangent   186
    Softmax   188
    Rectified linear unit   188
    Leaky ReLU   189
    Parametric ReLU   190
    Exponential linear unit   192
  The loss function   192
    Mean absolute error   193
    Mean squared error   193
    Root mean squared error   194
    The Huber loss   194
    Cross entropy   194
    Kullback-Leibler divergence   195
    Jensen-Shannon divergence   196
  Backpropagation   196
Training neural networks   198
  Parameter initialization   198
    All zeros   199
    Random initialization   199
    Xavier initialization   200
  The data   200
Deep neural networks   202
Summary   203

Chapter 8: Regularization   205
The need for regularization   206
Norm penalties   207
  L2 regularization   208
  L1 regularization   209

Early stopping 210
Parameter tying and sharing 211
Dataset augmentation 212
Dropout 213
Adversarial training 215
Summary 216

Chapter 9: Convolutional Neural Networks 217
   The inspiration behind ConvNets 218
   Types of data used in ConvNets 218
   Convolutions and pooling 220
      Two-dimensional convolutions 220
      One-dimensional convolutions 225
      1 × 1 convolutions 226
      Three-dimensional convolutions 227
      Separable convolutions 228
      Transposed convolutions 230
      Pooling 233
      Global average pooling 234
      Convolution and pooling size 235
   Working with the ConvNet architecture 235
   Training and optimization 239
   Exploring popular ConvNet architectures 241
      VGG-16 241
      Inception-v1 244
   Summary 246

Chapter 10: Recurrent Neural Networks 247
   The need for RNNs 248
   The types of data used in RNNs 248
   Understanding RNNs 249
      Vanilla RNNs 249
      Bidirectional RNNs 254
   Long short-term memory 256
   Gated recurrent units 258
   Deep RNNs 259
   Training and optimization 261
   Popular architecture 263
      Clockwork RNNs 263
   Summary 265

Section 3: Advanced Deep Learning Concepts Simplified

Chapter 11: Attention Mechanisms 269

Overview of attention   269
Understanding neural Turing machines   271
   Reading   272
   Writing   273
   Addressing mechanisms   273
      Content-based addressing mechanism   274
      Location-based address mechanism   274
Exploring the types of attention   275
   Self-attention   275
   Comparing hard and soft attention   275
   Comparing global and local attention   276
Transformers   276
Summary   281

Chapter 12: Generative Models   283
Why we need generative models   283
Autoencoders   284
   The denoising autoencoder   288
   The variational autoencoder   290
Generative adversarial networks   292
   Wasserstein GANs   296
Flow-based networks   298
   Normalizing flows   298
   Real-valued non-volume preserving   301
Summary   302

Chapter 13: Transfer and Meta Learning   305
Transfer learning   306
Meta learning   308
   Approaches to meta learning   308
   Model-based meta learning   310
      Memory-augmented neural networks   310
      Meta Networks   312
   Metric-based meta learning   313
      Prototypical networks   314
      Siamese neural networks   314
   Optimization-based meta learning   316
      Long Short-Term Memory meta learners 316
      Model-agnostic meta learning   318
Summary   319

Chapter 14: Geometric Deep Learning   321
Comparing Euclidean and non-Euclidean data   322
   Manifolds   323
   Discrete manifolds   328
   Spectral decomposition   329

Graph neural networks   330
Spectral graph CNNs   333
Mixture model networks   334
Facial recognition in 3D   335
Summary   337

Other Books You May Enjoy   339

Index   343

Preface

Most programmers and data scientists struggle with mathematics, either having overlooked or forgotten core mathematical concepts. This book helps you understand the math that's required to understand how various neural networks work so that you can go on to building better **deep learning** (**DL**) models.

You'll begin by learning about the core mathematical and modern computational techniques used to design and implement DL algorithms. This book will cover essential topics, such as linear algebra, eigenvalues and eigenvectors, the singular value decomposition concept, and gradient algorithms, to help you understand how to train deep neural networks. Later chapters focus on important neural networks, such as the linear neural network, multilayer perceptrons, and radial basis function networks, with a primary focus on helping you learn how each model works. As you advance, you will delve into the math used for normalization, multi-layered DL, forward propagation, optimization, and backpropagation techniques to understand what it takes to build full-fledged DL models. Finally, you'll explore **convolutional neural network** (**CNN**), **recurrent neural network** (**RNN**), and **generative adversarial network** (**GAN**) models and their implementation.

By the end of this book, you'll have built a strong foundation in neural networks and DL mathematical concepts, which will help you to confidently research and build custom DL models.

Who this book is for

This book is for data scientists, machine learning developers, aspiring DL developers, and anyone who wants to gain a deeper understanding of how DL algorithms work by learning the mathematical concepts that form their foundation. Having knowledge of the basics of machine learning is required to gain a better understanding of the topics covered in the book. Having a strong mathematical background is not essential but would be quite helpful in grasping some of the concepts.

What this book covers

Chapter 1, *Linear Algebra*, will give you an understanding of the inner workings of linear algebra, which is essential for understanding how deep neural networks work. In particular, you will learn about multi-dimensional linear equations, how matrices are multiplied together, and various methods of decomposing/factorizing matrices. These concepts will be critical for developing an intuition for how forward propagation works in neural networks.

Chapter 2, *Vector Calculus*, will cover all the main concepts of calculus, where you will start by learning the fundamentals of single variable calculus and build toward an understanding of multi-variable and ultimately vector calculus. The concepts of this chapter will help you better understand the math that underlies the training process of neural networks, particularly how backpropagation works.

Chapter 3, *Probability and Statistics*, will teach you the essentials of both probability and statistics and how they are related to each other. In particular, the focus will be on understanding different types of distributions, the importance of the central limit theorem, and how estimations are made. This chapter is critical to developing an understanding of what exactly it is that neural networks are learning.

Chapter 4, *Optimization*, will explain what exactly optimization is and several methods of it that are used in practice, such as least squares, gradient descent, Newton's method, and genetic algorithms. The methods covered in this chapter are essential to understanding how neural networks learn during their training phase.

Chapter 5, *Graph Theory*, will teach you about graph theory, which is used to model relationships between objects, and will also help in your understanding of the different types of neural network architectures. Later in the book, the concepts from this chapter will be very useful for understanding how graph neural networks work.

Chapter 6, *Linear Neural Networks*, will cover the most basic type of neural network and teach you how a model learns to find linear relationships from data through regression. You will also learn that this type of model has limitations, which is where the need for neural networks arises.

Chapter 7, *Feedforward Neural Networks*, will show you how all the concepts covered in the previous chapters are brought together to form modern-day neural networks, including coverage of how they are structured, how and what they learn, and what makes them so powerful.

Chapter 8, *Regularization*, will show you the various methods of regularization, such as dropout and norm penalties, that are used extensively in practice to help our models to generalize to test data so that they work well once deployed.

Chapter 9, *Convolutional Neural Networks*, will explain CNNs, which are a variant of feedforward neural networks and are particularly effective for tasks related to computer vision, as well as time series analysis.

Chapter 10, *Recurrent Neural Networks*, will explain RNNs, which are another variant of feedforward neural networks that have recurrent connections, which gives them the ability to learn relationships in sequences such as those in time series and language.

Chapter 11, *Attention Mechanisms*, will show a relatively recent breakthrough in deep learning known as attention. This has led to the creation of transformer models, which have resulted in phenomenal results in tasks related to natural language processing.

Chapter 12, *Generative Models*, is where the focus will be switched from neural networks that learn to predict classes given data to models that learn to synthetically create data. You will learn about various models, such as autoencoders, GANs, and flow-based networks.

Chapter 13, *Transfer and Meta Learning*, will teach you about two separate but related concepts known as transfer learning and meta learning. Their goals respectively are to transfer what one model has learned to another to help it work on a similar task and to create networks that can use existing knowledge to learn new tasks or learn how to learn.

Chapter 14, *Geometric Deep Learning*, will explain another relatively new concept in DL, which extends the power of deep neural networks from the Euclidean domain to the non-Euclidean domain.

To get the most out of this book

It is expected that most of you have had prior experience with implementing machine learning models and have at least a basic understanding of how they work. It is also assumed that many of you have some prior experience with calculus, linear algebra, probability, and statistics; having this prior experience will help you get the most out of this book.

For those of you who do have prior experience with the mathematics covered in the first five chapters and have a background in machine learning, you are welcome to skip ahead to the content from Chapter 7, *Feedforward Neural Networks*, onward and keep with the flow of the book from there.

However, for the reader who lacks the aforementioned experience, it is recommended that you stay with the flow and order of the book and pay particular attention to understanding the concepts covered in the first five chapters, moving on to the next chapter or section only when you feel comfortable with what you have learned. It is important that you do not rush or be hasty, as DL is a vast and complex field that should not be taken lightly.

Lastly, to become a very good DL practitioner, it is important that you keep learning and going over the fundamental concepts, as these can often be forgotten quite easily. After having gone through all the chapters in the book and through all the chapters, I recommend trying to read the code for and/or implementing a few architectures and trying to recall what you have learned in this book because doing so will help ground your concepts even further and help you to learn much faster.

Download the color images

We also provide a PDF file that has color images of the screenshots/diagrams used in this book. You can download it here: `https://static.packt-cdn.com/downloads/9781838647292_ColorImages.pdf`.

Conventions used

There are a number of text conventions used throughout this book.

Bold: Indicates a new term, an important word, or words that you see onscreen. For example, words in menus or dialog boxes appear in the text like this. Here is an example: "This is known as the **antiderivative**, and we define it formally as a function."

 Warnings or important notes appear like this.

 Tips and tricks appear like this.

Get in touch

Feedback from our readers is always welcome.

General feedback: If you have questions about any aspect of this book, mention the book title in the subject of your message and email us at customercare@packtpub.com.

Errata: Although we have taken every care to ensure the accuracy of our content, mistakes do happen. If you have found a mistake in this book, we would be grateful if you would report this to us. Please visit www.packtpub.com/support/errata, selecting your book, clicking on the Errata Submission Form link, and entering the details.

Piracy: If you come across any illegal copies of our works in any form on the Internet, we would be grateful if you would provide us with the location address or website name. Please contact us at copyright@packt.com with a link to the material.

If you are interested in becoming an author: If there is a topic that you have expertise in and you are interested in either writing or contributing to a book, please visit authors.packtpub.com.

Reviews

Please leave a review. Once you have read and used this book, why not leave a review on the site that you purchased it from? Potential readers can then see and use your unbiased opinion to make purchase decisions, we at Packt can understand what you think about our products, and our authors can see your feedback on their book. Thank you!

For more information about Packt, please visit packt.com.

Section 1: Essential Mathematics for Deep Learning

In this section, you will learn how to use the core mathematical and modern computational techniques that are used to design and implement deep learning algorithms.

This section is comprised of the following chapters:

- Chapter 1, *Linear Algebra*
- Chapter 2, *Vector Calculus*
- Chapter 3, *Probability and Statistics*
- Chapter 4, *Optimization*
- Chapter 5, *Graph Theory*

1
Linear Algebra

In this chapter, we will be covering the main concepts of linear algebra, and the concepts learned here will serve as the backbone on which we will learn all the concepts in the chapters to come, so it is important that you pay attention.

It is very important for you to know that these chapters cannot be substituted for an education in mathematics; they exist merely to help you better grasp the concepts of deep learning and how various architectures work and to develop an intuition for why that is, so you can become a better practitioner in the field.

At its core, algebra is nothing more than the study of mathematical symbols and the rules for manipulating these symbols. The field of algebra acts as a unifier for all of mathematics and provides us with a way of thinking. Instead of using numbers, we use letters to represent variables.

Linear algebra, however, concerns only linear transformations and vector spaces. It allows us to represent information through vectors, matrices, and tensors, and having a good understanding of linear algebra will take you a long way on your journey toward getting a very strong understanding of deep learning. It is said that a mathematical problem can only be solved if it can be reduced to a calculation in linear algebra. This speaks to the power and usefulness of linear algebra.

This chapter will cover the following topics:

- Comparing scalars and vectors
- Linear equations
- Matrix operations
- Vector spaces and subspaces
- Linear maps
- Matrix decompositions

Comparing scalars and vectors

Scalars are regular numbers, such as 7, 82, and 93,454. They only have a magnitude and are used to represent time, speed, distance, length, mass, work, power, area, volume, and so on.

Vectors, on the other hand, have magnitude and direction in many dimensions. We use vectors to represent velocity, acceleration, displacement, force, and momentum. We write vectors in bold—such as *a* instead of *a*—and they are usually an array of multiple numbers, with each number in this array being an element of the vector.

We denote this as follows:

$$\mathbf{x} = \begin{bmatrix} x_1 \\ x_2 \\ \vdots \\ x_n \end{bmatrix}$$

Here, $\mathbf{x} \in \mathbb{R}^n$ shows the vector is in n-dimensional real space, which results from taking the Cartesian product of $\mathbb{R}$ n times; $x_i \in \mathbb{R}$ shows each element is a real number; i is the position of each element; and, finally, $n \in \mathbb{N}$ is a natural number, telling us how many elements are in the vector.

As with regular numbers, you can add and subtract vectors. However, there are some limitations.

Let's take the vector we saw earlier (x) and add it with another vector (y), both of which are in $\mathbb{R}^n$, so that the following applies:

$$\begin{bmatrix} x_1 \\ x_2 \\ \vdots \\ x_n \end{bmatrix} + \begin{bmatrix} y_1 \\ y_2 \\ \vdots \\ y_n \end{bmatrix} = \begin{bmatrix} x_1 + y_1 \\ x_2 + y_2 \\ \vdots \\ x_n + y_n \end{bmatrix}$$

However, we cannot add vectors with vectors that do not have the same dimension or scalars.

Note that when $n = 2$ in $\mathbb{R}^n$, we reduce to 2-dimensions (for example, the surface of a sheet of paper), and when $n = 3$, we reduce to 3-dimensions (the real world).

We can, however, multiply scalars with vectors. Let λ be an arbitrary scalar, which we will multiply with the vector $\mathbf{x} \in \mathbb{R}^n$, so that the following applies:

$$\lambda\mathbf{x} = \lambda \begin{bmatrix} x_1 \\ x_2 \\ \vdots \\ x_n \end{bmatrix} = \begin{bmatrix} \lambda x_1 \\ \lambda x_2 \\ \vdots \\ \lambda x_n \end{bmatrix}$$

As we can see, λ gets multiplied by each x_i in the vector. The result of this operation is that the vector gets scaled by the value of the scalar.

For example, let $\lambda = 3$, and $\mathbf{x} = \begin{bmatrix} 1 \\ 0 \\ 1 \end{bmatrix}$. Then, we have the following:

$$\lambda\mathbf{x} = 3 \begin{bmatrix} 1 \\ 0 \\ 1 \end{bmatrix} = \begin{bmatrix} 1 \\ 0 \\ 1 \end{bmatrix} + \begin{bmatrix} 1 \\ 0 \\ 1 \end{bmatrix} + \begin{bmatrix} 1 \\ 0 \\ 1 \end{bmatrix} = \begin{bmatrix} 3 \\ 0 \\ 3 \end{bmatrix}$$

While this works fine for multiplying by a whole number, it doesn't help when working with fractions, but you should be able to guess how it works. Let's see an example.

Let $\lambda = \dfrac{1}{4}$, and $\mathbf{x} = \begin{bmatrix} 1 \\ 0 \\ 1 \end{bmatrix}$. Then, we have the following:

$$\lambda\mathbf{x} = \frac{1}{4} \begin{bmatrix} 1 \\ 0 \\ 1 \end{bmatrix} = \begin{bmatrix} \frac{1}{4} \\ 0 \\ \frac{1}{4} \end{bmatrix}$$

There is a very special vector that we can get by multiplying any vector by the scalar, 0. We denote this as $\mathbf{0}$ and call it the **zero vector** (a vector containing only zeros).

Linear equations

Linear algebra, at its core, is about solving a set of linear equations, referred to as **a system of equations**. A large number of problems can be formulated as a system of linear equations.

We have two equations and two unknowns, as follows:

$$x - 2y = 1$$
$$2x + y = 7$$

Both equations produce straight lines. The solution to both these equations is the point where both lines meet. In this case, the answer is the point (3, 1).

But for our purposes, in linear algebra, we write the preceding equations as a vector equation that looks like this:

$$x \begin{bmatrix} 1 \\ 2 \end{bmatrix} + y \begin{bmatrix} -2 \\ 1 \end{bmatrix} = \begin{bmatrix} 1 \\ 7 \end{bmatrix} = \mathbf{b}$$

Here, **b** is the result vector.

Placing the point (3, 1) into the vector equation, we get the following:

$$3 \begin{bmatrix} 1 \\ 2 \end{bmatrix} + 1 \begin{bmatrix} -2 \\ 1 \end{bmatrix} = \begin{bmatrix} 1 \\ 7 \end{bmatrix}$$
$$\begin{bmatrix} 3 \\ 6 \end{bmatrix} + \begin{bmatrix} -2 \\ 1 \end{bmatrix} = \begin{bmatrix} 1 \\ 7 \end{bmatrix}$$
$$\begin{bmatrix} 3-2 \\ 6+1 \end{bmatrix} = \begin{bmatrix} 1 \\ 7 \end{bmatrix}$$
$$\begin{bmatrix} 1 \\ 7 \end{bmatrix} = \begin{bmatrix} 1 \\ 7 \end{bmatrix}$$

As we can see, the left-hand side is equal to the right-hand side, so it is, in fact, a solution! However, I personally prefer to write this as a coefficient matrix, like so:

$$\mathbf{A} = \begin{bmatrix} 1 & -2 \\ 2 & 1 \end{bmatrix}$$

Using the coefficient matrix, we can express the system of equations as a matrix problem in the form $\mathbf{Av} = \mathbf{b}$, where the column vector v is the variable vector. We write this as shown:

$$\begin{bmatrix} 1 & -2 \\ 2 & 1 \end{bmatrix} \begin{bmatrix} x \\ y \end{bmatrix} = \begin{bmatrix} 1 \\ 7 \end{bmatrix}.$$

Going forward, we will express all our problems in this format.

To develop a better understanding, we'll break down the multiplication of matrix A and vector v. It is easiest to think of it as a linear combination of vectors. Let's take a look at the following example with a 3x3 matrix and a 3x1 vector:

$$\begin{bmatrix} a & b & c \\ d & e & f \\ g & h & i \end{bmatrix} \begin{bmatrix} v_1 \\ v_2 \\ v_3 \end{bmatrix} = \begin{bmatrix} av_1 + bv_2 + cv_3 \\ dv_1 + ev_2 + fv_3 \\ gv_1 + hv_2 + iv_3 \end{bmatrix} = v_1 \begin{bmatrix} a \\ d \\ g \end{bmatrix} + v_2 \begin{bmatrix} b \\ e \\ h \end{bmatrix} + v_3 \begin{bmatrix} c \\ f \\ i \end{bmatrix}$$

It is important to note that matrix and vector multiplication is only possible when the number of columns in the matrix is equal to the number of rows (elements) in the vector.

For example, let's look at the following matrix:

$$\begin{bmatrix} a & b & c & d \\ e & f & g & h \\ i & j & k & l \end{bmatrix} \begin{bmatrix} v_1 \\ v_2 \\ v_3 \\ v_4 \end{bmatrix}$$

This can be multiplied since the number of columns in the matrix is equal to the number of rows in the vector, but the following matrix cannot be multiplied as the number of columns and number of rows are not equal:

$$\begin{bmatrix} a & b & c \\ d & e & f \\ g & h & i \\ j & k & l \end{bmatrix} \begin{bmatrix} v_1 \\ v_2 \\ v_3 \\ v_4 \end{bmatrix}$$

Let's visualize some of the operations on vectors to create an intuition of how they work. Have a look at the following screenshot:

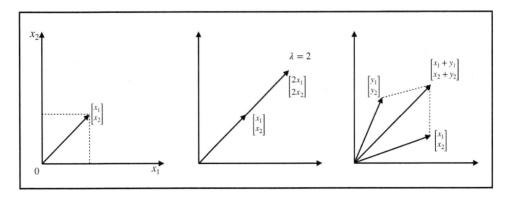

The preceding vectors we dealt with are all in $\mathbb{R}^2$ (in 2-dimensional space), and all resulting combinations of these vectors will also be in $\mathbb{R}^2$. The same applies for vectors in $\mathbb{R}^3$, $\mathbb{R}^5$, and $\mathbb{R}^n$.

There is another very important vector operation called the dot product, which is a type of multiplication. Let's take two arbitrary vectors in $\mathbb{R}^2$, **v** and **w**, and find its dot product, like this:

$$\mathbf{v} = \begin{bmatrix} v_1 \\ v_2 \end{bmatrix} \text{ and } \mathbf{w} = \begin{bmatrix} w_1 \\ w_2 \end{bmatrix}$$

The following is the product:

$$\mathbf{v} \cdot \mathbf{w} = v_1 w_1 + v_2 w_2.$$

Let's continue, using the same vectors we dealt with before, as follows:

$$\mathbf{v} = \begin{bmatrix} 1 \\ 2 \end{bmatrix} \text{ and } \mathbf{w} = \begin{bmatrix} -2 \\ 1 \end{bmatrix}$$

And by taking their dot product, we get zero, which tells us that the two vectors are perpendicular (there is a 90° angle between them), as shown here:

$$\mathbf{v} \cdot \mathbf{w} = \begin{bmatrix} 1 \\ 2 \end{bmatrix} \cdot \begin{bmatrix} -2 \\ 1 \end{bmatrix} = -2 + 2 = 0$$

The most common example of a perpendicular vector is seen with the vectors that represent the x axis, the y axis, and so on. In $\mathbb{R}^2$, we write the x axis vector as $i = \begin{bmatrix} 1 \\ 0 \end{bmatrix}$ and the y axis vector as $j = \begin{bmatrix} 0 \\ 1 \end{bmatrix}$. If we take the dot product $i \bullet j$, we find that it is equal to zero, and they are thus perpendicular.

By combining i and j into a 2x2 matrix, we get the following identity matrix, which is a very important matrix:

$$I = \begin{bmatrix} 1 & 0 \\ 0 & 1 \end{bmatrix}$$

The following are some of the scenarios we will face when solving linear equations of the type $\mathbf{Av} = \mathbf{b}$:

- Let's consider the matrix $\begin{bmatrix} 1 & 3 \\ 3 & 9 \end{bmatrix}$ and the equations $1v_1 + 3v_2 = 9$ and $3v_1 + 9v_2 = 0$. If we do the algebra and multiply the first equation by 3, we get $3v_1 + 9v_2 = 27$. But the second equation is equal to zero, which means that these two equations do not intersect and therefore have no solution. When one column is dependent on another—that is, is a multiple of another column—all combinations of $\begin{bmatrix} 1 \\ 3 \end{bmatrix}$ and $\begin{bmatrix} 3 \\ 9 \end{bmatrix}$ lie in the same direction. However, seeing as $\begin{bmatrix} 9 \\ 0 \end{bmatrix}$ is not a combination of the two aforementioned column vectors and does not lie on the same line, it cannot be a solution to the equation.

- Let's take the same matrix as before, but this time, $\mathbf{b} = \begin{bmatrix} 5 \\ 15 \end{bmatrix}$. Since $\mathbf{b}$ is on the line and is a combination of the dependent vectors, there is an infinite number of solutions. We say that $\mathbf{b}$ is in the column space of A. While there is only one specific combination of $\mathbf{v}$ that produces $\mathbf{b}$, there are infinite combinations of the column vectors that result in the zero vector ($\mathbf{0}$). For example, for any value, a, we have the following:

$$3a \begin{bmatrix} 1 \\ 3 \end{bmatrix} - 1a \begin{bmatrix} 3 \\ 9 \end{bmatrix} = \begin{bmatrix} 0 \\ 0 \end{bmatrix}$$

This leads us to another very important concept, known as the complete solution. The complete solution is all the possible ways to produce $\mathbf{b} = \begin{bmatrix} 5 \\ 15 \end{bmatrix}$. We write this as $\mathbf{A}(\mathbf{v}_n + \mathbf{v}_p) = \mathbf{b}$, where $\mathbf{v}_{complete} = \mathbf{v}_n + \mathbf{v}_p = \begin{bmatrix} 3a \\ -1a \end{bmatrix} + \begin{bmatrix} 2 \\ 1 \end{bmatrix}$.

Solving linear equations in *n*-dimensions

Now that we've dealt with linear equations in 2-dimensions and have developed an understanding of them, let's go a step further and look at equations in 3-dimensions.

Earlier, our equations produced curves in the 2-dimensional space (*xy*-plane). Now, the equations we will be dealing with will produce planes in 3-dimensional space (*xyz*-plane).

Let's take an arbitrary 3x3 matrix, as follows:

$$\begin{bmatrix} a & b & c \\ d & e & f \\ g & h & i \end{bmatrix}$$

We know from earlier in having dealt with linear equations in two dimensions that our solution $\mathbf{b}$, as before, is a linear combination of the three column vectors, so that $v_1 (\text{column 1}) + v_2 (\text{column 2}) + v_3 (\text{column 3}) = \mathbf{b}$.

The equation $av_1 + bv_2 + cv_3 = b_1$ (equation 1) produces a plane, as do $dv_1 + ev_2 + fv_3 = b_2$ (equation 2), and $gv_1 + hv_2 + iv_3 = b_3$ (equation 3).

When two planes intersect, they intersect at a line; however, when three planes intersect, they intersect at a point. That point is the vector $\mathbf{v} = \begin{bmatrix} v_1 \\ v_2 \\ v_3 \end{bmatrix}$, which is the solution to our problem.

However, if the three planes do not intersect at a point, there is no solution to the linear equation. This same concept of solving linear equations can be extended to many more dimensions.

Suppose now that we have a system with 15 linear equations and 15 unknown variables. We can use the preceding method and, according to it, we need to find the point that satisfies all the 15 equations—that is, where they intersect (if it exists).

It will look like this:

$$v_1(\text{column } 1) + v_2(\text{column } 2) + \cdots + v_{15}(\text{column } 15) = \mathbf{b}$$

As you can tell, that's a lot of equations we have to deal with, and the greater the number of dimensions, the harder this becomes to solve.

Solving linear equations using elimination

One of the best ways to solve linear equations is by a systematic method known as **elimination**. This is a method that allows us to systematically eliminate variables and use substitution to solve equations.

Let's take a look at two equations with two variables, as follows:

$$x - 2y = 1$$
$$2x + y = 7$$

After elimination, this becomes the following:

$$x - 2y = 1$$
$$5y = 5$$

As we can see, the x variable is no longer in the second equation. We can plug the y value back into the first equation and solve for x. Doing this, we find that $x = 3$ and $y = 1$.

We call this **triangular factorization**. There are two types—lower triangular and upper triangular. We solve the upper triangular system from top to bottom using a process known as **back substitution**, and this works for systems of any size.

 While this is an effective method, it is not fail-proof. We could come across a scenario where we have more equations than variables, or more variables than equations, which are unsolvable. Or, we could have a scenario such as $0x = 7$, and, as we know, dividing by zero is impossible.

Let's solve three equations with three variables, as follows:

$$\begin{aligned}
2x + 2y - 4z &= -2 \qquad &(1) \\
3x - 9y - 5z &= 10 \qquad &(2) \\
-2x - 4y + 6z &= 6 \qquad &(3)
\end{aligned}$$

We will use upper triangular factorization and eliminate variables, starting with y and then z. Let's start by putting this into our matrix form, as follows:

$$\begin{bmatrix} 2 & 2 & -4 \\ 3 & -9 & -5 \\ -2 & -4 & 6 \end{bmatrix} \begin{bmatrix} x \\ y \\ z \end{bmatrix} = \begin{bmatrix} -2 \\ 10 \\ 6 \end{bmatrix}$$

For our purposes and to make things simpler, we will drop v, the column vector, and get the following result:

$$\begin{bmatrix} 2 & 2 & -4 \\ 3 & -9 & -5 \\ -2 & -4 & 6 \end{bmatrix} = \begin{bmatrix} -2 \\ 10 \\ 6 \end{bmatrix}$$

Then, exchange row 2 and row 3 with each other, like this:

$$\begin{bmatrix} 2 & 2 & -4 \\ -2 & -4 & 6 \\ 3 & -9 & -5 \end{bmatrix} = \begin{bmatrix} -2 \\ 6 \\ 10 \end{bmatrix}$$

Then, add row 2 and row 1 together to eliminate the first value in row 2, like this:

$$\begin{bmatrix} 2 & 2 & -4 \\ 0 & -2 & 2 \\ 3 & -9 & -5 \end{bmatrix} = \begin{bmatrix} -2 \\ 4 \\ 10 \end{bmatrix}$$

Next, multiply row 1 by 3/2 and subtract it from row 3, like this:

$$\begin{bmatrix} 2 & 2 & -4 \\ 0 & -2 & 2 \\ 0 & -12 & 1 \end{bmatrix} = \begin{bmatrix} -2 \\ 4 \\ 13 \end{bmatrix}$$

Finally, multiply row 2 by 6 and subtract it from row 3, like this:

$$\begin{bmatrix} 2 & 2 & -4 \\ 0 & -2 & 2 \\ 0 & 0 & -11 \end{bmatrix} = \begin{bmatrix} -2 \\ 4 \\ -11 \end{bmatrix}$$

As you can notice, the values in the matrix now form a triangle pointing upward, which is why we call it upper triangular. By substituting the values back into the previous equation backward (from bottom to top), we can solve, and find that $x = 2$, $y = -1$, and $z = 1$.

In summary, $\mathbf{Av} = \mathbf{b}$ becomes $\mathbf{Uv} = \mathbf{c}$, as illustrated here:

$$\begin{bmatrix} 2 & 2 & -4 \\ 3 & -9 & -5 \\ -2 & -4 & 6 \end{bmatrix} \begin{bmatrix} x \\ y \\ z \end{bmatrix} = \begin{bmatrix} -2 \\ 10 \\ 6 \end{bmatrix} \longrightarrow \begin{bmatrix} 2 & 2 & -4 \\ 0 & -2 & 2 \\ 0 & 0 & -22 \end{bmatrix} \begin{bmatrix} x \\ y \\ z \end{bmatrix} = \begin{bmatrix} -2 \\ 4 \\ -22 \end{bmatrix}$$

$$\mathbf{A} \qquad \mathbf{v} = \mathbf{b} \longrightarrow \qquad \mathbf{U} \qquad \mathbf{v} = \mathbf{c}$$

Note: The values across the diagonal in the triangular factorized matrix are called pivots, and when factorized, the values below the diagonal are all zeros.

To check that our found solution is right, we solve $\mathbf{Ax} = \mathbf{b}$, using our found values for x, y, and z, like this:

$$\begin{bmatrix} 2 & 2 & -4 \\ 3 & -9 & -5 \\ -2 & -4 & 6 \end{bmatrix} \begin{bmatrix} 2 \\ -1 \\ 1 \end{bmatrix} = \begin{bmatrix} -2 \\ 10 \\ 6 \end{bmatrix}$$

This then becomes the following equation:

$$2 \begin{bmatrix} 2 \\ 3 \\ -2 \end{bmatrix} - 1 \begin{bmatrix} 2 \\ -9 \\ -4 \end{bmatrix} + 1 \begin{bmatrix} -4 \\ -5 \\ 6 \end{bmatrix} = \begin{bmatrix} -2 \\ 10 \\ 6 \end{bmatrix}$$

$$\begin{bmatrix} -2 \\ 10 \\ 6 \end{bmatrix} = \begin{bmatrix} -2 \\ 10 \\ 6 \end{bmatrix}$$

And as we can see, the left-hand side is equal to the right-hand side.

After upper triangular factorization, an arbitrary 4x4 matrix will look like this:

$$\mathbf{U} = \begin{bmatrix} x & x & x & x \\ 0 & x & x & x \\ 0 & 0 & x & x \\ 0 & 0 & 0 & x \end{bmatrix}$$

We could take this a step further and factorize the upper triangular matrix until we end up with a matrix that contains only the pivot values along the diagonal, and zeros everywhere else. This resulting matrix **P** essentially fully solves the problem for us without us having to resort to forward or backward substitution, and it looks like this:

$$\mathbf{P} = \begin{bmatrix} x & 0 & 0 & 0 \\ 0 & x & 0 & 0 \\ 0 & 0 & x & 0 \\ 0 & 0 & 0 & x \end{bmatrix}$$

But as you can tell, there are a lot of steps involved in getting us from **A** to **P**.

There is one other very important factorization method called **lower-upper (LU) decomposition**. The way it works is we factorize **A** into an upper triangular matrix **U**, and record the steps of Gaussian elimination in a lower triangular matrix **L**, such that **A** = **LU**.

Let's revisit the matrix we upper-triangular factorized before and put it into LU factorized form, like this:

$$\begin{bmatrix} 2 & 2 & -4 \\ -2 & -4 & 6 \\ 3 & -9 & -5 \end{bmatrix} = \begin{bmatrix} 1 & 0 & 0 \\ -1 & 1 & 0 \\ \frac{3}{2} & 6 & 1 \end{bmatrix} \begin{bmatrix} 2 & 2 & -4 \\ 0 & -2 & 2 \\ 0 & 0 & -11 \end{bmatrix}$$

If we multiply the two matrices on the right, we will get the original matrix **A**. But how did we get here? Let's go through the steps, as follows:

1. We start with **A** = I**A**, so that the following applies:

$$\begin{bmatrix} 2 & 2 & -4 \\ -2 & -4 & 6 \\ 3 & -9 & -5 \end{bmatrix} = \begin{bmatrix} 1 & 0 & 0 \\ 0 & 1 & 0 \\ 0 & 0 & 1 \end{bmatrix} \begin{bmatrix} 2 & 2 & -4 \\ -2 & -4 & 6 \\ 3 & -9 & -5 \end{bmatrix}$$

2. We add -1 to what was the identity matrix at $l_{2,1}$ to represent the operation (row 2)-(-1)(row 1), so it becomes the following:

$$\begin{bmatrix} 2 & 2 & -4 \\ -2 & -4 & 6 \\ 3 & -9 & -5 \end{bmatrix} = \begin{bmatrix} 1 & 0 & 0 \\ -1 & 1 & 0 \\ 0 & 0 & 1 \end{bmatrix} \begin{bmatrix} 2 & 2 & -4 \\ 0 & -2 & 2 \\ 3 & -9 & -5 \end{bmatrix}$$

3. We then add $\dfrac{3}{2}$ to the matrix at $l_{3,1}$ to represent the $(\text{row 3}) - \dfrac{3}{2}(\text{row 1})$ operation, so it becomes the following:

$$\begin{bmatrix} 2 & 2 & -4 \\ -2 & -4 & 6 \\ 3 & -9 & -5 \end{bmatrix} = \begin{bmatrix} 1 & 0 & 0 \\ -1 & 1 & 0 \\ \frac{3}{2} & 0 & 1 \end{bmatrix} \begin{bmatrix} 2 & 2 & -4 \\ 0 & -2 & 2 \\ 0 & -12 & 1 \end{bmatrix}$$

4. We then add 6 to the matrix at $l_{3,2}$ to represent the operation (row 3)-6(row 2), so it becomes the following:

$$\begin{bmatrix} 2 & 2 & -4 \\ -2 & -4 & 6 \\ 3 & -9 & -5 \end{bmatrix} = \begin{bmatrix} 1 & 0 & 0 \\ -1 & 1 & 0 \\ \frac{3}{2} & 6 & 1 \end{bmatrix} \begin{bmatrix} 2 & 2 & -4 \\ 0 & -2 & 2 \\ 0 & 0 & -11 \end{bmatrix}$$

This is the LU factorized matrix we saw earlier.

You might now be wondering what this has to do with solving $\mathbf{Av} = \mathbf{b}$, which is very valid. The elimination process tends to work quite well, but we have to additionally apply all the operations we did on $\mathbf{A}$ to b as well, and this involves extra steps. However, LU factorization is only applied to $\mathbf{A}$.

Let's now take a look at how we can solve our system of linear equations using this method.

For simplicity, we drop the variables vector and write $\mathbf{A}$ and $\mathbf{b}$ as follows:

$$\begin{bmatrix} 2 & 2 & -4 \\ -2 & -4 & 6 \\ 3 & -9 & -5 \end{bmatrix} = \begin{bmatrix} -2 \\ 6 \\ 10 \end{bmatrix}$$

But even this can get cumbersome to write as we go, so we will instead write it in the following way for further simplicity:

$$\begin{bmatrix} \mathbf{A} & \mathbf{b} \end{bmatrix} = \begin{bmatrix} \mathbf{LU} & \mathbf{b} \end{bmatrix}$$

We then multiply both sides by $\mathbf{L}^{-1}$ and get the following result:

$$\begin{bmatrix} \mathbf{U} & \mathbf{L}^{-1}\mathbf{b} \end{bmatrix} = \begin{bmatrix} \mathbf{U} & \mathbf{c} \end{bmatrix}$$

This tells us that $\mathbf{b} = \mathbf{L}\mathbf{c}$, and we already know from the preceding equation that $\mathbf{U}\mathbf{v} = \mathbf{c}$ (so $\mathbf{v} = \mathbf{U}^{-1}\mathbf{c}$). And by using back substitution, we can find the vector $\mathbf{v}$.

In the preceding example, you may have noticed some new notation that I have not yet introduced, but not to worry—we will observe all the necessary notation and operations in the next section.

Matrix operations

Now that we understand how to solve systems of linear equations of the type $\mathbf{A}\mathbf{v} = \mathbf{b}$ where we multiplied a matrix with a column vector, let's move on to dealing with the types of operations we can do with one or more matrices.

Adding matrices

As with scalars and vectors, sometimes we may have to add two or more matrices together, and the process of doing so is rather straightforward. Let's take two $\mathbb{R}^{m \times n}$ matrices, A and B, and add them:

$$
\begin{bmatrix} a_{1,1} & a_{1,2} & & a_{1,n} \\ a_{2,1} & a_{2,2} & \cdots & a_{2,n} \\ & \vdots & \ddots & \\ a_{m,1} & a_{m,2} & & a_{m,n} \end{bmatrix} + \begin{bmatrix} b_{1,1} & b_{1,2} & & b_{1,n} \\ b_{2,1} & b_{2,2} & \cdots & b_{2,n} \\ & \vdots & \ddots & \\ b_{m,1} & b_{m,2} & & b_{m,n} \end{bmatrix} = \begin{bmatrix} a_{1,1} + b_{1,1} & a_{1,2} + b_{1,2} & & a_{1,n} + b_{1,n} \\ a_{2,1} + b_{2,1} & a_{2,2} + b_{2,2} & \cdots & a_{2,n} + b_{2,n} \\ & \vdots & \ddots & \\ a_{m,1} + b_{m,1} & a_{m,2} + b_{m,1} & & a_{m,n} + b_{m,n} \end{bmatrix}
$$

It is important to note that we can only add matrices that have the same dimensions, and, as you have probably noticed, we add the matrices element-wise.

Multiplying matrices

So far, we have only multiplied a matrix by a column vector. But now, we will multiply a matrix A with another matrix B.

There are four simple rules that will help us in multiplying matrices, listed here:

- Firstly, we can only multiply two matrices when the number of columns in matrix A is equal to the number of rows in matrix B.
- Secondly, the first row of matrix A multiplied by the first column of matrix B gives us the first element in the matrix AB, and so on.

- Thirdly, when multiplying, order matters—specifically, $AB \neq BA$.
- Lastly, the element at row i, column j is the product of the ith row of matrix A and the jth column of matrix B.

Let's multiply an arbitrary 4x5 matrix with an arbitrary 5x6 matrix, as follows:

$$\begin{bmatrix} a_{1,1} & a_{1,2} & a_{1,3} & a_{1,4} & a_{1,5} \\ a_{2,1} & a_{2,2} & a_{2,3} & a_{2,4} & a_{2,5} \\ a_{3,1} & a_{3,2} & a_{3,3} & a_{3,4} & a_{3,5} \\ a_{4,1} & a_{4,2} & a_{4,3} & a_{4,4} & a_{4,5} \end{bmatrix} \begin{bmatrix} b_{1,1} & b_{1,2} & b_{1,3} & b_{1,4} & b_{1,5} & b_{1,6} \\ b_{2,1} & b_{2,2} & b_{2,3} & b_{2,4} & b_{2,5} & b_{2,6} \\ b_{3,1} & b_{3,2} & b_{3,3} & b_{3,4} & b_{3,5} & b_{3,6} \\ b_{4,1} & b_{4,2} & b_{4,3} & b_{4,4} & b_{4,5} & b_{4,6} \\ b_{5,1} & b_{5,2} & b_{5,3} & b_{5,4} & b_{5,5} & b_{5,6} \end{bmatrix}$$

This results in a 4x6 matrix, like this:

$$\begin{bmatrix} (AB)_{1,1} & (AB)_{1,2} & (AB)_{1,3} & (AB)_{1,4} & (AB)_{1,5} & (AB)_{1,6} \\ (AB)_{2,1} & (AB)_{2,2} & (AB)_{2,3} & (AB)_{2,4} & (AB)_{2,5} & (AB)_{2,6} \\ (AB)_{3,1} & (AB)_{3,2} & (AB)_{3,3} & (AB)_{3,4} & (AB)_{3,5} & (AB)_{3,6} \\ (AB)_{4,1} & (AB)_{4,2} & (AB)_{4,3} & (AB)_{4,4} & (AB)_{4,5} & (AB)_{4,6} \end{bmatrix}$$

From that, we can deduce that in general, the following applies:

$$(AB)_{i,j} = a_{i,1} \times b_{1,j} + a_{i,2} \times b_{2,j} + a_{i,3} \times b_{3,j} + a_{i,4} \times b_{4,j} + a_{i,5} \times b_{5,j}$$

Let's take the following two matrices and multiply them, like this:

$$A = \begin{bmatrix} 1 & 2 & -1 \\ 1 & 0 & 3 \\ 2 & 1 & 4 \end{bmatrix} \quad B = \begin{bmatrix} 1 & 0 & 0 \\ 0 & 1 & 0 \\ 0 & 0 & 1 \end{bmatrix}$$
and

This will give us the following matrix:

$$AB = \begin{bmatrix} 1 & 2 & -1 \\ 1 & 0 & 3 \\ 2 & 1 & 4 \end{bmatrix} \begin{bmatrix} 1 & 0 & 0 \\ 0 & 1 & 0 \\ 0 & 0 & 1 \end{bmatrix} = \begin{bmatrix} 1 & 2 & -1 \\ 1 & 0 & 3 \\ 2 & 1 & 4 \end{bmatrix}.$$

 Note: In this example, the matrix B is the identity matrix, usually written as I.

The identity matrix has two unique properties in matrix multiplication. When multiplied by any matrix, it returns the original matrix unchanged, and the order of multiplication does not matter—so, $AI = IA = A$.

For example, let's use the same matrix A from earlier, and multiply it by another matrix B, as follows:

$$\mathbf{AB} = \begin{bmatrix} 1 & 2 & -1 \\ 1 & 0 & 3 \\ 2 & 1 & 4 \end{bmatrix} \begin{bmatrix} 2 & -1 & 3 & 1 \\ 2 & 1 & 0 & 4 \\ -3 & 2 & -1 & 1 \end{bmatrix} = \begin{bmatrix} 9 & -1 & 4 & 8 \\ -7 & 5 & 0 & 4 \\ -6 & 7 & 2 & 10 \end{bmatrix}$$

Another very special matrix is the inverse matrix, which is written as A^{-1}. And when we multiply A with A^{-1}, we receive I, the identity matrix.

As mentioned before, the order in which we multiply matters. We must keep the matrices in order, but we do have some flexibility. As we can see in the following equation, the parentheses can be moved:

$$\mathbf{ABC} = (\mathbf{AB})\mathbf{C} = \mathbf{A}(\mathbf{BC})$$

This is the first law of matrix operations, known as **associativity**.

The following are three important laws that cannot be broken:

- **commutativity**: $\mathbf{A} + \mathbf{B} = \mathbf{B} + \mathbf{A}$
- **distributivity**: $c(\mathbf{A} + \mathbf{B}) = c\mathbf{A} + c\mathbf{B}$ or $\mathbf{A}(\mathbf{B} + \mathbf{C}) = \mathbf{AB} + \mathbf{AC}$
- **associativity**: $(\mathbf{A} + \mathbf{B}) + \mathbf{C} = \mathbf{A} + (\mathbf{B} + \mathbf{C})$

As proof that $AB \neq BA$, let's take a look at the following example:

$$\mathbf{AB} = \begin{bmatrix} 2 & 1 \\ 0 & 2 \end{bmatrix} \begin{bmatrix} 1 & 1 \\ 3 & 2 \end{bmatrix} = \begin{bmatrix} 5 & 4 \\ 6 & 4 \end{bmatrix}$$

$$\mathbf{BA} = \begin{bmatrix} 1 & 1 \\ 3 & 2 \end{bmatrix} \begin{bmatrix} 2 & 1 \\ 0 & 2 \end{bmatrix} = \begin{bmatrix} 2 & 3 \\ 6 & 7 \end{bmatrix}$$

This conclusively shows that the two results are not the same.

We know that we can raise numbers to powers, but we can also raise matrices to powers.

If we raise the matrix A to power p, we get the following:

$$\mathbf{A}^p = \mathbf{AAA}\cdots\mathbf{A} \text{ (multiplying the matrix by itself } p \text{ times)}$$

There are two additional power laws for matrices—$(\mathbf{A}^p)(\mathbf{A}^q) = \mathbf{A}^{p+q}$ and $(\mathbf{A}^p)^q = \mathbf{A}^{pq}$.

Inverse matrices

Let's revisit the concept of inverse matrices and go a little more in depth with them. We know from earlier that $AA^{-1} = I$, but not every matrix has an inverse.

There are, again, some rules we must follow when it comes to finding the inverses of matrices, as follows:

- The inverse only exists if, through the process of upper or lower triangular factorization, we obtain all the pivot values on the diagonal.
- If the matrix is invertible, it has only one unique inverse matrix—that is, if $AB = I$ and $AC = I$, then $B = C$.
- If A is invertible, then to solve $Av = b$ we multiply both sides by A^{-1} and get $AA^{-1}v = A^{-1}b$, which finally gives us $= A^{-1}b$.
- If v is nonzero and $b = 0$, then the matrix does not have an inverse.
- 2 x 2 matrices are invertible only if $ad - bc \neq 0$, where the following applies:

$$\begin{bmatrix} a & b \\ c & d \end{bmatrix}^{-1} = \frac{1}{ad-bc}\begin{bmatrix} d & -b \\ -c & a \end{bmatrix}$$

  And $ad - bc$ is called the **determinant** of A. A^{-1} involves dividing each element in the matrix by the determinant.

- Lastly, if the matrix has any zero values along the diagonal, it is non-invertible.

Sometimes, we may have to invert the product of two matrices, but that is only possible when both the matrices are individually invertible (follow the rules outlined previously).

For example, let's take two matrices A and B, which are both invertible. Then, $(\mathbf{AB})^{-1} = \mathbf{B}^{-1}\mathbf{A}^{-1}$ so that $(\mathbf{AB})(\mathbf{B}^{-1}\mathbf{A}^{-1}) = \mathbf{A}I\mathbf{A}^{-1} = \mathbf{AA}^{-1} = I$.

Note: Pay close attention to the order of the inverse—it too must follow the order. The left-hand side is the mirror image of the right-hand side.

Matrix transpose

Let's take an $\mathbb{R}^{m \times n}$ matrix A. If the matrix's transpose is B, then the dimensions of B are $\mathbb{R}^{n \times m}$, such that: $a_{i,j} = b_{j,i}$. Here is the matrix A:

$$
A = \begin{bmatrix} a_{1,1} & a_{1,2} & & a_{1,n} \\ a_{2,1} & a_{2,1} & \cdots & a_{2,n} \\ & \vdots & \ddots & \\ a_{m,1} & a_{m,2} & & a_{m,n} \end{bmatrix}
$$

Then, the matrix B is as given:

$$
B = \begin{bmatrix} a_{1,1} & a_{2,1} & & a_{n,1} \\ a_{1,2} & a_{2,2} & \cdots & a_{n,2} \\ & \vdots & \ddots & \\ a_{1,m} & a_{2,m} & & a_{n,m} \end{bmatrix}.
$$

Essentially, we can think of this as writing the columns of A as the rows of the transposed matrix, B.

We usually write the transpose of A as A^T.

A symmetric matrix is a special kind of matrix. It is an $n \times n$ matrix that, when transposed, is exactly the same as before we transposed it.

The following are the properties of inverses and transposes:

- $AA^{-1} = I = A^{-1}A$
- $(AB)^{-1} = B^{-1}A^{-1}$
- $(A + B)^{-1} \neq A^{-1} + B^{-1}$

- $(\mathbf{A}^{\mathrm{T}})^{\mathrm{T}} = \mathbf{A}$
- $(\mathbf{A} + \mathbf{B})^{\mathrm{T}} = \mathbf{A}^{\mathrm{T}} + \mathbf{B}^{\mathrm{T}}$
- $(\mathbf{AB})^{\mathrm{T}} = \mathbf{B}^{\mathrm{T}}\mathbf{A}^{\mathrm{T}}$

 If A is an invertible matrix, then so is A^{T}, and so $(A^{-1})^{T} = (A^{T})^{-1} = A^{-T}$.

Permutations

In the example on solving systems of linear equations, we swapped the positions of rows 2 and 3. This is known as a **permutation**.

When we are doing triangular factorization, we want our pivot values to be along the diagonal of the matrix, but this won't happen every time—in fact, it usually won't. So, instead, what we do is swap the rows so that we get our pivot values where we want them.

But that is not their only use case. We can also use them to scale individual rows by a scalar value or add rows to or subtract rows from other rows.

Let's start with some of the more basic permutation matrices that we obtain by swapping the rows of the identity matrix. In general, we have $n!$ possible permutation matrices that can be formed from an nxn identity matrix. In this example, we will use a 3×3 matrix and therefore have six permutation matrices, and they are as follows:

- $\mathbf{P}_{123} = \begin{bmatrix} 1 & 0 & 0 \\ 0 & 1 & 0 \\ 0 & 0 & 1 \end{bmatrix}$ This matrix makes no change to the matrix it is applied on.

- $\mathbf{P}_{132} = \begin{bmatrix} 1 & 0 & 0 \\ 0 & 0 & 1 \\ 0 & 1 & 0 \end{bmatrix}$ This matrix swaps rows two and three of the matrix it is applied on.

- $\mathbf{P}_{213} = \begin{bmatrix} 0 & 1 & 0 \\ 1 & 0 & 0 \\ 0 & 0 & 1 \end{bmatrix}$ This matrix swaps rows one and two of the matrix it is applied on.

$$\mathbf{P}_{231} = \begin{bmatrix} 0 & 1 & 0 \\ 0 & 0 & 1 \\ 1 & 0 & 0 \end{bmatrix}$$

- This matrix shifts rows two and three up one and moves row one to the position of row three of the matrix it is applied on.

$$\mathbf{P}_{312} = \begin{bmatrix} 0 & 0 & 1 \\ 1 & 0 & 0 \\ 0 & 1 & 0 \end{bmatrix}$$

- This matrix shifts rows one and two down one and moves row three to the row-one position of the matrix it is applied on.

$$\mathbf{P}_{321} = \begin{bmatrix} 0 & 0 & 1 \\ 0 & 1 & 0 \\ 1 & 0 & 0 \end{bmatrix}$$

- This matrix swaps rows one and three of the matrix it is applied on.

It is important to note that there is a particularly fascinating property of permutation matrices that states that if we have a matrix $\mathbf{A} \in \mathbb{R}^{n \times n}$ and it is invertible, then there exists a permutation matrix that when applied to A will give us the LU factor of A. We can express this like so:

$$\mathbf{PA} = \mathbf{LU}$$

Vector spaces and subspaces

In this section, we will explore the concepts of vector spaces and subspaces. These are very important to our understanding of linear algebra. In fact, if we do not have an understanding of vector spaces and subspaces, we do not truly have an understanding of how to solve linear algebra problems.

Spaces

Vector spaces are one of the fundamental settings for linear algebra, and, as the name suggests, they are spaces where all vectors reside. We will denote the vector space with V.

The easiest way to think of dimensions is to count the number of elements in the column vector. Suppose we have $\mathbf{x} = (x_1, x_2, \cdots, x_7)$, then $\mathbf{x} \in \mathbb{R}^7$. $\mathbb{R}^1$ is a straight line, $\mathbb{R}^2$ is all the possible points in the xy-plane, and $\mathbb{R}^3$ is all the possible points in the xyz-plane—that is, 3-dimensional space, and so on.

The following are some of the rules for vector spaces:

- There exists in V an additive identity element such that $\mathbf{x} + \mathbf{0} = \mathbf{x}$ for all $\mathbf{x} \in V$.
- For all $\mathbf{x} \in V$, there exists an additive inverse such that $\mathbf{x} + (-\mathbf{x}) = \mathbf{0}$.
- For all $\mathbf{x} \in V$, there exists a multiplicative identity such that $1\mathbf{x} = \mathbf{x}$.
- Vectors are commutative, such that for all $\mathbf{x}, \mathbf{y} \in V$, $\mathbf{x} + \mathbf{y} = \mathbf{y} + \mathbf{x}$.
- Vectors are associative, such that $(\mathbf{x} + \mathbf{y}) + \mathbf{z} = \mathbf{x} + (\mathbf{y} + \mathbf{z})$.
- Vectors have distributivity, such that $\alpha(\mathbf{x} + \mathbf{y}) = \alpha\mathbf{x} + \alpha\mathbf{y}$ and $(\alpha + \beta)\mathbf{x} = \alpha\mathbf{x} + \beta\mathbf{y}$ for all $\mathbf{x}, \mathbf{y} \in V$ and for all $\alpha, \beta \in \mathbb{R}$.

A set of vectors is said to be linearly independent if $\alpha_1 \mathbf{v}_1 + \cdots + \alpha_n \mathbf{v}_n = \mathbf{0}$, which implies that $\alpha_1 = \alpha_2 = \cdots = \alpha_n = 0$.

Another important concept for us to know is called **span**. The span of $\mathbf{v}_1, \cdots, \mathbf{v}_n \in V$ is the set of all linear combinations that can be made using the n vectors. Therefore, $\text{span}\{\mathbf{v}_1, \cdots, \mathbf{v}_n\} = \{\mathbf{v} \in V : \exists \alpha_1, \cdots, \alpha_n \mid \alpha_1 \mathbf{v}_1 + \cdots + \alpha_n \mathbf{v}_n = \mathbf{v}\}$ if the vectors are linearly independent and span V completely; then, the vectors $\mathbf{v}_1, \cdots, \mathbf{v}_n$ are the basis of V.

Therefore, the dimension of V is the number of basis vectors we have, and we denote it $dimV$.

Subspaces

Subspaces are another very important concept that state that we can have one or many vector spaces inside another vector space. Let's suppose V is a vector space, and we have a subspace $S \subseteq V$. Then, S can only be a subspace if it follows the three rules, stated as follows:

- $\mathbf{0} \in S$
- $\mathbf{x}, \mathbf{y} \in S$ and $\mathbf{x} + \mathbf{y} \in S$, which implies that S is closed under addition
- $\mathbf{x} \in S$ and $\alpha \in \mathbb{R}$ so that $\alpha\mathbf{x} \in S$, which implies that S is closed under scalar multiplication

If $U, W \in V$, then their sum is $U + W = \{\mathbf{u} + \mathbf{w} \mid \mathbf{u} \in U, \mathbf{w} \in W\}$, where the result is also a subspace of V.

The dimension of the sum $U + W$ is as follows:

$$\dim(U + W) = \dim U + \dim W - \dim(U \cap W)$$

Linear maps

A linear map is a function $T : V \to W$, where V and W are both vector spaces. They must satisfy the following criteria:

- $T(\mathbf{x} + \mathbf{y}) = T\mathbf{x} + T\mathbf{y}$, for all $\mathbf{x}, \mathbf{y} \in V$
- $T(\alpha \mathbf{x}) = \alpha T\mathbf{x}$, for all $\mathbf{x} \in V$ and $\alpha \in \mathbb{R}$

Linear maps tend to preserve the properties of vector spaces under addition and scalar multiplication. A linear map is called a **homomorphism of vector spaces;** however, if the homomorphism is invertible (where the inverse is a homomorphism), then we call the mapping an **isomorphism**.

When V and W are isomorphic, we denote this as $V \cong W$, and they both have the same algebraic structure.

If V and W are vector spaces in $\mathbb{R}^n$, and $\dim V = \dim W = n$, then it is called a **natural isomorphism**. We write this as follows:

$$\varphi : V \to W$$
$$\alpha_1 \mathbf{v}_1 + \alpha_n \mathbf{v}_n \mapsto \alpha_1 \mathbf{w}_1 + \alpha_n \mathbf{w}_n$$

Here, $\mathbf{v}_1, \cdots, \mathbf{v}_n$ and $\mathbf{w}_1, \cdots, \mathbf{w}_n$ are the bases of V and W. Using the preceding equation, we can see that $V \cong W$, which tells us that φ is an isomorphism.

Let's take the same vector spaces V and W as before, with bases $\mathbf{v}_1, \cdots, \mathbf{v}_n$ and $\mathbf{w}_1, \cdots, \mathbf{w}_m$ respectively. We know that $T : V \to W$ is a linear map, and the matrix T that has entries A_{ij}, where $i = 1, \cdots, m$ and $j = 1, \cdots, n$ can be defined as follows:

$$T\mathbf{v}_j = A_{1,j}\mathbf{w}_1 + \cdots + A_{m,j}\mathbf{w}_m.$$

From our knowledge of matrices, we should know that the jth column of A contains Tv_j in the basis of W.

Thus, $\mathbf{A} \in \mathbb{R}^{m \times n}$ produces a linear map $T : \mathbb{R}^n \to \mathbb{R}^m$, which we write as $T\mathbf{x} = \mathbf{A}\mathbf{x}$.

Image and kernel

When dealing with linear mappings, we will often encounter two important terms: the image and the kernel, both of which are vector subspaces with rather important properties.

The **kernel** (sometimes called the **null space**) is 0 (the zero vector) and is produced by a linear map, as follows:

$$\ker(T) = \{\mathbf{v} \in V \mid T\mathbf{v} = \mathbf{0}\}$$

And the **image** (sometimes called the **range**) of T is defined as follows:

$$\mathrm{Im}(T) = \{\mathbf{w} \in W \mid \exists \mathbf{v} \in V \text{ such that } T\mathbf{v} = \mathbf{w}\}.$$

V and W are also sometimes known as the **domain** and **codomain** of T.

It is best to think of the kernel as a linear mapping that maps the vectors $\mathbf{v} \in V$ to $\mathbf{0} \in W$. The image, however, is the set of all possible linear combinations of $\mathbf{v} \in V$ that can be mapped to the set of vectors $\mathbf{w} \in W$.

The **Rank-Nullity theorem** (sometimes referred to as the **fundamental theorem of linear mappings**) states that given two vector spaces V and W and a linear mapping $T : V \rightarrow W$, the following will remain true:

$$\dim(\ker(T)) + \dim(\mathrm{Im}(T)) = \dim(V).$$

Metric space and normed space

Metrics help define the concept of distance in Euclidean space (denoted by $\mathbb{E}^n$). Metric spaces, however, needn't always be vector spaces. We use them because they allow us to define limits for objects besides real numbers.

So far, we have been dealing with vectors, but what we don't yet know is how to calculate the length of a vector or the distance between two or more vectors, as well as the angle between two vectors, and thus the concept of orthogonality (perpendicularity). This is where Euclidean spaces come in handy. In fact, they are the fundamental space of geometry. This may seem rather trivial at the moment, but their importance will become more apparent to you as we get further on in the book.

In Euclidean space, we tend to refer to vectors as points.

A metric on a set S is defined as a function $d : S \times S \to \mathbb{R}$ and satisfies the following criteria:

- $d(x, y) \geq 0$, and when $x = y$ then $d(x, y) = 0$
- $d(x, y) = d(y, x)$
- $d(x, z) \leq d(x, y) + d(y, z)$ (known as the **triangle inequality**)

For all $x, y, z \in S$.

That's all well and good, but how exactly do we calculate distance?

Let's suppose we have two points, (x_1, y_1) and (x_2, y_2); then, the distance between them can be calculated as follows:

$$d(x, y) = \sqrt{(x_1 - y_1)^2 + (x^2 - y_2)^2}$$

And we can extend this to find the distance of points in $\mathbb{R}^n$, as follows:

$$d(x, y) = \sqrt{\sum_{i}^{n} (x_i - y_i)^2}$$

While metrics help with the notion of distance, norms define the concept of length in Euclidean space.

A norm on a vector space is a function $\|\mathbf{v}\| : V \to \mathbb{R}$, and satisfies the following conditions:

- $\|\mathbf{x}\| \geq 0$, and when $\mathbf{x} = \mathbf{0}$ then $\|\mathbf{x}\| = 0$
- $\|\alpha\mathbf{x}\| = |\alpha| \|\mathbf{x}\|$
- $\|\mathbf{x} + \mathbf{y}\| \leq \|\mathbf{x}\| + \|\mathbf{y}\|$ (also known as the triangle inequality)

For all $\mathbf{x}, \mathbf{y} \in V$ and $\alpha \in \mathbb{R}$.

It is important to note that any norm on the vector space creates a distance metric on the said vector space, as follows:

$$d(\mathbf{x}, \mathbf{y}) = \|\mathbf{x} - \mathbf{y}\|$$

This satisfies the rules for metrics, telling us that a normed space is also a metric space.

In general, for our purposes, we will only be concerned with four norms on $\mathbb{R}^n$, as follows:

- $$\|\mathbf{x}\|_1 = \sum_{i=1}^{n} |x_i|$$

- $$\|\mathbf{x}\|_2 = \sqrt{\sum_{i=1}^{n} x_i^2}$$

- $$\|\mathbf{x}\|_p = (\sum_{i=1}^{n} |x_i|^p)^{\frac{1}{p}}$$

- $$\|\mathbf{x}\|_\infty = \max_{1 \le i \le n} |x_i|$$ (this applies only if $p \ge 1$)

If you look carefully at the four norms, you can notice that the 1- and 2-norms are versions of the p-norm. The ∞-norm, however, is a limit of the p-norm, as p tends to infinity.

Using these definitions, we can define two vectors to be orthogonal if the following applies:

$$\|\mathbf{u} + \mathbf{v}\|^2 = \|\mathbf{u}\|^2 + \|\mathbf{v}\|^2$$

Inner product space

An inner product on a vector space is a function $\langle v_1, v_2 \rangle : V \times V \to \mathbb{R}$, and satisfies the following rules:

- $\langle \mathbf{x}, \mathbf{x} \rangle \ge 0$
- $\langle \mathbf{x} + \mathbf{y}, \mathbf{z} \rangle = \langle \mathbf{x}, \mathbf{z} \rangle + \langle \mathbf{y}, \mathbf{z} \rangle$ and $\langle \alpha \mathbf{x}, \mathbf{y} \rangle = \alpha \langle \mathbf{x}, \mathbf{y} \rangle$
- $\langle \mathbf{x}, \mathbf{y} \rangle = \langle \mathbf{y}, \mathbf{x} \rangle$

For all $\mathbf{x}, \mathbf{y}, \mathbf{z} \in V$ and $\alpha \in \mathbb{R}$.

It is important to note that any inner product on the vector space creates a norm on the said vector space, which we see as follows:

$$\|\mathbf{x}\| = \sqrt{\langle \mathbf{x}, \mathbf{x} \rangle}$$

We can notice from these rules and definitions that all inner product spaces are also normed spaces, and therefore also metric spaces.

Another very important concept is orthogonality, which in a nutshell means that two vectors are perpendicular to each other (that is, they are at a right angle to each other) from Euclidean space.

Two vectors are orthogonal if their inner product is zero—that is, $\langle \mathbf{x}, \mathbf{y} \rangle = 0$. As a shorthand for perpendicularity, we write $\mathbf{x} \perp \mathbf{y}$.

Additionally, if the two orthogonal vectors are of unit length—that is, $\|\mathbf{x}\| = \|\mathbf{y}\| = 1$, then they are called **orthonormal**.

In general, the inner product in $\mathbb{R}^n$ is as follows:

$$\langle \mathbf{x}, \mathbf{y} \rangle = \sum_{i=1}^{n} x_i y_i = \mathbf{x}^\mathrm{T} \mathbf{y}$$

Matrix decompositions

Matrix decompositions are a set of methods that we use to describe matrices using more interpretable matrices and give us insight to the matrices' properties.

Determinant

Earlier, we got a quick glimpse of the determinant of a square 2x2 matrix when we wanted to determine whether a square matrix was invertible. The determinant is a very important concept in linear algebra and is used frequently in the solving of systems of linear equations.

 Note: The determinant only exists when we have square matrices.

Notationally, the determinant is usually written as either $\det(\mathbf{A})$ or $|\mathbf{A}|$.

Let's take an arbitrary *n×n* matrix A, as follows:

$$\mathbf{A} = \begin{bmatrix} a_{1,1} & a_{1,2} & \cdots & a_{1,n} \\ a_{2,1} & a_{2,2} & \cdots & a_{2,n} \\ \vdots & \vdots & \ddots & \vdots \\ a_{n,1} & a_{n,2} & \cdots & a_{n,n} \end{bmatrix}$$

We will also take its determinant, as follows:

$$\det(\mathbf{A}) = \begin{vmatrix} a_{1,1} & a_{1,2} & \cdots & a_{1,n} \\ a_{2,1} & a_{2,2} & \cdots & a_{2,n} \\ \vdots & \vdots & \ddots & \vdots \\ a_{n,1} & a_{n,2} & \cdots & a_{n,n} \end{vmatrix}$$

The determinant reduces the matrix to a real number (or, in other words, maps A onto a real number).

We start by checking if a square matrix is invertible. Let's take a 2x2 matrix, and from the earlier definition, we know that the matrix applied to its inverse produces the identity matrix. It works no differently than when we multiply a with $\frac{1}{a}$ (only true when $a \neq 0$), which produces 1, except with matrices. Therefore, $AA^{-1} = I$.

Let's go ahead and find the inverse of our matrix, as follows:

$$\mathbf{A}^{-1} = \frac{1}{a_{1,1}a_{2,2} - a_{1,2}a_{2,1}} \begin{bmatrix} a_{2,2} & -a_{1,2} \\ -a_{2,1} & a_{1,1} \end{bmatrix}$$

A is invertible only when $a_{1,1}a_{2,2} - a_{1,2}a_{2,1} \neq 0$, and this resulting value is what we call the **determinator**.

Now that we know how to find the determinant in the 2x2 case, let's move on to a 3x3 matrix and find its determinant. It looks like this:

$$\det(\mathbf{A}) = \begin{vmatrix} a_{1,1} & a_{1,2} & a_{1,3} \\ a_{2,1} & a_{2,2} & a_{2,3} \\ a_{3,1} & a_{3,2} & a_{3,3} \end{vmatrix} = a_{1,1}\begin{vmatrix} a_{2,2} & a_{2,3} \\ a_{3,2} & a_{3,3} \end{vmatrix} - a_{1,2}\begin{vmatrix} a_{2,1} & a_{2,3} \\ a_{3,1} & a_{3,3} \end{vmatrix} + a_{1,3}\begin{vmatrix} a_{2,1} & a_{2,2} \\ a_{3,1} & a_{3,2} \end{vmatrix}$$

This produces the following:

$$\det(\mathbf{A}) = a_{1,1}a_{2,2}a_{3,3} + a_{1,2}a_{2,3}a_{3,1} + a_{1,3}a_{2,1}a_{3,2} - a_{1,1}a_{2,3}a_{3,2} - a_{1,2}a_{2,1}a_{3,3} - a_{1,3}a_{2,2}a_{3,1}$$

I know that probably looks more intimidating, but it's really not. Take a moment to look carefully at what we did and how this would work for a larger *n×n* matrix.

If we have an *n×n* matrix and if it can be triangularly factorized (upper or lower), then its determinant will be the product of all the pivot values. For the sake of simplicity, we will represent all triangularly factorizable matrices with *T*. Therefore, the determinant can be written like so:

$$\det(\mathbf{T}) = \prod_{i=1}^{n} \mathbf{T}_{i,i}$$

Looking at the preceding 3×3 matrix example, I'm sure you've figured out that computing the determinant for matrices where *n* > 3 is quite a lengthy process. Luckily, there is a way in which we can simplify the calculation, and this is where the Laplace expansion comes to the rescue.

When we want to find the determinant of an n×n matrix, the Laplace expansion finds the determinant of (n×1)×(n×1) matrices and does so repeatedly until we get to 2×2 matrices. In general, we can calculate the determinant of an n×n matrix using 2×2 matrices.

Let's again take an *n*-dimensional square matrix, where $\mathbf{A} \in \mathbb{R}^{n \times n}$. We then expand for all $i = 1, \cdots, n$, as follows:

- Expansion along row *i*:

$$\det(\mathbf{A}) = \sum_{j=1}^{n}(-1)^{i+j}a_{i,j}\det(\mathbf{A}_{i,j})$$

- Expansion along row *j*:

$$\det(\mathbf{A}) = \sum_{j=1}^{n}(-1)^{i+j}a_{j,i}\det(\mathbf{A}_{j,i})$$

And $\mathbf{A}_{i,j} \in \mathbb{R}^{(n-1)\times(n-1)}$ is a sub-matrix of $\mathbf{A} \in \mathbb{R}^{n \times n}$, which we get after removing row *i* and column *j*.

For example, we have a 3x3 matrix, as follows:

$$\mathbf{A} = \begin{bmatrix} 1 & 4 & 3 \\ 3 & 2 & 1 \\ 2 & 0 & 1 \end{bmatrix}$$

We want to find its determinant using the Laplace expansion along the first row. This results in the following:

$$\begin{vmatrix} 1 & 4 & 3 \\ 3 & 2 & 1 \\ 2 & 0 & 1 \end{vmatrix} = (-1)^{1+1} \times 1 \begin{vmatrix} 2 & 1 \\ 0 & 1 \end{vmatrix} + (-1)^{1+2} \times 4 \begin{vmatrix} 3 & 1 \\ 2 & 1 \end{vmatrix} + (-1)^{1+3} \times 3 \begin{vmatrix} 3 & 2 \\ 2 & 0 \end{vmatrix}$$

We can now use the preceding equation from the 2x2 case and calculate the determinant for A, as follows:

$$1(2 - 0) - 4(3 - 2) + 3(-4) = -14$$

Here are some of the very important properties of determinants that are important to know:

- $\det(I) = 1$
- $\det(\mathbf{A}^T) = \det(\mathbf{A})$
- $\det(\mathbf{AB}) = \det(\mathbf{A})\det(\mathbf{B})$
- $\det(\mathbf{A}^{-1}) = \det(\mathbf{A})^{-1}$
- $\det(\alpha\mathbf{A}) = \alpha^n \det(\mathbf{A})$

There is one other additional property of the determinant, and it is that we can use it to find the volume of an object in $\mathbb{R}^n$ whose vertices are formed by the column vectors in the matrix.

As an example, let's take a parallelogram in $\mathbb{R}^2$ with the vectors $a = \begin{bmatrix} 4 \\ 0 \end{bmatrix}$ and $b = \begin{bmatrix} 0 \\ 3 \end{bmatrix}$. By taking the determinant of the 2x2 matrix, we find the area of the shape (we can only find the volume for objects in $\mathbb{R}^3$ or higher), as follows:

$$\text{area} = |\det(\mathbf{A})| = 4 \times 3 - 0 \times 0 = 12$$

You are welcome to try it for any 3x3 matrix for yourselves as practice.

Eigenvalues and eigenvectors

Let's imagine an arbitrary real n×n matrix, A. It is very possible that when we apply this matrix to some vector, they are scaled by a constant value. If this is the case, we say that the nonzero n-dimensional vector is an eigenvector of A, and it corresponds to an eigenvalue λ. We write this as follows:

$$\mathbf{Ax} = \lambda\mathbf{x}$$

Note: The zero vector (0) cannot be an eigenvector of A, since $A0 = 0$ = $\lambda0$ for all λ.

Let's consider again a matrix A that has an eigenvector $\mathbf{x}$ and a corresponding eigenvalue λ. Then, the following rules will apply:

- If we have a matrix A and it has been shifted from its current position to $\mathbf{A} + \gamma I$, then it has the eigenvector $\mathbf{x}$ and the corresponding eigenvalue $\lambda + \gamma$, for all $\gamma \in \mathbb{R}$, so that $(\mathbf{A} + \gamma I)\mathbf{x} = (\lambda + \gamma)\mathbf{x}$.
- If the matrix A is invertible, then $\mathbf{x}$ is also an eigenvector of the inverse of the matrix, $\mathbf{A}^{-1}$, with the corresponding eigenvalue λ^{-1}.
- $\mathbf{A}^k\mathbf{x} = \lambda^k\mathbf{x}$ for any $k \in \mathbb{Z}$.

We know from earlier in the chapter that whenever we multiply a matrix and a vector, the direction of the vector is changed, but this is not the case with eigenvectors. They are in the same direction as A, and thus $\mathbf{x}$ remains unchanged. The eigenvalue, being a scalar value, tells us whether the eigenvector is being scaled, and if so, how much, as well as if the direction of the vector has changed.

Another very fascinating property the determinant has is that it is equivalent to the product of the eigenvalues of the matrix, and it is written as follows:

$$\det(\mathbf{A}) = \prod_i \lambda_i(\mathbf{A})$$

But this isn't the only relation that the determinant has with eigenvalues. We can rewrite $\mathbf{Ax} = \lambda\mathbf{x}$ in the form $(\mathbf{A} - \lambda I)\mathbf{x} = 0$. And since this is equal to zero, this means it is a non-invertible matrix, and therefore its determinant too must be equal to zero. Using this, we can use the determinant to find the eigenvalues. Let's see how.

Suppose we have $\mathbf{A} \in \mathbb{R}^{2 \times 2}$. Then, its determinant is shown as follows:

$$\det(\mathbf{A} - \lambda I) = \begin{vmatrix} a - \lambda & b \\ c & d - \lambda \end{vmatrix} = (a - \lambda)(d - \lambda) - bc = 0$$

We can rewrite this as the following quadratic equation:

$$\det(\mathbf{A} - \lambda I) = \lambda^2 - (a + d)\lambda + (ad - bc) = 0$$

We know that the quadratic equation will give us both the eigenvalues λ_1, λ_2. So, we plug our values into the quadratic formula and get our roots.

Another interesting property is that when we have triangular matrices such as the ones we found earlier in this chapter, their eigenvalues are the pivot values. So, if we want to find the determinant of a triangular matrix, then all we have to do is find the product of all the entries along the diagonal.

Trace

Given an $n \times n$ matrix A, the sum of all the entries on the diagonal is called the **trace**. We write it like so:

$$\text{tr}(\mathbf{A}) = \sum_{i=1}^{n} A_{i,i}$$

The following are four important properties of the trace:

- $\text{tr}(\mathbf{A} + \mathbf{B}) = \text{tr}(\mathbf{A}) + \text{tr}(\mathbf{B})$
- $\text{tr}(\alpha \mathbf{A}) = \alpha \text{tr}(\mathbf{A})$
- $\text{tr}(\mathbf{A}^{\mathrm{T}}) = \text{tr}(\mathbf{A})$
- $\text{tr}(\mathbf{ABCD}) = \text{tr}(\mathbf{CDAB}) = \text{tr}(\mathbf{DABC}) = \text{tr}(\mathbf{BCDA})$

A very interesting property of the trace is that it is equal to the sum of its eigenvalues, so that the following applies:

$$\text{tr}(\mathbf{A}) = \sum_{i} \lambda_i(\mathbf{A})$$

Orthogonal matrices

The concept of orthogonality arises frequently in linear algebra. It's really just a fancy word for perpendicularity, except it goes beyond two dimensions or a pair of vectors.

But to get an understanding, let's start with two column vectors $\mathbf{x}, \mathbf{y} \in \mathbb{R}^n$. If they are orthogonal, then the following holds:

$$\mathbf{x}^T \mathbf{y} = x_1 y_1 + x_2 y_2 + \cdots + x_n y_n = 0.$$

Orthogonal matrices are a special kind of matrix where the columns are pairwise orthonormal. What this means is that we have a matrix $\mathbf{Q} \in \mathbb{R}^{n \times n}$ with the following property:

$$\mathbf{Q}^T \mathbf{Q} = \mathbf{Q} \mathbf{Q}^T = I$$

Then, we can deduce that $\mathbf{Q}^T = \mathbf{Q}^{-1}$ (that is, the transpose of Q is also the inverse of Q).

As with other types of matrices, orthogonal matrices have some special properties.

Firstly, they preserve inner products, so that the following applies:

$$(\mathbf{Qx})^T (\mathbf{Qy}) = \mathbf{x}^T \mathbf{Q}^T \mathbf{Qy} = \mathbf{x}^T I \mathbf{y} = \mathbf{x}^T \mathbf{y}.$$

This brings us to the second property, which states that 2-norms are preserved for orthogonal matrices, which we see as follows:

$$\|\mathbf{Qx}\|_2 = \sqrt{(\mathbf{Qx})^T (\mathbf{Qx})} = \sqrt{\mathbf{x}^T \mathbf{x}} = \|\mathbf{x}\|_2$$

When multiplying by orthogonal matrices, you can think of it as a transformation that preserves length, but the vector may be rotated about the origin by some degree.

The most well-known orthogonal matrix that is also orthonormal is a special matrix we have dealt with a few times already. It is the identity matrix *I*, and since it represents a unit of length in the direction of axes, we generally refer to it as the standard basis.

Diagonalization and symmetric matrices

Let's suppose we have a matrix $\mathbf{A} \in \mathbb{R}^{n \times n}$ that has n eigenvectors. We put these vectors into a matrix X that is invertible and multiply the two matrices. This gives us the following:

$$\mathbf{AX} = \mathbf{A}\begin{bmatrix} \mathbf{x}_1 & \mathbf{x}_2 & \cdots & \mathbf{x}_n \end{bmatrix} = \begin{bmatrix} \mathbf{Ax}_1 & \mathbf{Ax}_2 & \cdots & \mathbf{Ax}_n \end{bmatrix}$$

We know from $\mathbf{Ax} = \lambda \mathbf{x}$ that when dealing with matrices, this becomes $\mathbf{AX} = \mathbf{X\Lambda}$, where $\mathbf{\Lambda} = \mathrm{diag}(\lambda_1, \cdots, \lambda_n)$ and each x_i has a unique λ_i. Therefore, $\mathbf{A} = \mathbf{X\Lambda X}^{-1}$.

Let's move on to symmetric matrices. These are special matrices that, when transposed, are the same as the original, implying that $\mathbf{A} = \mathbf{A}^{\mathrm{T}}$ and for all (i, j), $\mathbf{A}_{i,j} = \mathbf{A}_{j,i}$. This may seem rather trivial, but its implications are rather strong.

The spectral theorem states that if a matrix $\mathbf{A} \in \mathbb{R}^{n \times n}$ is a symmetric matrix, then there exists an orthonormal basis for $\mathbb{R}^n$, which contains the eigenvectors of A.

This theorem is important to us because it allows us to factorize symmetric matrices. We call this **spectral decomposition** (also sometimes referred to as **Eigendecomposition**).

Suppose we have an orthogonal matrix Q, with the orthonormal basis of eigenvectors $\mathbf{q}_1, \cdots, \mathbf{q}_n$ and $\mathbf{\Lambda} = \mathrm{diag}(\lambda_1, \cdots, \lambda_n)$ being the matrix with corresponding eigenvalues.

From earlier, we know that $\mathbf{Aq}_i = \lambda_i \mathbf{q}_i$ for all $I = 1, \cdots, n$; therefore, we have the following:

$$\mathbf{AQ} = \mathbf{Q\Lambda}$$

 Note: Λ comes after Q because it is a diagonal matrix, and the λ_is need to multiply the individual columns of Q.

By multiplying both sides by Q^T, we get the following result:

$$\mathbf{A} = \mathbf{Q\Lambda Q}^{\mathrm{T}}$$

Singular value decomposition

Singular Value Decomposition (SVD) is widely used in linear algebra and is known for its strength, particularly arising from the fact that every matrix has an SVD. It looks like this:

$$\mathbf{A} = \mathbf{U}\mathbf{\Sigma}\mathbf{V}^{\mathrm{T}}$$

For our purposes, let's suppose $\mathbf{A} \in \mathbb{R}^{m \times n}$, $\mathbf{U} \in \mathbb{R}^{m \times m}$, $\mathbf{\Sigma} \in \mathbb{R}^{m \times n}$, and $\mathbf{V} \in \mathbb{R}^{n \times n}$, and that U, V are orthogonal matrices, whereas Σ is a matrix that contains singular values (denoted by σ_i) of A along the diagonal.

Σ in the preceding equation looks like this:

$$\mathbf{A} = \mathbf{U} \begin{bmatrix} \sigma_1 & \cdots & 0 \\ \vdots & \ddots & \vdots \\ 0 & \cdots & \sigma_n \end{bmatrix} \mathbf{V}^{\mathrm{T}}$$

We can also write the SVD like so:

$$\mathbf{A} = \sum_{i=1}^{r} \sigma_i \mathbf{u}_i \mathbf{v}_i^{\mathrm{T}}$$

Here, u_i, v_i are the column vectors of U, V.

Cholesky decomposition

As I'm sure you've figured out by now, there is more than one way to factorize a matrix, and there are special methods for special matrices.

The Cholesky decomposition is square root-like and works only on symmetric positive definite matrices.

This works by factorizing A into the form LL^T. Here, L, as before, is a lower triangular matrix.

Do develop some intuition. It looks like this:

$$
\begin{bmatrix} a_{1,1} & a_{1,2} & \cdots & a_{1,n} \\ a_{2,1} & a_{2,2} & \cdots & a_{2,n} \\ \vdots & \vdots & \ddots & \vdots \\ a_{n,1} & a_{n,2} & \cdots & a_{n,n} \end{bmatrix} = \begin{bmatrix} l_{1,1} & 0 & \cdots & 0 \\ l_{2,1} & l_{2,2} & \cdots & 0 \\ \vdots & \vdots & \ddots & \vdots \\ l_{n,1} & l_{n,2} & \cdots & l_{n,n} \end{bmatrix} \begin{bmatrix} l_{1,1} & l_{1,2} & \cdots & l_{1,n} \\ 0 & l_{2,2} & \cdots & l_{2,n} \\ \vdots & \vdots & \ddots & \vdots \\ 0 & 0 & \cdots & l_{n,n} \end{bmatrix}
$$

However, here, L is called a **Cholesky factor**.

Let's take a look at the case where $\mathbf{A} \in \mathbb{R}^{3 \times 3}$.

We know from the preceding matrix that $\mathbf{A} = \mathbf{L}\mathbf{L}^{\mathrm{T}}$; therefore, we have the following:

$$
\begin{bmatrix} a_{1,1} & a_{2,1} & a_{3,1} \\ a_{2,1} & a_{2,2} & a_{3,2} \\ a_{3,1} & a_{3,2} & a_{3,3} \end{bmatrix} = \begin{bmatrix} l_{1,1} & 0 & 0 \\ l_{2,1} & l_{2,2} & 0 \\ l_{3,1} & l_{3,2} & l_{3,3} \end{bmatrix} \begin{bmatrix} l_{1,1} & l_{2,1} & l_{3,1} \\ 0 & l_{2,2} & l_{3,2} \\ 0 & 0 & l_{3,3} \end{bmatrix}
$$

Let's multiply the upper and lower triangular matrices on the right, as follows:

$$
\mathbf{A} = \begin{bmatrix} l_{1,1}^2 & l_{2,1}l_{1,1} & l_{3,1}l_{1,1} \\ l_{2,1}l_{1,1} & l_{2,1}^2 l_{2,2}^2 & l_{3,1}l_{2,1} + l_{3,2}l_{2,2} \\ l_{3,1}l_{1,1} & l_{3,1}l_{2,1} + l_{3,2}l_{2,2} & l_{3,1}^2 + l_{3,2}^2 + l_{3,3}^2 \end{bmatrix}
$$

Writing out A fully and equating it to our preceding matrix gives us the following:

$$
\begin{bmatrix} a_{1,1} & a_{2,1} & a_{3,1} \\ a_{2,1} & a_{2,2} & a_{3,2} \\ a_{3,1} & a_{3,2} & a_{3,3} \end{bmatrix} = \begin{bmatrix} l_{1,1}^2 & l_{2,1}l_{1,1} & l_{3,1}l_{1,1} \\ l_{2,1}l_{1,1} & l_{2,1}^2 l_{2,2}^2 & l_{3,1}l_{2,1} + l_{3,2}l_{2,2} \\ l_{3,1}l_{1,1} & l_{3,1}l_{2,1} + l_{3,2}l_{2,2} & l_{3,1}^2 + l_{3,2}^2 + l_{3,3}^2 \end{bmatrix}
$$

We can then compare, element-wise, the corresponding entries of A and LL^T and solve algebraically for $l_{i,j}$ as follows:

$$l_{1,1} = \sqrt{a_{1,1}}$$

$$l_{2,1} = \frac{1}{l_{1,1}} a_{2,1}$$

$$l_{2,2} = \sqrt{a_{2,2} - l_{2,1}^2}$$

$$l_{3,1} = \frac{1}{l_{1,1}} a_{3,1}$$

$$l_{3,2} = \frac{1}{l_{2,2}} (a_{3,2} - l_{3,1} l_{2,1})$$

$$l_{3,3} = \sqrt{a_{3,3} - l_{3,1}^2 + l_{3,2}^2}$$

We can repeat this process for any symmetric positive definite matrix, and compute the $l_{i,j}$ values given $a_{i,j}$.

Summary

With this, we conclude our chapter on linear algebra. So far, we have learned all the fundamental concepts of linear algebra, such as matrix multiplication and factorization, that will lead you on your way to gaining a deep understanding of how **deep neural networks (DNNs)** work and are designed, and what it is that makes them so powerful.

In the next chapter, we will be learning about calculus and will combine it with the concepts learned earlier on in this chapter to understand vector calculus.

2
Vector Calculus

Most of you will likely have had some exposure to calculus in the past, be it in high school, college, or university, and were likely hoping to never have to deal with it again. However, calculus is not only one of the most profound discoveries in mathematics; it also plays a vital role in deep learning.

In this chapter, we will start by introducing core concepts of calculus using single variable calculus, and then we will move on to multivariable calculus and extend everything we learned in multivariable calculus to gain an understanding of vector calculus and its relation to deep learning.

This chapter will cover the following topics:

- Single variable calculus
- Multivariable calculus
- Vector calculus

Single variable calculus

At its core, calculus is nothing more than the study of relationships and change. Having a keen grasp of calculus will help you better understand how deep learning algorithms work and how to make them work better for you as a practitioner.

Let's move on to understanding what makes calculus such a powerful tool. We start with single variable calculus, which is about functions that take in a single input and produce a single output.

Derivatives

To start with, let's imagine a straight line with the following equation:

$$y = \pm mx \ (\pm b)$$

In the equation, the following aspects apply:

- y is a function of x, often written simply as $f(x)$ (which is the notation we will be predominantly using in the remainder of the book). In the preceding equation, the output value y is dependent on the input value x.
- The m value is the gradient, which tells us how steep the straight line is, or what its rate of change is (that is, how much does a change in the x value affect the y value).
- The $\pm$ value tells us whether the line is moving upward or downward.
- The $\pm b$ value tells us by how much the line is above or below the origin.
- The m and b values in a straight line are constant throughout.

Now that you know what the equation of a straight line looks like, you're probably wondering how to find it for an arbitrary straight line.

We start by first picking two points, (x_1, y_1) and (x_2, y_2), that lay on the line, and plug their values into the formula $m = \dfrac{y_2 - y_1}{x_2 - x_1}$. After having found the value for m, we find the value of b by using the line equation and plugging into it the value for m and one (x, y) point on the line, and solve for b.

Well, that was very simple and straightforward. However, there are far more complex equations out there that aren't as straightforward—those that relate to curves (nonlinear functions), as illustrated in the following image:

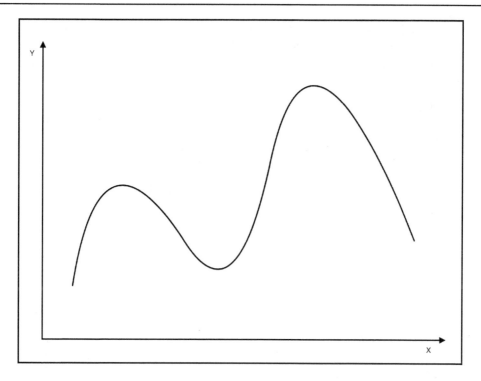

Imagine a picture of a couple of hills or camel humps. If you trace the surface of them, you will have a curve, and as you may have no doubt noticed, they go up and then down and then back up, and the process repeats itself.

From the preceding image of the curve, you can easily tell that the gradient is not constant, as it was in the previous example with the straight line. We could sketch straight lines along the curve and calculate their slopes to understand how the curve moves. However, there is a simpler method than this tedious one.

At the very core of calculus are two concepts, as follows:

- **Differentiation** helps us understand how much a function output changes with respect to changing input.
- **Integration** helps us understand the impact of this change in inputs between certain points.

We will begin initially by taking an in-depth look at differentiation. The primary equation for finding the derivative of a function is shown here:

$$\frac{df}{dx} = f'(x) = \lim_{h \to 0} \frac{f(x+h) - f(x)}{h}$$

I know there are a few new symbols here and it looks complicated, but it's really very simple. What this equation is doing is finding the derivative of the function *f* with respect to the variable in the denominator *x*. This isn't too different from the earlier equation we saw (which we used to calculate the gradient of a straight line). We subtract two values, *f(x+h)* and *f(x)*, and divide it by its difference, *h*. But what does $\lim_{h\to 0}$ have to do with this? This tells us that we want the two points on the curve to be as close to each other as possible so that when we are sketching the gradient on the curve, it looks like a straight line at one point on the curve. This allows us to better visualize and understand the effect of the change, as can be seen in the following screenshot:

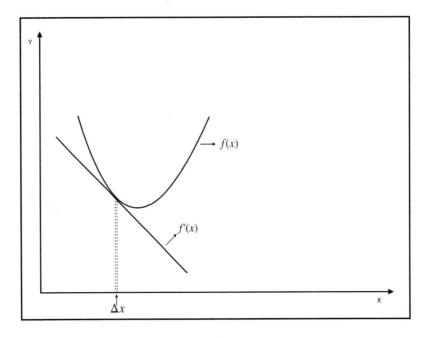

See the following example:

$$f(x) = 4x - 7$$
$$f'(x) = \lim_{h\to 0} \frac{[4(x+h) - 7] - [4(x) - 7]}{h}$$
$$f'(x) = \lim_{h\to 0} \frac{4x + 4h - 7 - 4x + 7}{h}$$
$$f'(x) = \lim_{h\to 0} \frac{4h}{h}$$
$$f'(x) = 4$$

Now that we understand what a derivative is and how to find it for any function, let's move on to some important rules of differentiation.

Sum rule

The sum rule states that the derivative of the sum of two functions is the same as the sum of the individual derivatives of the two functions, as can be seen in the following equation:

$$\frac{d}{dx}(f(x) + g(x)) = \frac{df(x)}{dx} + \frac{dg(x)}{dx}$$

Let's suppose we have $f(x) = 3x^4 + 12x^2 + 8$ and $g(x) = 2x^2 - 11x + 2$.

From this, we can see that the following equation,

$\frac{df(x)}{dx} + \frac{dg(x)}{dx} = (12x^3 + 24x) + (4x - 11) = 12x^3 + 28x - 11$, is the same as this one:

$\frac{d}{dx}(f(x) + g(x)) = \frac{d}{dx}(3x^4 + 14x^2 - 11x + 10) = 12x^3 + 28x - 11$.

Power rule

The power rule helps to find the derivative of a function where the variable has an exponent. Simply put, you multiply the power by the constant in front of the variable, and reduce the power by 1. Let's see what an example of this looks like, using the power rule $f'(x) = 2 \times 4x^{2-1} = 8x$, as follows:

$$f(x) = 4x^2$$
$$f'(x) = \lim_{h \to 0} \frac{4(x+h)^2 - 4(x)^2}{h}$$
$$f'(x) = \lim_{h \to 0} \frac{4(x^2 + 2xh + h^2) - 4(x^2)}{h}$$
$$f'(x) = \lim_{h \to 0} \frac{4x^2 + 8xh + 4h^2 - 4x^2}{h}$$
$$f'(x) = \lim_{h \to 0} \frac{8xh + 4h^2}{h}$$
$$f'(x) = \lim_{h \to 0} 8x + 4h$$
$$f'(x) = 8x$$

 Note that not every function will have a derivative, at least not in the function's domain.

There are certain functions—such as $f(x) = \frac{1}{x}$ or $f(x) = e^x$ —that are not as straightforward as the ones we saw earlier. The function $f(x) = \frac{1}{x}$ is not differentiable at x = 0 because its value is undefined. This is known as **discontinuity**.

The same applies to $f(x) = e^x$; however, e (known as **Euler's number**) has a very interesting property whereby the function is equal to its derivative—that is, $f(x) = f'(x)$.

Trigonometric functions

In high school or university, you likely studied trigonometry and encountered the sine, cosine, and tangent functions. More important to us are the sine and cosine functions, which you will encounter often and which we will look at here. These functions can be seen in the following image:

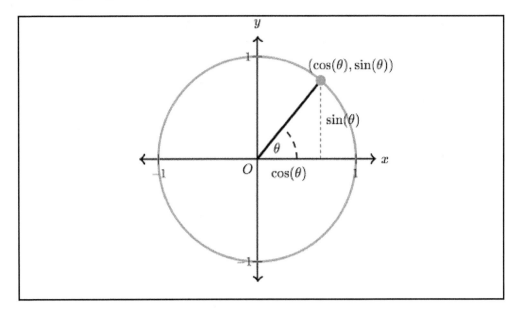

Here, sine is $f(x) = \sin(x)$ and cosine is $f(x) = \cos(x)$.

The sine and cosine functions are related, and the derivative will show us how.

If $y = \sin(x)$, then $\dfrac{dy}{dx} = \cos(x)$. However, if $y = \cos(x)$, then $\dfrac{dy}{dx} = -\sin(x)$.

The derivatives create a loop, which we can see as follows:

$$\sin(x) \xrightarrow{\frac{d}{dx}} \cos(x) \xrightarrow{\frac{d}{dx}} -\sin(x) \xrightarrow{\frac{d}{dx}} -\cos(x) \xrightarrow{\frac{d}{dx}} \sin(x)$$

First and second derivatives

Now that we know how to find the derivative of a function, it is important to know that we can take the derivative more than once.

The first derivative, as we know, gives us the gradient (slope of the tangent line) of a function at any given point (*x*) on the curve—in other words, whether the curve's altitude (that is, *y* or *f(x)*) is increasing or decreasing. A positive slope tells us *f(x)* is increasing as *x* increases and a negative slope tells us *f(x)* is decreasing as *x* increases, and a slope of 0 tells us nothing about the curve's direction, other than that it is likely at a turning point (local minimum or local maximum). This can be written as follows:

- If $\frac{d}{dx} f(t) > 0$, then *f(x)* is increasing at *x = t*.
- If $\frac{d}{dx} f(t) < 0$, then *f(x)* is decreasing at *x = t*.
- If $\frac{d}{dx} f(t) = 0$, then *x=t* is a critical point of *f(x)*.

For example, let $f(x) = 4x^3 - 12x^2 + 9x - 4$. The derivative of this function is shown here:

$$\frac{dy}{dx} = 12x^2 - 24x + 9$$

At *x = 0*, the derivative is 9, which tells us the function is increasing at this point. But at *x = 1* the derivative is -3 telling us that the function is decreasing at this point.

The second derivative is the derivative of the derivative of the function. We write this as $f''(x)$ or $\frac{d^2y}{dx^2}$. As before, where the first derivative told us whether the function was increasing or decreasing, the second derivative gives us the same information about the first derivative—whether it is increasing or decreasing.

If the second derivative is positive, then as *x* increases, the first derivative is increasing; and if the second derivative is negative, then as *x* increases, the first derivative is decreasing.

To help us visualize this, when the second derivative is positive, the curve is concave up (parabola open upward) at a point, whereas when it is negative, the curve is concave down (parabola open downward). And as before, when the second derivative is equal to zero, we learn nothing new. This point could be a local maximum, a local minimum, or an inflection point. This is written as follows:

- If $\frac{d^2}{dx^2} f(t) > 0$, then $f(x)$ is concave up at $x=t$.

- If $\frac{d^2}{dx^2} f(t) < 0$, then $f(x)$ is concave down at $x=t$.

- If $\frac{d^2}{dx^2} f(t) = 0$, then at $x=t$ we obtain no new information about $f(x)$.

For example, let's take the second derivative of the same function we used, as follows:

$$\frac{d^2 y}{dx^2} = 24x - 24$$

At $x = 0$, the second derivative is -24, which tells us the function is concave down here. But at $x = 2$, it is equal to 24, telling us the function is concave up.

Earlier, we learned that when x is a critical point of a function we learn nothing new about the function at that point, but we can use it to find out whether it is a local maximum or a local minimum. These rules can be written as follows:

- If $\frac{d}{dx} f(t) = 0$ and $\frac{d^2}{dx^2} f(t) > 0$, then $f(x)$ has a local minimum at $x=t$.

- If $\frac{d}{dx} f(t) = 0$ and $\frac{d^2}{dx^2} f(t) < 0$, then $f(x)$ has a local maximum at $x=t$.

- If $\frac{d}{dx} f(t) = 0$ and $\frac{d^2}{dx^2} f(t) = 0$, then at $x=t$ we learn nothing new about $f(x)$.

Product rule

The product rule gives us a straightforward method to find the derivative of the product of two functions. Let's take two arbitrary functions, $f(x)$ and $g(x)$, and multiply them. So, $y = f(x)g(x)$. The derivative is $\frac{dy}{dx} = f(x)g'(x) + f'(x)g(x)$.

Let's explore this in more detail to understand how this works. Have a look at the following equation:

$$\lim_{dx \to 0} \frac{dy}{dx} = \lim_{dx \to 0} \frac{f(x)(g(x+dx) - g(x)) + (f(x+dx) - f(x))g(x)}{dx}$$

We can rewrite the derivative, as follows:

$$\lim_{dx \to 0} f(x) \frac{(g(x+dx) - g(x))}{dx} + g(x) \frac{(f(x+dx) - f(x))}{dx}$$

This can be further simplified as $\lim_{x \to 0} f(x)g'(x) + f'(x)g(x)$, which is the same as before.

Quotient rule

The quotient rule allows us to find the derivative of a function that is being divided by another function. This can be derived from the product rule. As before, we take two functions $f(x)$ and $g(x)$, but now, we will divide them. So, $y = \frac{f(x)}{g(x)}$. The derivative is $\frac{dy}{dx} = \frac{f(x)g'(x) - f'(x)g(x)}{g(x)^2}$.

Suppose we have $f(x) = 4x^2 + 7$ and $g(x) = 2x^3 - 11$. Then, we have the following:

$$y = \frac{f(x)}{g(x)} = \frac{4x^2 + 7}{2x^3 - 11}$$

By finding the derivatives of f(x) and g(x) and plugging them into the preceding equation, we get the following:

$$\frac{dy}{dx} = \frac{(4x^2 + 7)(6x^2) - (2x^3 - 11)(8x)}{(2x^3 - 11)^2}$$

If we expand it, we find the derivative.

Chain rule

The chain rule applies to functions that take in another function as input. Let's consider $F(x) = f(g(x))$, which is often written as $(f \circ g)(x)$ and read as f of g of x. This means that the output of $g(x)$ will become the input to the function f.

The derivative of this will be written as follows:

$$\frac{dF}{dx} = \frac{df}{dg} \times \frac{dg}{dx}$$

This is the same as $F'(x) = f'(g(x))g'(x)$.

For example, suppose we have $f(g) = 7g^2 - 9$ and $g(x) = e^{x^2}$. We then differentiate the two functions and get $f'(g) = 14g$ and $g'(x) = 2xe^{x^2}$.

By plugging this into the preceding formula, we get $28xe^{2x^2}$.

Antiderivative

We now know what derivatives are and how to find them, but now, suppose we know the rate of change (*F*) of the population (*f*), and we want to find what the population will be at some point in time. What we have to do is find a function *F* whose derivative is *f*. This is known as the **antiderivative**, and we define it formally as a function *F* is called an antiderivative of *f* on $[a, b]$ if $F'(x) = f(x)$ for all $a \leq x \leq b$.

Suppose we have a function $f(x) = x^n$, then $F(x) = \frac{1}{n+1}x^{n+1} + c$ (where *c* is some constant), from which we can confirm that $F'(x) = x^n = f(x)$.

The following table shows some important functions and their antiderivatives that we will encounter often:

Function	Antiderivative
$cf(x)$	$cF(x)$
$f(x) + g(x)$	$F(x) + G(x)$
x^n	$\dfrac{x^{n+1}}{n+1}$
$\dfrac{1}{x}$	$\ln|x|$
e^x	e^x
$\cos x$	$\sin x$
$\sin x$	$-\cos x$

$\dfrac{1}{\sqrt{1-x^2}}$	$\sin^{-1} x$
$\dfrac{1}{1+x^2}$	$\tan^{-1} x$

Let's suppose we have the following function:

$$f'(x) = 4\sin x + \frac{2x^5 - \sqrt{x}}{x}$$

We want to find its antiderivative. I know this probably looks like a difficult equation, but by using the preceding table, we can make this very easy for ourselves. Let's see how.

First, we rewrite the function so it becomes the following:

$$f'(x) = 4\sin x + 2x^4 - x^{-\frac{1}{2}}$$

And so, the antiderivative is as follows:

$$f(x) = 4(-\cos x) + 2\frac{x^5}{5} - \frac{x^{\frac{1}{2}}}{\frac{1}{2}} + c$$

To make things easier, we rewrite this, as follows:

$$f(x) = -4\cos x + \frac{2}{5}x^5 - 2\sqrt{x} + c$$

And there you have it.

You may now be wondering whether or not we can find what the value of c is, and if so, how. Let's go through another example, and see how.

Suppose we have a function that is the second derivative, and we want to find the antiderivative of the antiderivative—that is, the original function. We have the following:

$$f''(x) = 12x^2 + 6x - 4 \text{ and } f(0) = 4 \text{ and } f(1) = 1$$

Then, the first antiderivative is as follows:

$$f'(x) = 4x^3 + 3x^2 - 4x + c$$

And so, the second antiderivative is as follows:

$$f(x) = x^4 + x^3 - 2x^2 + cx + d$$

Here, we want to find the values of c and d. We can do this simply by plugging in the preceding values and solving for the unknowns, as follows:

$$f(0) = (0)^4 + (0)^3 - 2(0)^2 + c(0) + d = 4;\text{ therefore, } d = 4$$

We can also do this:

$$f(1) = (1)^4 + (1)^3 - 2(1)^2 + c(1) + 4 = 1;\text{ therefore, } c = -3$$

Thus, our function looks like this:

$$f(x) = x^4 + x^3 - 2x^2 - 3x + 4$$

Integrals

So far, we have studied derivatives, which is a method for extracting information about the rate of change of a function. But as you may have realized, integration is the reverse of the earlier problems.

In integration, we find the area underneath a curve. For example, if we have a car and our function gives us its velocity, the area under the curve will give us the distance it has traveled between two points.

Let's suppose we have the curve $y = f(x)$, and the area under the curve between $x = a$ (the lower limit) and $x = b$ (the upper limit, also written as [a, b]) is S. Then, we have the following:

$$S = \int_a^b f(x)\mathrm{d}x$$

The diagramatical representation of the curve is as follows:

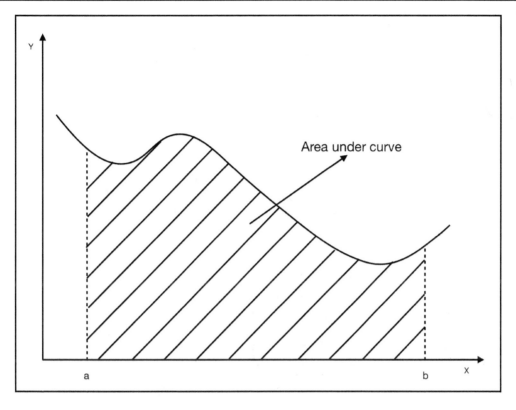

This can also be written as follows:

$$\lim_{n \to \infty} \sum_{i=1}^{n} f(x_i^*)\triangle x = \lim_{n \to \infty} \left[f(x_1^*)\triangle x + f(x_2^*)\triangle x + \cdots + f(x_n^*)\triangle x \right]$$

In the preceding function, the following applies: $\triangle x = \dfrac{b-a}{n}$, and x_i^* is in the subinterval $[x_{i-1}, x_i]$.

The function looks like this:

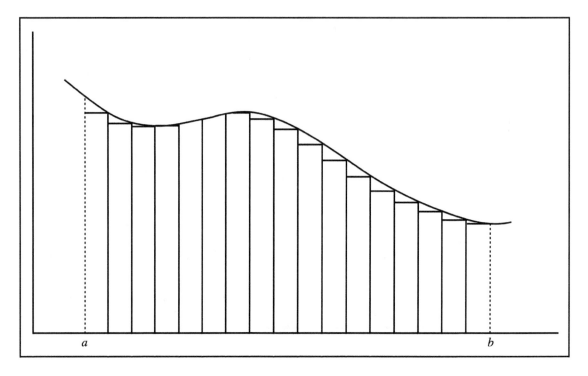

The integral gives us an approximation of the area under the curve such that for some, ε > 0 (ε is assumed to be a small value), the following formula applies:

$$\left| \int_a^b f(x)\mathrm{d}x - \sum_{i=1}^n f(x_i^*)\triangle x \right| < \epsilon$$

Now, let's suppose our function lies both above and below the x axis, thus taking on positive and negative values, like so:

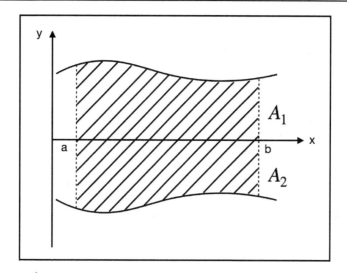

As we can see from the preceding screenshot, the portions above the x axis (A_1) have a positive area, and the portions below the x axis (A_2) have a negative area. Therefore, the following formula applies:

$$S = \int_a^b f(x)\mathrm{d}x = A_1 - A_2$$

Working with sums is an important part of evaluating integrals, and understanding this requires some new rules for sums. Look at the following examples:

- $$\sum_{i=1}^{n} i = \frac{n(n+1)}{2}$$

- $$\sum_{i=1}^{n} i^2 = \frac{n(n+1)(2n+1)}{6}$$

- $$\sum_{i=1}^{n} i^3 = \left[\frac{n(n+1)}{2}\right]^2$$

- $$\sum_{i=1}^{n} c = nc$$

$$\sum_{i=1}^{n} ca_i = c \sum_{i=1}^{n} a_i$$

$$\sum_{i=1}^{n} (a_i + b_i) = \sum_{i=1}^{n} a_i + \sum_{i=1}^{n} b_i$$

$$\sum_{i=1}^{n} (a_i - b_i) = \sum_{i=1}^{n} a_i - \sum_{i=1}^{n} b_i$$

Now, let's explore some of the important properties of integrals, which will help us as we go deeper into the chapter. Look at the following examples:

$$\int_{a}^{b} f(x)dx = - \int_{b}^{a} f(x)dx$$

$$\int_{a}^{b} f(x)dx = 0 \quad \text{, when } a = b$$

$$\int_{a}^{b} c\,dx = c(b - a) \quad \text{, where } c \text{ is a constant}$$

$$\int_{a}^{b} [f(x) + g(x)]dx = \int_{a}^{b} f(x)dx + \int_{a}^{b} g(x)dx$$

$$\int_{a}^{b} [f(x) - g(x)]dx = \int_{a}^{b} f(x)dx - \int_{a}^{b} g(x)dx$$

$$\int_{a}^{b} c\,f(x)dx = c \int_{a}^{b} f(x)dx$$

Now, suppose we have the function $y = f(x)$, which looks like this:

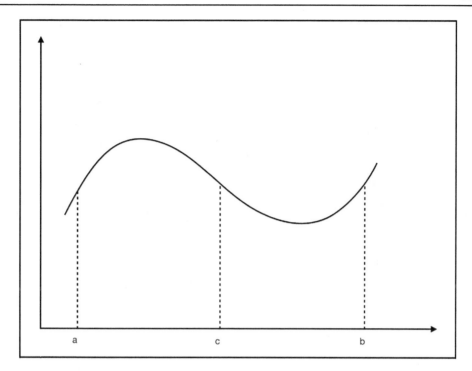

Then, we get the following property:

$$\int_a^c f(x)\mathrm{d}x + \int_c^b f(x)\mathrm{d}x = \int_a^b f(x)\mathrm{d}x$$

This property only works for functions that are continuous and have adjacent intervals.

The fundamental theorem of calculus

The fundamental theorem of calculus is the most important theorem in calculus and is named very appropriately since it establishes a relationship between differential calculus and integral calculus. Let's see how.

Suppose that $f(x)$ is continuous on $[a, b]$ and differentiable at (a, b), and that $F(x)$ is the antiderivative of $f(x)$. Then, we have the following:

$$\int_a^b f(x)\mathrm{d}x = F(b) - F(a)$$

Let's rewrite the preceding equation a bit so it becomes this equation:

$$\int_a^x f(t)\mathrm{d}t = F(x) - F(a)$$

All we have done here is replace x with t and b with x. And we know that F(x)-F(a) is also a function. From this, we can derive the following property:

$$\frac{\mathrm{d}}{\mathrm{d}x}(F(x) - F(a)) = F'(x) = f(x)$$

We can derive the preceding property since F(a) is a constant and thus has the derivative zero.

By shifting our point of view a bit, we get the following function:

$$G(x) = \int_a^x f(t)\mathrm{d}t$$

Therefore, we get $G'(x) = f(x)$.

In summary, if we integrate our function *f* and then differentiate it, we end up with the original function *f*.

Substitution rule

Obviously, being able to find the antiderivative of a function is important, but the anti-differentiation formulas do not tell us how to evaluate every type of integral—for example, what to do when we have functions such as the following one:

$$f(x) = \int 2x\sqrt{x^2 + 1}\,\mathrm{d}x$$

This isn't as straightforward as the examples we saw earlier. In this case, we need to introduce a new variable to help us out and make the problem more manageable.

Let's make our new variable u, and $u = x^2 + 1$, and the differential of u is then $du = 2x \, dx$. This changes the problem into the following:

$$f(u) = \int \sqrt{u} \, du$$

This is clearly a lot simpler. The antiderivative of this becomes the following:

$$\frac{2}{3} u^{\frac{3}{2}} + c$$

And by plugging in the original value $u = x^2 + 1$, we get the following:

$$\frac{2}{3}(x^2 + 1)^{\frac{3}{2}} + c$$

And there we have it.

This method is very useful, and works when we have problems that can be written in the following form:

$$\int f(g(x))g'(x) \, dx$$

If $F' = f$, then the following applies:

$$\int F'(g(x))g'(x) = F(g(x)) + c$$

That equation might be looking somewhat similar to you. And it should. It is the chain rule from differentiation.

Areas between curves

We know that integration gives us the ability to find the area underneath a curve between two points. But now, suppose we want to find the area that lies between two graphs, as in the following screenshot:

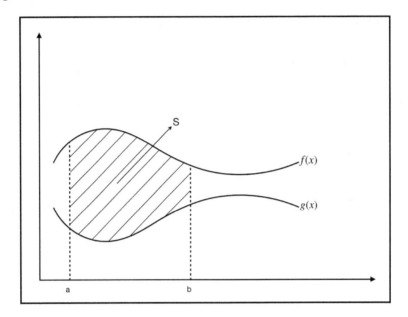

Our region S, as we can see, lies between the curves *f(x)* and *g(x)* in between the two vertical lines *x = a* and *x = b*. Therefore, we can take an approximation of the area between the curves to be the following:

$$A = \lim_{n \to \infty} \sum_{i=1}^{n} (f(x_i^*) - g(x_i^*)) \triangle x$$

We can rewrite this as an integral, in the following form:

$$A = \int_a^b (f(x) - g(x)) dx$$

To visualize this better and create an intuition of what is happening, we have the following image:

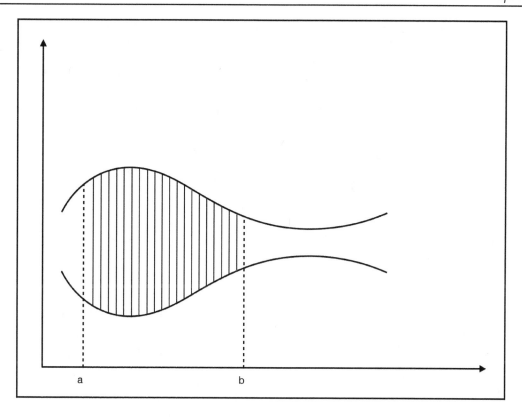

Integration by parts

By now, we know that for every rule in differentiation, there is a corresponding rule in integration since they have an inverse relationship.

In the earlier section on differentiation, we encountered the product rule. In integration, the corresponding rule is known as integration by parts.

As a recap, the product rule states that if f and g are differentiable, then the following applies:

$$\frac{d}{dx}(f(x)g(x)) = f(x)g'(x) + g(x)f'(x)$$

And so, in integration, this becomes the following:

$$\int (f(x)g'(x) + g(x)f'(x))dx = f(x)g(x)$$

We can rewrite this, as follows:

$$\int f(x)g'(x)dx = f(x)g(x) - \int g(x)f'(x)dx$$

We can combine this formula with the fundamental theorem of calculus and obtain the following equation:

$$\int_a^b f(x)g'(x)dx = f(x)g(x)\big|_a^b - \int_a^b g(x)f'(x)dx$$

We can use this to evaluate the integral between the interval [a, b].

 Note: The term $f(x)g(x)\big|_a^b$ merely states that we plug in the value b in place of x and evaluate it, and then subtract it from the evaluation at a.

We can also use the preceding substitution method for integration by parts to make our lives easier when calculating the integral. We make $u = f(x)$ and $v = g(x)$; then, the differentials are $du = f'(x)dx$ and $dv = g'(x)dx$. And so, the formula becomes this:

$$\int u\, dv = uv - \int v\, du$$

Multivariable calculus

Now that we have gone through single variable calculus and understand what calculus is about, it is time for us to go a step deeper and look at multivariable calculus. Multivariable calculus has a lot of similarities with single variable calculus, except—as the name suggests—here, we will be dealing with functions that accept two or more variables as input.

Multivariable calculus is used everywhere in the real world and has applications in every field and industry, from healthcare to economics, to finance, to robotics, to aerospace, and so on. An example of this could be trying to model how air curves around an airplane, to understand how aerodynamic it is and where the design of the airplane body can be improved. This is something we would not be able to do with single variable calculus.

Partial derivatives

A partial derivative is a method we use to find the derivative of a function that depends on more than one variable, with respect to one of its variables, while keeping the others constant. This allows us to understand how a function is affected by a single variable instead of by all of them. Suppose we are modeling the price of a stock item, and the price depends on a number of different factors. We can vary one variable at a time to determine how much this change will affect the price of the stock item. This is different from taking a total derivative, where all the variables vary.

A multivariate function can have as many variables as you would look like, but to keep things simple, we will look at a function with two variables, as follows:

$$z = f(x, y) = 5y^3 + 7x^2y - 3y + 11$$

This function looks a lot more complicated than the ones we have previously dealt with. Let's break it down. When we take the partial derivative of a function with respect to x, we find the rate of change of z as x varies, while keeping y constant. The same applies when we differentiate with respect to any other variable.

Let's visually imagine the xy-plane (a flat surface) as being the set of acceptable points that can be used as input to our function. The output, z, can be thought of as how much we are elevated (or the height) from the xy-plane.

Let's start by first differentiating the function with respect to x, as follows:

$$\frac{\partial z}{\partial x} = \lim_{\triangle x \to 0} \frac{z(x + \triangle x, y) - z(x, y)}{h}$$

This gives us the following:

$$\frac{\partial z}{\partial x} = 14xy$$

Now, we will differentiate with respect to y, as follows:

$$\frac{\partial z}{\partial y} = \lim_{\triangle y \to 0} \frac{z(x, y + \triangle y) - z(x, y)}{h}$$

This gives us the following:

$$\frac{\partial z}{\partial y} = 15y^2 + 7x^2 - 3$$

As we saw earlier, in single variable differentiation, we can take second derivatives of functions (within reason, of course), but in multivariable calculus, we can also take mixed partial derivatives, as illustrated here:

$$\frac{\partial^2 z}{\partial x^2} = 14y$$
$$\frac{\partial^2 z}{\partial x \partial y} = \frac{\partial}{\partial x}\left(\frac{\partial z}{\partial y}\right) = 14x$$
$$\frac{\partial^2 z}{\partial y^2} = 30y$$

You may have noticed that when we take a mixed partial derivative, the order of the variables does not matter, and we get the same result whether we first differentiate with respect to x and then with respect to y, or vice versa.

We can also write this in another form that is often more convenient, and this is what we will be using in this book, going forward. The function is illustrated here:

$$f_x = \frac{\partial f}{\partial x}, f_{xy} = \frac{\partial^2 f}{\partial x \partial y}, f_y = \frac{\partial f}{\partial y}$$

Chain rule

Let's take an arbitrary function f that takes variables x and y as input, and there is some change in either variable so that $(x, y) \rightarrow (x + \triangle x, y + \triangle y)$. Using this, we can find the change in f using the following:

$$\triangle f = f(x + \triangle x, y + \triangle y) - f(x, y)$$

This leads us to the following equation:

$$\triangle f = \frac{\partial f}{\partial x}\triangle x + \frac{\partial f}{\partial y}\triangle y$$

Then, by taking the limit of the function as $\triangle x, \triangle y \rightarrow 0$, we can derive the chain rule for partial derivatives.

We express this as follows:

$$df = \frac{\partial f}{\partial x}dx + \frac{\partial f}{\partial y}dy$$

We now divide this equation by an additional small quantity (t) on which x and y are dependent, to find the gradient along $(x(t), y(t))$. The preceding equation then becomes this one:

$$\frac{df}{dt} = \frac{\partial f}{\partial x}\frac{dx}{dt} + \frac{\partial f}{\partial y}\frac{dy}{dt}$$

The differentiation rules that we came across earlier still apply here and can be extended to the multivariable case.

Integrals

As in the single variable case, we have antiderivatives and integrals for functions that depend on multiple variables as well. Earlier, we learned that an integral gives us the area under a curve $y = f(x)$ between an interval [a, b]. Now, instead of finding the area over an interval, we will be finding the volume under the graph $z = f(x, y)$ over a region. The equation looks like this:

$$\iint_R f(x, y) \, dA = \text{volume}$$

In the preceding equation, R is a region in the xy-plane. Think of R as being cut into multiple small rectangular regions, denoted ΔA. Then, we can approximate the volume as follows:

$$\iint_R f(x, y) \, dA = \sum_i \lim_{\Delta A \to 0} f(x_i, y_i)\Delta A_i$$

Additionally, $dA = dxdy$; thus, $\Delta A = \Delta x \Delta y$.

Note: A double integral is not the same as taking an integral twice.

Now, instead of calculating over small rectangular regions, let's divide the region into long, thin slices of a fixed width Δx. Sound familiar? It should, as this is very similar to what we did earlier in single variable integration.

Let's assign $\Delta x = S$, and now, our integral takes the following form:

$$\iint_R f(x,y)\,\mathrm{d}A = \int_c^d f(S,y)\,\mathrm{d}y$$

We then multiply the result by Δx.

We can now rewrite the integral, as follows:

$$\iint_R f(x,y)\,\mathrm{d}A = \int_a^b \left(\int_c^d f(x,y)\mathrm{d}y \right) \mathrm{d}x = \int_c^d \left(\int_a^b f(x,y)\mathrm{d}x \right) \mathrm{d}y$$

Here, $a \le x \le b$ and $c \le y \le d$.

Suppose that we have the function $z = 1 - x^2 - y^2$ and the boundaries of the region are defined over $0 \le x \le 1$ and $0 \le y \le 1$. Then, the integral is as follows:

$$Z = \int_0^1 \int_0^1 (1 - x^2 - y^2)\,\mathrm{d}x\,\mathrm{d}y$$

And by evaluating the inner integral, we get the following:

$$Z = \int_0^1 \left[(1 - y^2)x - \frac{1}{3}x^3 \right]_0^1 \mathrm{d}y = \frac{2}{3} - y^2$$

And by evaluating the outer integral, we get the following:

$$Z = \int_0^1 \left(\frac{2}{3} - y^2 \right) \mathrm{d}y = \left[\frac{2}{3}y - \frac{1}{3}y^3 \right]_0^1 = \frac{1}{3}$$

And there you have it. That is how we find integrals of multivariable functions.

Let's now suppose that we have a function $f(x,y) = g(x) \bullet h(y)$, and we evaluate the integral over the region where $a \le x \le b$ and $c \le y \le d$. Then, we have the following:

$$\iint_R f(x,y)\,\mathrm{d}A = \left(\int_a^b g(x)\,\mathrm{d}x \right) \times \left(\int_c^d h(y)\,\mathrm{d}y \right)$$

This is a direct result of the distributive law.

The region we have been integrating over so far has been rectangular, but this most likely will not always be the case. If the region is an irregular shape, then the limits of integration will vary at each slice.

The best way to deal with this is to write it as a function of the variable we are not integrating.

Let's suppose that we have $f(x, y) = x^2 + y^2$, and the set of points it exists on is $\{(x, y) : x^2 + y^2 \leq 1\}$, which tells us $-1 \leq x \leq 1$ and $-1 \leq y \leq 1$. We can now write this in the following form:

$$\{(x, y) : a \leq x \leq b, \ g(x) \leq y \leq h(x)\}$$

Here, as we can see, x is defined on the interval [a, b], and y exists between two functions of x—g(x) and h(x).

We know from trigonometry, particularly the Pythagorean theorem, that the smallest value for y will be $-\sqrt{1 - x^2}$ and the largest value will be $+\sqrt{1 - x^2}$.

We can now proceed to rewrite the preceding set of points, as follows:

$$\{(x, y) : -1 \leq x \leq 1, \ -\sqrt{1 - x^2} \leq y \leq \sqrt{1 - x^2}\}$$

Changing it up and writing it this way slices the unit disk into vertical lines spaced apart by a fixed width.

Then, our integral becomes this one:

$$\int_a^b \int_{g(x)}^{h(x)} f(x, y) \, dy \, dx$$

And because $f(x, y) = x^2 + y^2 = 1$, we can rewrite the preceding integral, like so:

$$\int_{-1}^1 \left[\int_{-\sqrt{1-x^2}}^{\sqrt{1-x^2}} 1 \, dy \right] dx$$

We then proceed by evaluating the inner integral and then the outer integral, like so:

$$F = \int_{-1}^{1} [y]_{-\sqrt{1-x^2}}^{\sqrt{1-x^2}} \, dx = \int_{-1}^{1} 2\sqrt{1-x^2} \, dx = \pi$$

We know this to be true from the area of a circle: $\pi r^2 = \pi(1)^2 = \pi$

Some important properties for double integrals are shown in the following list:

- $$\iint_R [f(x,y) + g(x,y)] dA = \iint_R f(x,y) \, dA + \iint_R g(x,y) \, dA$$

- $$\iint_R cf(x,y) \, dA = c \iint_R f(x,y) \, dA$$, where c is some constant

- $$\iint_R f(x,y) \, dA = \iint_{R_1} f(x,y) \, dA + \iint_{R_2} f(x,y) \, dA$$ if the R can be split into two
  regions, R_1 and R_2

- $$\iint_R f(x,y) \, dA \le \iint_R g(x,y) \, dA$$ when $f(x,y) \le g(x,y)$ for all $(x,y) \in R$

Let's now suppose we have a cylinder with a spherical top, as in the following diagram, and we want to find its volume. The region under the sphere is $x^2 + y^2 + z^2 = 9$ and inside the cylinder $x^2 + y^2 = 5$ and above z = 0, as follows:

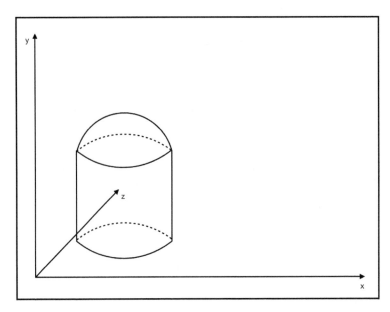

We know that we find the volume of a region as follows:

$$V = \iint_R f(x, y) \, dA$$

To evaluate this integral, we start by rewriting the equation of the sphere into $z = \sqrt{9 - (x^2 + y^2)}$, and the set of points where x and y are defined is $\{(x, y) : x^2 + y^2 \leq 5\}$.

We rewrite our points and define the limits of the region in terms of polar coordinates θ and the radius r, so that the equation looks like this:

$$0 \leq \theta \leq 2\pi \text{ and } 0 \leq r \leq \sqrt{5}$$

We can now rewrite z, as follows:

$$z = \sqrt{9 - (x^2 + y^2)} = \sqrt{9 - r^2}$$

So, the volume is as follows:

$$V = \int_0^{2\pi} \left(\int_0^{\sqrt{5}} \sqrt{9 - r^2} \right) dr \, d\theta$$

And by evaluating the inner and outer integrals, we get the following:

$$V = \int_0^{2\pi} \left[-\frac{1}{3} (9 - r^2)^{\frac{3}{2}} \right]_0^{\sqrt{5}} d\theta$$

$$V = \int_0^{2\pi} \frac{19}{3} \, d\theta = \frac{38\pi}{3}$$

We now know how to integrate our regions in $\mathbb{R}^2$ and find the volume under the graph. But what about when we have regions in $\mathbb{R}^3$? Earlier, we used a double integral for two-dimensional regions; so, naturally, for a three-dimensional region, we will use three integrals. We write this as follows:

$$\iiint_R f(x, y, z) \, dV$$

Suppose now that the region we integrate over is defined by $a \leq x \leq b$, $c \leq y \leq d$ and $r \leq z \leq s$. The triple integral then becomes the following:

$$\iiint_R f(x, y, z) \, dV = \int_r^s \int_c^d \int_a^b f(x, y, z) \, dx \, dy \, dz$$

Earlier on, we came across something called substitution, where we made our function equal to a variable to make it easier for us to find the derivative. We can also do the same in integration.

Suppose we have the following integral:

$$\int_a^b f(g(x))g'(x) \, dx$$

We can make $u = g(x)$, and the integral then becomes this:

$$\int_c^d f(u) \, du$$

Now, let's move on to double integrals, and see how we can transform regions to make them easier for us to deal with. To do this, we will need to call on our old friend the Jacobian matrix for help.

As a refresher, suppose we have $x = f(u, v)$ and $y = g(u, v)$. Then, the Jacobian matrix is as follows:

$$\frac{\partial(x, y)}{\partial(u, v)} = \begin{vmatrix} \frac{\partial x}{\partial u} & \frac{\partial x}{\partial v} \\ \frac{\partial y}{\partial u} & \frac{\partial y}{\partial v} \end{vmatrix}$$

Also, recall that the Jacobian matrix can also be thought of as the determinant. So, we can rewrite the preceding equation as follows:

$$\frac{\partial(x, y)}{\partial(u, v)} = \begin{vmatrix} \frac{\partial x}{\partial u} & \frac{\partial x}{\partial v} \\ \frac{\partial y}{\partial u} & \frac{\partial y}{\partial v} \end{vmatrix} = \frac{\partial x}{\partial u} \frac{\partial y}{\partial v} - \frac{\partial x}{\partial v} \frac{\partial y}{\partial u}$$

Suppose now that we want to integrate $f(x, y)$ over R. Now, let's make $x = g(u, v)$ and $y = h(u, v)$, and rename our region as S. The integral now looks like this:

$$\iint_R f(x, y) \, dA = \iint_S f(g(u, v), h(u, v)) \left| \frac{\partial(x, y)}{\partial(u, v)} \right| du \, dv$$

From this, we can easily observe that $dA = \left| \frac{\partial(x, y)}{\partial(u, v)} \right| du \, dv$.

Let's move on to triple integrals now. Suppose we have a function $f(x, y, z)$ and we want to integrate it over R. We start by making $x = g(u, v, w)$, $y = (u, v, w)$, and $z = k(u, v, w)$, and as before, we rename the new region as S. The Jacobian matrix is then the following one:

$$\frac{\partial(x, y, z)}{\partial(u, v, w)} = \begin{vmatrix} \frac{\partial x}{\partial u} & \frac{\partial x}{\partial v} & \frac{\partial x}{\partial w} \\ \frac{\partial y}{\partial u} & \frac{\partial y}{\partial v} & \frac{\partial y}{\partial w} \\ \frac{\partial z}{\partial u} & \frac{\partial z}{\partial v} & \frac{\partial z}{\partial w} \end{vmatrix}$$

The triple integral now looks like this:

$$\iiint_R f(x, y, z) \, dV = \iiint_S f(g(u, v, w), h(u, v, w), k(u, v, w)) \left| \frac{\partial(x, y, z)}{\partial(u, v, w)} \right| du \, dv \, dw$$

We now have a good enough understanding of multivariable calculus and are ready to dive into the wonderful world of vector calculus.

Vector calculus

When we find derivatives of functions with respect to vectors, we need to be a lot more diligent. And as we will see in `Chapter 2`, *Linear Algebra*, vectors and matrices are noncommutative and behave quite differently from scalars, and so we need to find a different way to differentiate them.

Derivatives

Earlier, we saw that functions are differentiated by using the limit of the variable in the quotient. But vectors, as we know, are not like scalars in that we cannot divide by vectors, which creates the need for new definitions for vector-valued functions.

We can define a vector function as a function $\mathbf{F} : \mathbb{R} \to \mathbb{R}^n$—that is, it takes in a scalar value as input and outputs a vector. So, the derivative of F is defined as follows:

$$\mathbf{F}' = \frac{d\mathbf{F}}{dx} = \lim_{\delta x \to 0} \frac{1}{\delta x}[\mathbf{F}(x + \delta x) - \mathbf{F}(x)]$$

In the preceding equation, δx is a small perturbation on x. Additionally, F is only differentiable if the following applies:

$$\delta \mathbf{F} = \mathbf{F}(x + \delta x) - \mathbf{F}(x) = \mathbf{F}'(x)\delta x$$

We can also write the preceding differential as follows:

$$d\mathbf{F} = \mathbf{F}'(x)\, dx$$

Generally, we differentiate vectors component-wise, so, the preceding differential becomes this:

$$\mathbf{F}'(x) = F_i'(x)\mathbf{e}_i$$

Here e_i is an orthonormal basis vector.

Some rules for vector differentiation are shown in the following list:

- $\frac{d}{dt}(f\mathbf{g}) = \frac{df}{dt}\mathbf{g} + f\frac{d\mathbf{g}}{dt}$

- $\frac{d}{dt}(\mathbf{f} \cdot \mathbf{g}) = \frac{d\mathbf{f}}{dt} \cdot \mathbf{g} + \mathbf{f} \cdot \frac{d\mathbf{g}}{dt}$

- $\frac{d}{dt}(\mathbf{f} \times \mathbf{g}) = \frac{d\mathbf{f}}{dt} \times \mathbf{g} + \mathbf{f} \times \frac{d\mathbf{g}}{dt}$

- $\frac{\partial}{\partial \mathbf{x}}(f(\mathbf{x})g(\mathbf{x})) = \frac{\partial f}{\partial \mathbf{x}}g(\mathbf{x}) + f(\mathbf{x})\frac{\partial g}{\partial \mathbf{x}}$

- $\frac{\partial}{\partial \mathbf{x}}(f(\mathbf{x}) + g(\mathbf{x})) = \frac{\partial f}{\partial \mathbf{x}} + \frac{\partial g}{\partial \mathbf{x}}$

- $\frac{\partial}{\partial \mathbf{x}}(f \circ g)(\mathbf{x}) = \frac{\partial}{\partial \mathbf{x}}(f(g(\mathbf{x}))) = \frac{\partial f}{\partial g}\frac{\partial g}{\partial \mathbf{x}}$

We know from earlier that we use the concept of limits to find the derivative of a function. So, let's see how we can find the limit of a vector. We use the concept of norms here. We say $\mathbf{v} \to \mathbf{c}$ iff $|\mathbf{v} - \mathbf{c}| \to 0$, and so, if $f(\mathbf{r}) = o(\mathbf{r})$, then as $\mathbf{r} \to \mathbf{0}$, $\dfrac{|f(\mathbf{r})|}{|\mathbf{r}|} \to 0$.

Generally, the derivative is calculated in all possible directions. But what if we want to find it in only one particular direction n (unit vector)? Then, assuming $\delta r = hn$, we have the following:

$$f(\mathbf{r} + h\mathbf{n}) - f(\mathbf{r}) = h(\nabla f \cdot \mathbf{n})$$

From this, we can derive the directional derivative to be the following:

$$\mathbf{n} \cdot \nabla f = \lim_{h \to 0} \frac{1}{h}[f(\mathbf{r} + h\mathbf{n}) - f(\mathbf{r})]$$

This gives us the rate of change of f in this direction.

Suppose now that we have $n = e_i$. Then, our directional derivative becomes the following:

$$\mathbf{e}_i \cdot \nabla f = \lim_{h \to 0} \frac{1}{h}[f(\mathbf{r} + h\mathbf{e}_i) - f(\mathbf{r})] = \frac{\partial f}{\partial x_i}$$

Therefore, we have the following:

$$\nabla f = \frac{\partial f}{\partial x_i}\mathbf{e}_i$$

And so, the condition of differentiability now becomes the following:

$$\delta f = \frac{\partial f}{\partial x_i}\delta x_i$$

We can express this in differential notation, as follows:

$$df = \nabla f \cdot d\mathbf{r} = \frac{\partial f}{\partial x_i}dx_i$$

This looks very similar to something we encountered earlier. It's the chain rule for partial derivatives.

Let's now take a function $f : \mathbb{R}^n \to \mathbb{R}$ that takes in a vector input $\mathbf{x} \in \mathbb{R}^n$ such that $\mathbf{x} = x_1, x_2, \ldots, x_{n-1}, x_n$. The partial derivatives of this function are written as follows:

$$\frac{\partial f}{\partial x_1} = \lim_{h \to 0} \frac{f(x_1 + h, x_2, \ldots, x_n) - f(\mathbf{x})}{h}$$

$$\vdots$$

$$\frac{\partial f}{\partial x_n} = \lim_{h \to 0} \frac{f(x_1, x_2, \ldots, x_n + h) - f(\mathbf{x})}{h}$$

We can then write this collectively as an $\mathbb{R}^{1 \times n}$ vector, which we write as follows:

$$\frac{df}{d\mathbf{x}} = \left[\frac{\partial f(\mathbf{x})}{\partial x_1}, \frac{\partial f(\mathbf{x})}{\partial x_2}, \ldots, \frac{\partial f(\mathbf{x})}{\partial x_n} \right]$$

Let's go a step further and imagine a vector function made of m different scalar functions, which take the vector x as input. We will write this as $y = f(x)$.

Expanding $y = f(x)$, we get the following:

$$y_1 = f_1(\mathbf{x})$$
$$y_2 = f_2(\mathbf{x})$$
$$\vdots$$
$$y_m = f_m(\mathbf{x})$$

Let's revisit the Jacobian matrix briefly. As you can see, it is simply an $(m \times n)$ matrix containing all the partial derivatives of the earlier vector function. We can see what this looks like here:

$$\frac{\partial \mathbf{y}}{\partial \mathbf{x}} = \begin{bmatrix} \frac{\partial}{\partial \mathbf{x}} f_1(\mathbf{x}) \\ \frac{\partial}{\partial \mathbf{x}} f_2(\mathbf{x}) \\ \vdots \\ \frac{\partial}{\partial \mathbf{x}} f_m(\mathbf{x}) \end{bmatrix} = \begin{bmatrix} \frac{\partial}{\partial x_1} f_1(\mathbf{x}) & \frac{\partial}{\partial x_2} f_1(\mathbf{x}) & \cdots & \frac{\partial}{\partial x_n} f_1(\mathbf{x}) \\ \frac{\partial}{\partial x_1} f_2(\mathbf{x}) & \frac{\partial}{\partial x_2} f_2(\mathbf{x}) & \cdots & \frac{\partial}{\partial x_n} f_2(\mathbf{x}) \\ \vdots & & \ddots & \\ \frac{\partial}{\partial x_1} f_m(\mathbf{x}) & \frac{\partial}{\partial x_2} f_m(\mathbf{x}) & \cdots & \frac{\partial}{\partial x_n} f_m(\mathbf{x}) \end{bmatrix}$$

Let's go a step further and extend this definition to multiple functions. Here, we have y, which is the sum of two functions f and g, each taking in a different vectorial input, which gives us the following:

$$y = f(a) + g(b)$$

And for the sake of simplicity, f, g, a, and b are all n-dimensional, which results in an $n \times n$ matrix, as follows:

$$
\begin{bmatrix} y_1 \\ y_2 \\ \vdots \\ y_{n-1} \\ y_n \end{bmatrix} = \begin{bmatrix} y_1(\mathbf{a}) + g_1(\mathbf{b}) \\ y_2(\mathbf{a}) + g_2(\mathbf{b}) \\ \vdots \\ y_{n-1}(\mathbf{a}) + g_{n-1}(\mathbf{b}) \\ y_n(\mathbf{a}) + g_n(\mathbf{b}) \end{bmatrix}
$$

We can differentiate this matrix with respect to a or b and find the Jacobian matrix(es) for each.

By differentiating with respect to a, we get the following:

$$
J_{\mathbf{a}} = \frac{\partial \mathbf{y}}{\partial \mathbf{a}} = \begin{bmatrix} \frac{\partial}{\partial a_1}(y_1(\mathbf{a}) + g_1(\mathbf{b})) & \frac{\partial}{\partial a_2}(y_1(\mathbf{a}) + g_1(\mathbf{b})) & \cdots & \frac{\partial}{\partial a_n}(y_1(\mathbf{a}) + g_1(\mathbf{b})) \\ \frac{\partial}{\partial a_1}(y_2(\mathbf{a}) + g_2(\mathbf{b})) & \frac{\partial}{\partial a_2}(y_2(\mathbf{a})) + g_2(\mathbf{b}) & \cdots & \frac{\partial}{\partial a_n}(y_2(\mathbf{a}) + g_2(\mathbf{b})) \\ & \vdots & \ddots & \\ \frac{\partial}{\partial a_1}(y_n(\mathbf{a}) + g_n(\mathbf{b})) & \frac{\partial}{\partial a_2}(y_n(\mathbf{a}) + g_n(\mathbf{b})) & \cdots & \frac{\partial}{\partial a_n}(y_n(\mathbf{a}) + g_n(\mathbf{b})) \end{bmatrix}
$$

By differentiating with respect to b, we get the following:

$$
J_{\mathbf{b}} = \frac{\partial \mathbf{y}}{\partial \mathbf{b}} = \begin{bmatrix} \frac{\partial}{\partial b_1}(y_1(\mathbf{a}) + g_1(\mathbf{b})) & \frac{\partial}{\partial b_2}(y_1(\mathbf{a}) + g_1(\mathbf{b})) & \cdots & \frac{\partial}{\partial b_n}(y_1(\mathbf{a}) + g_1(\mathbf{b})) \\ \frac{\partial}{\partial b_1}(y_2(\mathbf{a}) + g_2(\mathbf{b})) & \frac{\partial}{\partial b_2}(y_2(\mathbf{a})) + g_2(\mathbf{b}) & \cdots & \frac{\partial}{\partial b_n}(y_2(\mathbf{a}) + g_2(\mathbf{b})) \\ & \vdots & \ddots & \\ \frac{\partial}{\partial b_1}(y_n(\mathbf{a}) + g_n(\mathbf{b})) & \frac{\partial}{\partial b_2}(y_n(\mathbf{a}) + g_n(\mathbf{b})) & \cdots & \frac{\partial}{\partial b_n}(y_n(\mathbf{a}) + g_n(\mathbf{b})) \end{bmatrix}
$$

We can do the same for any type of element-wise operation on the two functions.

As in single variable and multivariable calculus, we have a chain rule for vector differentiation as well.

Let's take the composition of two vector functions that take in a vector input $f(g(x))$, and so the gradient of this will be $\frac{\partial f}{\partial g}\frac{\partial g}{\partial x}$, which looks similar to what we encountered before. Let's expand this further, as follows:

$$\frac{\partial}{\partial \mathbf{x}}\mathbf{f}(\mathbf{g}(\mathbf{x})) = \begin{bmatrix} \frac{\partial f_1}{\partial g_1} & \frac{\partial f_1}{\partial g_2} \\ \frac{\partial f_2}{\partial g_1} & \frac{\partial f_2}{\partial g_2} \end{bmatrix} \begin{bmatrix} \frac{\partial g_1}{\partial x_1} & \frac{\partial g_1}{\partial x_2} \\ \frac{\partial g_2}{\partial x_1} & \frac{\partial g_2}{\partial x_2} \end{bmatrix}$$

In the majority of cases, for arguments in the Jacobian matrix where $i \neq j$, the argument tends to be zero, which leads us to the following definitions:

$$\frac{\partial \mathbf{f}}{\partial \mathbf{g}} = diag\left(\frac{\partial f_i}{\partial g_i}\right)$$

$$\frac{\partial \mathbf{g}}{\partial \mathbf{x}} = diag\left(\frac{\partial g_i}{\partial x_i}\right)$$

And so, the following applies:

$$\frac{\partial}{\partial \mathbf{x}}\mathbf{f}(\mathbf{g}(\mathbf{x})) = diag\left(\frac{\partial f_i}{\partial g_i}\right) diag\left(\frac{\partial g_i}{\partial x_i}\right) = diag\left(\frac{\partial f_i}{\partial g_i}\frac{\partial g_i}{\partial x_i}\right)$$

As we can see, this is a diagonal matrix.

Vector fields

We define a vector field as a function $\mathbf{F} : \mathbb{R}^n \rightarrow \mathbb{R}^m$, and it can only be differentiated if the following applies:

$$\delta \mathbf{F} = \mathbf{F}(\mathbf{x} + \delta \mathbf{x}) - \mathbf{F}(\mathbf{x}) = M\delta \mathbf{x}$$

Here, $M \in \mathbb{R}^{n \times m}$ is the derivative of F.

We can think of M as a matrix that maps one vector to another, and we can now express F as follows:

$$dy_j = \frac{\partial F_j}{\partial x_i}dx_i$$

Here, $y_j = F_j(\mathbf{x})$ for all $j = 1, \cdots, m$, and therefore, the derivative of F is this:

$$M_{j,i} = \frac{\partial y_j}{\partial x_i}$$

Earlier on in single and multivariable calculus, we learned the importance of the chain rule, so it should be no surprise that we have it in vector calculus as well. And it goes as follows.

Suppose we have $g : \mathbb{R}^p \to \mathbb{R}^n$ and $f : \mathbb{R}^n \to \mathbb{R}^m$ and the coordinates are $u_a \in \mathbb{R}^p$, $x_i \in \mathbb{R}^n$, and $y_r \in \mathbb{R}^m$. Then, the chain rule gives us the following:

$$\frac{\partial y_r}{\partial u_a} = \frac{\partial y_r}{\partial x_i} \frac{\partial x_i}{\partial u_a}$$

We can rewrite this in matrix form, as follows:

$$M(f \circ g)_{r,a} = M(f)_{r,i} M(g)_{i,a}$$

Inverse functions

Inverse functions are a rather fascinating class of functions in that if we have two functions and we apply them on each other, we receive the identity. Mathematically, we define this as follows:

Suppose we have $f, g : \mathbb{R}^n \to \mathbb{R}^n$. Then, they are only inverse functions if $f \circ g = g \circ f = \text{identity}$. For example, we could have $f(\mathbf{u}) = \mathbf{v}$ and $g(\mathbf{v}) = \mathbf{u}$. Therefore, $M(f \circ g) = I$, which tells us that $M(g) = M(f)^{-1}$.

Here is another cool property that this has:

$$\det M(f) \det M(g) = 1$$

Summary

And with that, we conclude our chapter on calculus. So far, we have learned about the fundamental concepts of single variable, multivariable, and vector calculus, and what it is that makes them so useful.

In the next chapter, we will move on to probability and statistics, and see how what we learned in linear algebra and calculus carries over into these fields.

3
Probability and Statistics

In this chapter, we will cover two of the most important areas of mathematics—probability and statistics. These are two terms that you've likely come across a number of times in your everyday life. People use it to justify just about everything that occurs or when they're trying to prove a point. Once you are done with this chapter, you will have a firm grasp of both of them and will understand how they both are related and how they differ.

This chapter will cover the following topics:

- Understanding the concepts in probability
- Essential concepts in statistics

Understanding the concepts in probability

Probability theory is one of the most important fields of mathematics and is essential to the understanding and creation of deep neural networks. We will explore the specifics of this statement in the coming chapters. For now, however, we will focus our effort toward gaining an intricate understanding of this field.

We use probability theory to create an understanding of how likely it is that a certain event will occur. Generally speaking, probability theory is about understanding and dealing with uncertainty.

Classical probability

Let's suppose we have a random variable that maps the results of random experiments to the properties that interest us. The aforementioned random variable measures the likelihood (probability) of one or more sets of outcomes taking place. We call this the **probability distribution**. Consider probability distribution as the foundation of the concepts we will study in this chapter.

There are three ideas that are of great importance in probability theory—probability space, random variables, and probability distribution. Let's start by defining some of the more basic, yet important, concepts.

The sample space is the set of all the possible outcomes. We denote this with Ω. Suppose we have n likely outcomes—then, we have $\omega_1, \omega_2, \cdots, \omega_n \in \Omega$, where w_i is a possible outcome. The subset of the sample space (Ω) is called an **event**.

Probability has a lot to do with sets, so let's go through some of the notation so that we can get a better grasp of the concepts and examples to come.

Suppose we have two events, A and B, $\subseteq \Omega$. We have the following axioms:

- The complement of A is A^c, so $\mathbb{P}(A^C) = 1 - \mathbb{P}(A)$.
- If either A or B occurs, this is written as $A \cup B$ (read as A union B).
- If both A and B occur, this is written as $A \cap B$ (read as A intersect B).
- If A and B are mutually exclusive (or disjoint), then we write $A \cap B = \emptyset$
- If the occurrence of A implies the occurrence of B, this is written as $A \subseteq B$ (so, $\mathbb{P}(A) \leq \mathbb{P}(B)$).

Say we have an event, $A \in \Omega$, and $\omega_1, \omega_2, \cdots, \omega_n \in \Omega$. In this case, the probability of A occurring is defined as follows:

$$\mathbb{P}(A) = \frac{\text{number of outcomes in A}}{\text{number of outcomes in } \Omega} = \frac{|A|}{N}$$

This is the number of times A can occur divided by the total number of possible outcomes in the sample space.

Let's go through a simple example of flipping a coin. Here, the sample space consists of all the possible outcomes of flipping the coin. Say we are dealing with two coin tosses instead of one and h means heads and t means tails. So, the sample space is $\Omega = \{hh, ht, th, tt\}$.

All of the possible results of the experiment make up the event space, $\mathcal{A}$. On finishing the experiment, we observe whether the outcome, $\omega \in \Omega$, is in A.

Since, in each event, $A \in \mathcal{A}$, we denote $P(A)$ as the probability that the event will happen and we read $P(A)$ as the probability of A occurring.

Continuing on from the previous axioms, $\mathbb{P}$ must satisfy the following:

- $0 \le \mathbb{P}(A) \le 1$ for all cases of $A \in \mathcal{A}$
- $\mathbb{P}(\Omega) = 1$

- If the events $A_1, A_2, \ldots$ are disjoint and countably additive—that is, $A_i \cap A_j \ne \emptyset$ for all cases of i, j—we then have $\mathbb{P}\left(\bigcup_i A_i\right) = \sum_i \mathbb{P}(A_i)$.

The triple $(\Omega, \mathcal{A}, \mathbb{P})$ terms are known as the **probability space**.

As a rule of thumb, when $\mathbb{P}(A) = 1$, then event A happens almost surely and when $\mathbb{P}(A) = 0$, then event A happens almost never.

Using the preceding axioms, we can derive the following:

$$\mathbb{P}(A) + \mathbb{P}(A^C) = \mathbb{P}(A \cup A^C) = \mathbb{P}(\Omega) = 1$$

So, $\mathbb{P}(\emptyset) = 0$.

Additionally, if we have two events, A and B, then we can deduce the following:

$$\mathbb{P}(A \cup B) = \mathbb{P}(A) + \mathbb{P}(B) - \mathbb{P}(A \cap B).$$

Continuing on from the preceding axioms, $\mathbb{P}$ must satisfy the following:

$$0 \le \mathbb{P}(A) \le 1 \text{ for all } A \in \mathcal{A}$$

To find the probability of anything, we usually have to count things. Let's say we have a bucket filled with tennis balls and we pick a ball from the bucket r times; so, there are n_1 possibilities for the first pick, n_2 for the next pick, and so on. The total number of choices ends up being $n_1 \times n_2 \times \ldots \times n_r$.

Sampling with or without replacement

Let's now assume that there is a total of n items in the bucket and we must pick r of them. Then, let $R = \{1, 2, \ldots, r\}$ be the list of items picked and let $N = \{1, 2, \ldots, n\}$ be the total number of items. This can be written as a function, as follows:

$$f : R \to N$$

Here, *f(i)* is the ith item.

Sampling with replacement is when we pick an item at random and then put it back so that the item can be picked again.

However, sampling without replacement refers to when we choose an item and don't put it back, so we cannot pick it again. Let's see an example of both.

Say we need to open the door to our office and we have a bag containing *n* keys; they all look identical, so there's no way of differentiating between them.

The first time we try picking a key, we replace each one after trying it, and we manage to find the correct key on the rth trial, implying we got it wrong *r-1* times. The probability is then as follows:

$$\frac{(n-1)(n-1)\cdots(n-1)(1)}{n^r} = \frac{(n-1)^{r-1}}{n^r}$$

Now, we know that our earlier strategy wasn't the smartest, so this time we try it again but without replacement and eliminate each key that doesn't work. Now, the probability is as follows:

$$\frac{(n-1)(n-2)\cdots(n-r+1)(1)}{n(n-1)\cdots(n-r+1)} = \frac{1}{n}$$

Multinomial coefficient

We know from the binomial theorem (which you likely learned in high school) that the following is true:

$$(x+y)^n = x^n + \binom{n}{1}x^{n-1}y + \binom{n}{2}x^{n-2}y^2 + \cdots + y^n$$

Then, the trinomial is as follows:

$$(x+y+z)^n \sum_{n_1,n_2,n_3} \binom{n}{n_1,n_2,n_3} x^{n_1}y^{n_2}z^{n_3}$$

Say we have n pieces of candy and there are blue- and red-colored candies. The different ways that we can pick the candies is defined as $\binom{n}{k}$, which is read as n choose k.

The multinomial coefficient is as follows:

$$\binom{n}{n_1, n_2, \cdots, n_k} = \binom{n}{n_1}\binom{n-n_1}{n_2} \cdots \binom{n-n_1-\cdots-n_{k-1}}{n_k} = \frac{n!}{n_1! n_2! \cdots n_k!}$$

This way, we spread n items over k positions, where the ith position has n_i items.

For example, say we're playing cards and we have four players. A deck of cards has 52 cards and we deal 13 cards to each player. So, the number of possible ways that we can distribute the cards is as follows:

$$\binom{52}{13, 13, 13, 13} = \frac{52!}{(13!)^4} = 5.36 \times 10^{28}$$

This is absolutely massive!

This is where Stirling's formula comes to the rescue. It allows us to approximate the answer.

Stirling's formula

For the sake of argument, let's say $\log n! \sim n \log n$.

We know that the following is true:

$$\log n! = \sum_{k=1}^{n} \log k$$

However, we now claim the following:

$$\int_1^n \log x \, dx \le \sum_1^n \log k \le \int_1^{n+1} \log x \, dx$$

This can be illustrated as follows:

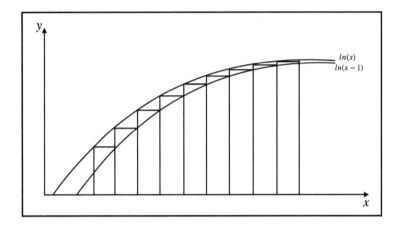

Now, by evaluating the integral, we get the following:

$$n \log n - n + 1 \leq \log n! \leq (n+1) \log(n+1) - n$$

We now divide both sides by $n \log n$ and take the limit as $n \to \infty$. We observe that both sides tend to 1. So, we have the following:

$$\frac{\log n!}{n \log n} \to 1$$

Stirling's formula states that as $n \to \infty$, the following is true:

$$\log\left(\frac{n! e^n}{n^{n+\frac{1}{2}}}\right) = \log \sqrt{2\pi} + O\left(\frac{1}{n}\right)$$

Furthermore, we have the following:

$$n! \sim \sqrt{2\pi} n^{n+\frac{1}{2}} e^{-n}$$

 We will avoid looking into the proof for Sterling's formula, but if you're interested in learning more, then I highly recommend looking it up.

Independence

Events are independent when they are not related to each other; that is, the outcome of one has no bearing on the outcome of another.

Suppose we have two independent events, A and B. Then, we can test the following:

$$\mathbb{P}(A \cap B) = \mathbb{P}(A)\mathbb{P}(B)$$

If this is not true, then the events are dependent.

Imagine you're at a casino and you're playing craps. You throw two dice—their outcomes are independent of each other.

An interesting property of independence is that if A and B are independent events, then so are A and B^C.

Let's take a look and see how this works:

$$\begin{aligned}
\mathbb{P}(A \cap B^C) &= \mathbb{P}(A) - \mathbb{P}(A \cap B) \\
&= \mathbb{P}(A) - \mathbb{P}(A)\mathbb{P}(B) \\
&= \mathbb{P}(A)(1 - \mathbb{P}(B)) \\
&= \mathbb{P}(A)\mathbb{P}(B^C)
\end{aligned}$$

When we have multiple events, A_1, A_2, ..., A_n, we call them mutually independent when $\mathbb{P}(A_1 \cap A_2 \cap \cdots \cap A_n) = \mathbb{P}(A_1)\mathbb{P}(A_2)\cdots\mathbb{P}(A_n)$ for all cases of n ≥ 2.

Let's suppose we conduct two experiments in a lab; we model them independently as $\Omega_1 = \{\alpha_1, \alpha_2, \cdots\}$ and $\Omega_2 = \{\beta_1, \beta_2, \cdots\}$ and the probabilities of each are $\mathbb{P}(\alpha_i) = p_i$ and $\mathbb{P}(\beta_i) = q_i$, respectively. If the two are independent, then we have the following:

$$\mathbb{P}(\alpha_i \beta_j) = p_i q_j$$

This is for all cases of i and j, and our new sample space is $\Omega = \Omega_1 \times \Omega_2$.

Now, say A and B are events in the Ω_1 and Ω_2 experiments, respectively. We can view them as subspaces of the new sample space, Ω, by calculating $A \times \Omega_2$ and $B \times \Omega_1$, which leads to the following:

$$\mathbb{P}(A \cap B) = \sum_{\alpha_i \in A, \beta_i \in B} p_i q_i = \sum_{\alpha_i \in A} p_i \sum_{\beta_i \in B} q_i = \mathbb{P}(A)\mathbb{P}(B)$$

Even though we normally define independence as different (unrelated) results in the same experiment, we can extend this to an arbitrary number of independent experiments as well.

Discrete distributions

Discrete refers to when our sample space is countable, such as in the cases of coin tosses or rolling dice.

In discrete probability distributions, the sample space is $\Omega = \{\omega_1, \omega_2, \cdots, \omega_n\}$ and $p_i = \mathbb{P}(\{\omega_i\})$.

The following are the six different kinds of discrete distributions that we often encounter in probability theory:

- Bernoulli distribution
- Binomial distribution
- Geometric distribution
- Hypergeometric distribution
- Poisson distribution

Let's define them in order.

For the Bernoulli distribution, let's use the example of a coin toss, where our sample space is $\Omega = \{H, T\}$ (where H is heads and T is tails) and $p \in [0, 1]$ (that is, $0 \leq p \leq 1$). We denote the distribution as $B(1, p)$, such that the following applies:

$$\mathbb{P}(H) = p \text{ and } \mathbb{P}(T) = 1 - p$$

But now, let's suppose the coin is flipped n times, each with the aforementioned probability of p for the outcome being heads. Then, the binomial distribution, denoted as $B(n, p)$, states the following:

$$\mathbb{P}(THHTT \cdots H) = (1 - p)pp(1 - p)(1 - p) \cdots p$$

Therefore, we have the following:

$$\mathbb{P}(\text{four heads}) = \binom{n}{4} p^4 (1 - p)^{n-4}$$

Generally, the binomial distribution is written as follows:

$$\mathbb{P}(k \text{ heads}) = \binom{n}{k} p^k (1-p)^{n-k}$$

The geometric distribution does not keep any memory of past events and so is memoryless. Suppose we flip our coin again; this distribution does not give us any indication as to when we can expect a heads result or how long it will take. So, we write the probability of getting heads after getting tails k times as follows:

$$p_k = (1-p)^k p$$

Let's say we have a bucket filled with balls of two colors—red and black (which we will denote as r and b, respectively). From the bucket, we have picked out n balls and we want to figure out the probability that k of the balls are black. For this, we use the hypergeometric distribution, which looks as follows:

$$\mathbb{P}(k \text{ black}) = \frac{\binom{b}{k}\binom{r}{n-k}}{\binom{b+r}{n}}$$

The Poisson distribution is a bit different from the other distributions. It is used to model rare events that occur at a rate, λ. It is denoted as $P(\lambda)$ and is written as follows:

$$p_k = \frac{\lambda^k}{k!} e^{-\lambda}$$

This is true for all cases of $k \in \mathbb{N}$.

Conditional probability

Conditional probabilities are useful when the occurrence of one event leads to the occurrence of another. If we have two events, A and B, where B has occurred and we want to find the probability of A occurring, we write this as follows:

$$\mathbb{P}(A \mid B) = \frac{\mathbb{P}(A \cap B)}{\mathbb{P}(B)}$$

Here, $\mathbb{P}(B) > 0$.

However, if the two events, A and B, are independent, then we have the following:

$$\mathbb{P}(A \mid B) = \frac{\mathbb{P}(A \cap B)}{\mathbb{P}(B)} = \frac{\mathbb{P}(A)\mathbb{P}(B)}{\mathbb{P}(B)} = \mathbb{P}(A)$$

Additionally, if $\mathbb{P}(A \mid B) > \mathbb{P}(A)$, then it is said that B attracts A. However, if A attracts B^C, then it repels B.

The attraction between A and B is bidirectional; that is, A can only attract B if B also attracts A.

The following are some of the axioms of conditional probability:

- $\mathbb{P}(A \cap B) = \mathbb{P}(A \mid B)\mathbb{P}(B) = \mathbb{P}(B \mid A)\mathbb{P}(A)$
- $\mathbb{P}(A \cap B \cap C) = \mathbb{P}(A \mid B \cap C)\mathbb{P}(B \mid C)\mathbb{P}(C)$
- $\mathbb{P}(A \mid B \cap C) = \dfrac{\mathbb{P}(A \cap B \mid C)}{\mathbb{P}(B \mid C)}$
- $\mathbb{P}(\bullet \mid B)$ is a probability function that works only for subsets of B.
- $\mathbb{P}(B \mid B) = \dfrac{\mathbb{P}(B)}{\mathbb{P}(B)} = 1$
- If $A \subseteq B$, then $\mathbb{P}(A \mid B) = \dfrac{\mathbb{P}(A \cap B)}{\mathbb{P}(B)} \leq 1$

The following equation is known as **Bayes' rule**:

$$\mathbb{P}(A \mid B) = \frac{\mathbb{P}(B \mid A)\mathbb{P}(A)}{\mathbb{P}(B)}$$

This can also be written as follows:

$$\mathbb{P}(A \mid B) \propto \mathbb{P}(A)\mathbb{P}(B \mid A)$$

Here, we have the following:

- $\mathbb{P}(A)$ is called the prior.
- $\mathbb{P}(A \mid B)$ is the posterior.

- $\mathbb{P}(B \mid A)$ is the likelihood.
- $\mathbb{P}(B)$ acts as a normalizing constant.

The $\propto$ symbol is read as **proportional to**.

Often, we end up having to deal with complex events, and to effectively navigate them, we need to decompose them into simpler events.

This leads us to the concept of partitions. A partition is defined as a collection of events that together makes up the sample space, such that, for all cases of B_i, $\underset{i=1,\cdots,\infty}{\bigcup} B_i = \Omega$.

In the coin flipping example, the sample space is partitioned into two possible events—heads and tails.

If A is an event and B_i is a partition of Ω, then we have the following:

$$\mathbb{P}(A) = \sum_{i=1}^{\infty} \mathbb{P}(A \cap B_i) = \sum_{i=1}^{\infty} \mathbb{P}(A \mid B_i)\mathbb{P}(B_i)$$

We can also rewrite Bayes' formula with partitions so that we have the following:

$$\mathbb{P}(B_i \mid A) = \frac{\mathbb{P}(A \mid B_i)\mathbb{P}(B_i)}{\sum_j \mathbb{P}(A \mid B_j)\mathbb{P}(B_j)}$$

Here, $\mathbb{P}(B_i) \neq 0$.

Random variables

Random variables are variables that have a probability distribution attached to them that determines the values each one can have. We view the random variable as a function, $X: \Omega \to \Omega_x$, where $\Omega_X \in \mathbb{R}$ (or $\mathbb{N}$). The range of the X function is denoted by $X(\Omega) = \{X(\omega) : \omega \in \Omega\}$.

A discrete random variable is a random variable that can take on finite or countably infinite values.

Suppose we have $S \in \Omega_x$:

$$\mathbb{P}(X \in S) = \mathbb{P}(\{\omega \in \Omega : X(\omega) \in S\})$$

This is the probability that S is the set containing the result.

In the case of random variables, we look at the probability of a random variable having a certain value instead of the probability of obtaining a certain event.

If our sample space is countable, then we have the following:

$$\mathbb{P}(X \in S) = \sum_{\omega \in \Omega : X(\omega) \in S} p_\omega$$

Suppose we have a die and X is the result after a roll. Then, our sample space for X is $\Omega_x = \{1, 2, 3, 4, 5, 6\}$. Assuming this die is fair (unbiased), then we have the following:

$$\mathbb{P}(X = i) = \frac{1}{6}$$

When we have a finite number of possible outcomes and each outcome has an equivalent probability assigned to it, such that each outcome is just as likely as any other, we call this a discrete uniform distribution.

Let's say $X \sim B(n, p)$. Then, the probability that the value that X takes on is r is as follows:

$$\mathbb{P}(X = r) = \binom{n}{r} p^r (1 - p)^{n-r}$$

 Sometimes, in probability literature, $\mathbb{P}(X = x)$ is written as $\mathbb{P}_X(x)$.

A lot of the time, we may need to find the expected (average) value of a random variable. We do this using the following formula:

$$\mathbb{E}[X] = \sum_{\omega \in \Omega} p_\omega X(\omega)$$

We can also write the preceding equation in the following form:

$$\mathbb{E}[X] = \sum_{x \in \Omega_X} x\mathbb{P}(X = x)$$

The preceding two equations only work when our sample space is discrete (countable).

The following are some of the axioms for $\mathbb{E}[X]$:

- If $X \geq 0$, then $\mathbb{E}[X] \geq 0$.
- If $X \geq 0$ and $\mathbb{E}[X] = 0$, then $\mathbb{P}(X = 0) = 1$.
- $\mathbb{E}[X + Y] = \mathbb{E}[X] + \mathbb{E}[Y]$.
- $\mathbb{E}\left[\sum_{i=1}^{n} \alpha_i X_i + \beta\right] = \sum_{i=1}^{n} \alpha_i \mathbb{E}[X_i] + \beta$, given that α and β are constants and X_i is not independent.
- $\mathbb{E}\left[\prod_{i=1}^{n} X_i\right] = \prod_{i=1}^{n} \mathbb{E}[X_i]$, which holds for when X_i is independent.
- $\mathbb{E}[X]$ minimizes $\mathbb{E}[(X - c)^2]$ over c.

Suppose we have n random variables. Then, their expected value is as follows:

$$\mathbb{E}\left[\sum_{i=1}^{n} X_i\right] = \sum_{i=1}^{n} \mathbb{E}[X_i]$$

Now that we have a good understanding of the expectation of real-valued random variables, it is time to move on to defining two important concepts—variance and standard variables.

Variance

We define the variance of X as follows:

$$\mathrm{var}(X) = \mathbb{E}\left[(X - \mathbb{E}[X])^2\right]$$

The standard deviation of X is the square root of the variance:

$$\sqrt{\text{var}(X)}$$

We can think of this as how spread out or close values are from the expected (mean) value. If they are highly dispersed, then they have a high variance, but if they are grouped together, then they have a low variance.

Here are some properties for variance that are important to remember:

- $\text{var}(X) \geq 0$
- If $\text{var}(X) = 0$, then $\mathbb{P}(X = \mathbb{E}[X]) = 1$
- $\text{var}(\alpha + \beta X) = \beta^2 \text{var}(X)$
- $\text{var}(X) = \mathbb{E}[X^2] - (\mathbb{E}[X])^2$
- $\text{var}\left(\sum_{i=1}^{n} X_i\right) = \sum_{i=1}^{n} \text{var}(X_i)$, given that all the X_i values are independent.

Let's suppose that we now have n discrete random variables. Then, they are independent if we take the following:

$$\mathbb{P}(X_1 = x_1, X_2 = x_2, \cdots, X_n = x_n) = \mathbb{P}(X_1 = x_1)\mathbb{P}(X_2 = x_2) \cdots \mathbb{P}(X_n = x_n)$$

Now, let our n random variables be independent and **identically distributed (iid)**. We now have the following:

$$\text{var}\left(\frac{1}{n}\sum_{i=1}^{n} X_i\right) = \frac{1}{n}\text{var}(X_1)$$

This concept is very important, especially in statistics. It implies that if we want to reduce the variance in the results of our experiment, then we can repeat the experiment a number of times and the sample average will have a small variance.

For example, let's imagine two pieces of rope that have unknown lengths—a and b, respectively. Because the objects are ropes—and, therefore, are non-rigid—we can measure the lengths of the ropes, but our measurements may not be accurate. Let A be the measured value of rope a and B be the measured value of rope b so that we have the following:

$$\mathbb{E}\left[A\right] = a, \text{ and } \mathrm{var}(A) = \sigma^2$$
$$\mathbb{E}\left[B\right] = b, \text{ and } \mathrm{var}(B) = \sigma^2$$

We can increase the accuracy of our measurements by measuring $X = A + B$ and $Y = A - B$. Now, we can estimate a and b using the following:

$$\hat{a} = \frac{X+Y}{2}$$
$$\hat{b} = \frac{X-Y}{2}$$

Now, $\mathbb{E}\left[\hat{a}\right] = a$ and $\mathbb{E}\left[\hat{b}\right] = b$, which are both unbiased. Additionally, we can see that the variance has decreased in our measurement using the following:

$$\mathrm{var}(\hat{a}) = \frac{1}{4}\mathrm{var}(X+Y) = \frac{1}{4}2\sigma^2 = \frac{1}{2}\sigma^2$$

From this, we can clearly see that measuring the ropes together instead of separately has improved our accuracy significantly.

Multiple random variables

A lot of the time, we will end up dealing with more than one random variable. When we do have two or more variables, we can inspect the linear relationships between the random variables. We call this the covariance.

If we have two random variables, X and Y, then the covariance is defined as follows:

$$\mathrm{cov}(X,Y) = \mathbb{E}\left[(X - \mathbb{E}\left[X\right])(Y - \mathbb{E}\left[Y\right])\right]$$

The following are some of the axioms for the covariance:

- If c is a constant, then $\mathrm{cov}(X,c) = 0$
- $\mathrm{cov}(X, Y + c) = \mathrm{cov}(X,Y)$
- $\mathrm{cov}(X,Y) = \mathrm{cov}(Y,X)$
- $\mathrm{cov}(X,Y) = \mathbb{E}[XY] - \mathbb{E}[X]\mathbb{E}[Y]$
- $\mathrm{cov}(X,X) = \mathrm{var}(X)$
- $\mathrm{var}(X + Y) = \mathrm{var}(X) + \mathrm{var}(Y) + 2\mathrm{cov}(X,Y)$

- $\text{cov}(X, Y) = 0$, given that X and Y are independent (but it does not imply that the two are independent).
- $\text{cov}(aX + bY, Z) = a\,\text{cov}(X, Z) + b\,\text{cov}(Y, Z)$

However, sometimes, the covariance doesn't give us the full picture of the correlation between two variables. This could be a result of the variance of X and Y. For this reason, we normalize the covariance as follows and get the correlation:

$$\text{corr}(X, Y) = \frac{\text{cov}(X, Y)}{\sqrt{\text{var}(X)\text{var}(Y)}}$$

The resulting value will always lie in the [-1, 1] interval.

This leads us to the concept of conditional distributions, where we have two random variables, X and Y, that are not independent and we have the joint distribution, $\mathbb{P}(X = x, Y = y)$, from which we can get the probabilities, $\mathbb{P}(X = x)$ and $\mathbb{P}(Y = y)$. Then, our distribution is defined as follows:

$$\mathbb{P}(X = x) = \sum_{y \in \Omega_Y} \mathbb{P}(X = x, Y = y)$$

From this definition, we can find our conditional distribution of X given Y to be as follows:

$$\mathbb{P}(X = x \mid Y = y) = \frac{\mathbb{P}(X = x, Y = y)}{\mathbb{P}(Y = y)}$$

We may also want to find the conditional expectation of X given Y, which is as follows:

$$\mathbb{E}\left[X \mid Y = y\right] = \sum_{x \in \Omega_X} x\mathbb{P}\left(X = x \mid Y = y\right)$$

Now, if our random variables are independent, then, $\mathbb{E}[X \mid Y] = \mathbb{E}[X]$, which we know to be true because Y has no effect on X.

Continuous random variables

So far, we've looked at discrete outcomes in the sample space where we could find the probability of a certain outcome. But now, in the continuous space, we will find the probability of our outcome being in a particular interval or range.

Now, to find the distribution of X, we need to define a function, f, so that the probability of X must lie in the interval $[x, x + \delta x]$

Formally, a random variable, $X : \Omega \to \mathbb{R}$, is continuous if, in a function, $f : \mathbb{R} \to \mathbb{R}_{\geq 0}$ so that we have the following:

$$\mathbb{P}(a \leq X \leq b) = \int_a^b f(x)\mathrm{d}x$$

We call the function, f, the **probability density function (PDF)** and it must satisfy the following:

- $f \geq 0$
- $\int_{-\infty}^{\infty} f(x) = 1$

There is another distribution function that is important for us to know, known as the **cumulative distribution function**. If we have a random variable, X, that could be continuous or discrete, then, $F(x) = \mathbb{P}(X \leq x)$, where $F(x)$ is increasing so that x→∞ and F(x)→1.

When dealing with continuous random variables such as the following, we know that F is both continuous and differentiable:

$$F(x) = \int_{-\infty}^x f(z)\mathrm{d}z$$

So, when F is differentiable, then $F'(x) = f(x)$.

An important fact to note is that $\mathbb{P}(a < x \leq b) = F(b) - F(a)$.

This leads us to the concept of uniform distribution, which, in general, has the following PDF:

$$f(x) = \frac{1}{b - a}$$

So, we have the following:

$$F(x) = \int_a^x f(z)\mathrm{d}z = \frac{x - a}{b - a}$$

This is the case for $a \le x \le b$.

We write $X \sim U[a,b]$ if X follows a uniform distribution on the [a, b] interval.

Now, let's suppose our random variable is an exponential random variable and has the added λ parameter. Then, its PDF is $f(x) = \lambda e^{-\lambda x}$ and $F(x) = 1 - e^{-\lambda x}$ for all $x \ge 0$.

We write this as $X \sim \mathcal{E}(\lambda)$, so we have the following:

$$\mathbb{P}(a \le x \le b) = \int_a^b f(z)dz = e^{-\lambda a} - e^{-\lambda b}$$

It is also very important to note that the exponential random variable, such as the geometric random variable, is memory-less; that is, the past gives us no information about the future.

Just as in the discrete case, we can define the expectation and variance in the case of continuous random variables.

The expectation for a continuous random variable is defined as follows:

$$\mathbb{E}[X] = \int_{-\infty}^{\infty} x f(x)dx$$

But, say $X \sim \mathcal{E}(\lambda)$. Then, we have the following:

$$\mathbb{P}(X \ge x) = \int_x^{\infty} \lambda e^{-\lambda t} dt = e - \lambda x$$
$$\mathbb{E}[X] = \int_0^{\infty} e^{-\lambda x} dx = \frac{1}{\lambda}$$

In the case of continuous random variables, the variance is defined as follows:

$$\text{var}(X) = \mathbb{E}[(X - \mathbb{E}[X])^2] = \mathbb{E}[X^2] - (\mathbb{E}[X])^2$$

This gives us the following:

$$\text{var}(X) = \int_{-\infty}^{\infty} x^2 f(x)dx - \left(\int_{-\infty}^{\infty} x f(x)dx \right)^2$$

Now, for example, let's take $X \sim U[a, b]$. We can find the expected value of X as follows:

$$\mathbb{E}[X] = \int_a^b x \frac{1}{b-a} dx = \frac{a+b}{2}$$

Its variance can be found as follows:

$$\text{var}(X) = \int_a^b x^2 \frac{1}{b-a} dx - (\mathbb{E}[X])^2 = \frac{1}{12}(b-a)^2$$

Now, we have a good handle of expectation and variance in continuous distribution. Let's get acquainted with two additional terms that apply to PDFs—**mode** and **median**.

The mode in a PDF is the value that appears the most; however, it is also possible for the mode to appear more than once. For example, in a uniform distribution, all the x values can be considered as the mode.

Say we have a PDF, $f(x)$. Then, we denote the mode as $\hat{x}$, so $f(\hat{x}) \geq f(x)$ for all cases of x.

We define the median as follows:

$$\int_{-\infty}^{\hat{x}} f(x) dx = \int_{\hat{x}}^{\infty} f(x) dx = \frac{1}{2}$$

However, in a discrete case, the median is as follows:

$$\mathbb{P}(X \leq \hat{x}) \geq \frac{1}{2} \text{ and } \mathbb{P}(X \geq \hat{x}) \geq \frac{1}{2}$$

Many times, in probability, we take the sample mean instead of the mean. Suppose we have a distribution that contains all the values that X can take. From it, we randomly sample n values and average it so that we have the following:

$$\bar{X} = \frac{1}{n} \sum_{i=1}^{n} X_i$$

Joint distributions

So far, we have dealt with and learned about distributions that relate to one random variable; but now, say we have two random variables, X and Y. Then, their joint distribution is defined as $F(x, y) = \mathbb{P}(X \le x, Y \le y)$, such that $F : \mathbb{R}^2 \mapsto [0, 1]$.

In joint distributions, we usually tend to know the distribution of a set of variables, but sometimes, we may only want to know the distribution of a subset. We call this the marginal distribution. We define the marginal distribution of X as follows:

$$F_X(x) = \mathbb{P}(X \le x) = \mathbb{P}(X \le x, Y < \infty) = F(x, \infty) = \lim_{y \to \infty} F(x, y)$$

Let's say our n continuous random variables in A are jointly distributed and have the f PDF. Then, we have the following:

$$\mathbb{P}((X_1, \cdots, X_n) \in A) = \int_{(x_1, \cdots, x_n) \in A} f(x_1, \cdots, x_n) dx_1 \cdots dx_n$$

Here, $f(x_1, \cdots, x_n) \ge 0$ and $\int_{\mathbb{R}^n} f(x_1, \cdots, x_n) dx_1 \cdots dx_n = 1$.

Let's revisit an earlier example, where we have two variables, X and Y. If the variables are continuous, then their joint distribution is

$$F(x, y) = \mathbb{P}(X \le x, Y \le y) = \int_{-\infty}^{x} \int_{-\infty}^{y} f(x, y) dx dy \quad \text{and} \quad f(x, y) = \frac{\partial^2}{\partial x \partial y} F(x, y).$$

 If the random variables are jointly continuous, then they are individually continuous.

Now, let's suppose our n continuous random variables are independent. Then, $\mathbb{P}(X_1 \in A_1, X_2 \in A_2, \cdots, X_n \in A_n) = \mathbb{P}(X_1 \in A_1)\mathbb{P}(X_2 \in A_2) \cdots \mathbb{P}(X_n \in A_n)$ for all cases of $A_i \in \Omega_X$.

If F_{X_i} is a cumulative distribution function and f_{X_i} is the PDF, then $F(x_1, x_2, \cdots, x_n) = F_{X_1}(x_1)F_{X_2}(x_2) \cdots F_{X_n}(x_n)$ and $f(x_1, x_2, \cdots, x_n) = f_{X_1}(x_1)f_{X_2}(x_2) \cdots f_{X_n}(x_n)$.

More probability distributions

Earlier on in this chapter, we introduced several different types of distributions in the *Random variables* section. I am sure, at some point, that you thought to yourself *there must also be probability distributions for continuous random variables.*

Normal distribution

The following distribution is quite an important one and is known as the **normal distribution**. It looks like as follows:

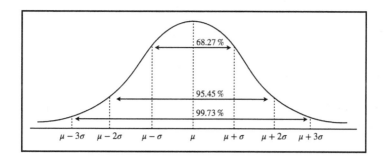

The normal distribution, written as $N(\mu, \sigma^2)$, has the $f(x) = \dfrac{1}{\sqrt{2\pi}\sigma}e^{-\frac{(x-\mu)^2}{2\sigma^2}}$ PDF for all cases of $-\infty < x < \infty$.

Additionally, we have the following:

$$\int_{-\infty}^{\infty} \frac{1}{\sqrt{2\pi\sigma^2}} e^{-\frac{(x-\mu)^2}{2\sigma^2}} \, \mathrm{d}x = 1$$

When the normal distribution has $\mu = 0$ and $\sigma^2 = 1$, it is called the **standard normal** and we denote $\phi(x)$ as its PDF and $\Phi(x)$ as its cumulative distribution function.

The normal distribution has some rather interesting properties, which are as follows:

- $\mathbb{E}[X] = \mu$
- $\mathrm{var}(X) = \sigma^2$

Assuming we have two independent random variables, $X \sim N(\mu_1, \sigma_1^2)$ and $Y \sim N(\mu_2, \sigma_2^2)$, then we have the following:

- $X + Y \sim N(\mu_1 + \mu_2, \sigma_1^2 + \sigma_2^2)$
- $aX \sim N(a\mu_1, a^2\sigma_1^2)$, where a is a constant

The reason this probability distribution is so important is because of its relation to the central limit theorem, which states that if we have a large number of independent and identically distributed random variables, then their distribution is approximately the same as the normal distribution.

Multivariate normal distribution

The normal distribution can also be extended for multiple random variables, which gives us the multivariate normal distribution.

Say we have n iid random variables sampled from $N(0, 1)$. Then, we define their joint density function as follows:

$$g(x_1, x_2, \cdots, x_n) = \prod_{i=1}^{n} \phi(x_i)$$

$$= \prod_{i=1}^{n} \frac{1}{\sqrt{2\pi}} e^{-\frac{1}{2}x_i^2}$$

$$= \frac{1}{(2\pi)^{\frac{n}{2}}} e^{-\frac{1}{2}\sum_{1}^{n} x_i^2}$$

$$= \frac{1}{(2\pi)^{\frac{n}{2}}} e^{-\frac{1}{2}\mathbf{x}^T\mathbf{x}}$$

Here, $\mathbf{x} = (x_1, \cdots, x_n)$.

Let's take this a step further. Now, let's suppose we have an invertible $n \times n$ matrix, A, and are interested in $\mathbf{Z} = \mu + \mathbf{AX}$. Then, $\mathbf{X} = \mathbf{A}^{-1}(\mathbf{Z} - \mu)$ and $|J| = |\det(A^{-1})| = \frac{1}{\det A}$. So, we have the following:

$$f(z_1, z_2, \cdots, z_n) = \frac{1}{(2\pi)^{\frac{n}{2}}} \frac{1}{\det A} e^{\left[-\frac{1}{2}(\mathbf{A}^{-1}(\mathbf{z}-\mu))^{\mathrm{T}}(\mathbf{A}^{-1}(\mathbf{z}-\mu))\right]}$$

$$= \frac{1}{(2\pi)^{\frac{n}{2}} \det A} e^{\left[-\frac{1}{2}(\mathbf{z}-\mu)^{\mathrm{T}}\Sigma^{-1}(\mathbf{z}-\mu)\right]}$$

$$= \frac{1}{(2\pi)^{\frac{n}{2}} \sqrt{\det \Sigma}} e^{\left[-\frac{1}{2}(\mathbf{z}-\mu)^{\mathrm{T}}\Sigma^{-1}(\mathbf{z}-\mu)\right]}$$

Here, $\Sigma = \mathbf{A}\mathbf{A}^{\mathrm{T}}$. Therefore, Z is the multivariate normal and is expressed as follows:

$$\mathbf{Z} = \begin{pmatrix} Z_1 \\ \vdots \\ Z_3 \end{pmatrix} \sim MVN(\mu, \Sigma)$$

You're likely wondering what this new matrix, Σ, represents. It is the covariance matrix where the ith and j^{th} entry is $\mathrm{cov}(Z_i, Z_j) = \mathbb{E}[(Z_i - \mu_i)(Z_j - \mu_j)]$.

In the case where the covariances are 0, which implies the variables are independent, then $\Sigma = \mathrm{diag}(\sigma_1^2, \cdots, \sigma_n^2)$.

Bivariate normal distribution

When $n = 2$ in the multivariate normal distribution, this is a special case known as the **bivariate normal**. Its covariance matrix is written as follows:

$$\Sigma = \begin{pmatrix} \sigma_1^2 & \rho\sigma_1\sigma_2 \\ \rho\sigma_1\sigma_2 & \sigma_2^2 \end{pmatrix}$$

The inverse of this is as follows:

$$\Sigma^{-1} = \frac{1}{1 - \rho^2} \begin{pmatrix} \sigma_1^{-2} & -\rho\sigma_1^{-1}\sigma_2^{-1} \\ -\rho\sigma_1^{-1}\sigma_2^{-1} & \sigma_2^{-2} \end{pmatrix}$$

In this case, the correlation between the two variables becomes the following:

$$\mathrm{corr}(X_1, X_2) = \frac{\mathrm{cov}(X_1, X_2)}{\sqrt{\mathrm{var}(X_1)\mathrm{var}(X_2)}} = \frac{\rho\sigma_1\sigma_2}{\sigma_1\sigma_2} = \rho$$

For the sake of simplicity, we will assume the mean is 0, so the joint PDF of the bivariate normal is as follows:

$$f(x_1, x_2) = \frac{1}{2\pi\sigma_1\sigma_2\sqrt{1-\rho^2}} e^{-\frac{1}{2(1-\rho^2)}\left(\frac{x_1^2}{\sigma_1^2} - \frac{2\rho x_1 x_2}{\sigma_1\sigma_2} + \frac{x_2^2}{\sigma_2^2}\right)}$$

Gamma distribution

Gamma distribution is a widely used distribution to model positive continuous variables with skewed distributions.

Gamma distribution is denoted by $\Gamma(n, \lambda)$ and has the following PDF:

$$f(x) = \frac{\lambda^n x^{n-1} e^{-\lambda x}}{(n-1)!}$$

With that, we conclude our section on probability. We will now start exploring statistics.

Essential concepts in statistics

While probability allows us to measure and calculate the odds of events or outcomes occurring, statistics allows us to make judgments and decisions given data generated by some unknown probability model. We use the data to learn the properties of the underlying probabilistic model. We call this process parametric inference.

Estimation

In estimation, our objective is given n iid samples with the same distribution as X (the probability model). If the PDF and **probability mass function (PMF)** is $f_X(x; \theta)$, we need to find θ.

Formally, we define a statistic as an estimate of θ.

A statistic is a function, T, of the data, $\mathbf{x} = (x_1, x_2, \cdots, x_n)$, so that our estimate is $\hat{\theta} = T(\mathbf{x})$. Therefore, $T(x)$ is the sampling distribution of the statistic and an estimator of θ.

Going forward, X will denote a random variable and x will denote an observed value.

Let's say we have $X_1, X_2, \cdots, X_n$, which are iid $N(\mu, 1)$. Then, a possible estimation for μ is as follows:

$$T(\mathbf{X}) = \frac{1}{n} \sum X_i$$

However, our estimate for a particular observed sample, **x**, is as follows:

$$T(\mathbf{x}) = \frac{1}{n} \sum x_i$$

A method we use to determine whether or not our estimator is good is the bias. The bias is defined as the difference between the true value and the expected value and is written as $\text{bias}(\hat{\theta}) = \mathbb{E}_\theta(\hat{\theta}) - \theta$. The estimator is unbiased if $\mathbb{E}_\theta(\hat{\theta}) = \theta$.

Mean squared error

The **mean squared error** (**MSE**) is a measure of how good an estimator is and is a better indicator of this than the bias. We write it as follows:

$$\text{MSE} = \mathbb{E}_\theta[(\hat{\theta} - \theta)^2]$$

However, sometimes, we use the root MSE, which is the square root of the MSE.

We can also express the MSE in terms of bias and variance, as follows:

$$\mathbb{E}[(\hat{\theta} - \theta)^2] = \text{var}(\hat{\theta}) + \text{bias}^2(\hat{\theta})$$

Sometimes, when we are trying to get a low MSE, it is in our best interest to have a biased estimator with low variance. We call this the **bias-variance trade-off**.

Sufficiency

A lot of the time, the purpose of conducting our experiments is to find the value of θ and to find the bigger picture. A sufficient statistic is one that gives us all the information we want about θ.

Lucky for us, the factorization theorem gives us the ability to find sufficient statistics. It states that T is sufficient for θ if we have the following:

$$f_{\mathbf{X}}(\mathbf{x} \mid \theta) = g(T(\mathbf{x}), \theta)h(\theta)$$

Here, g and h are arbitrary functions.

In general, if T is a sufficient statistic, then it does not lose any information about θ and the best statistic is the one that gives us the maximal reduction. We call this the minimal sufficient statistic; in its definition, $T(X)$ is minimal if—and only if—it is a function of every other statistic. So, if $T'(X)$ is sufficient, then $T'(X) = T'(Y) \Rightarrow T(X) = T(Y)$.

Suppose $T = T(X)$ is a statistic that satisfies $\dfrac{f_{\mathbf{X}}(\mathbf{x}; \theta)}{f_{\mathbf{X}}(\mathbf{y}; \theta)}$, which does not depend on θ if (and only if) $T(\mathbf{x}) = T(\mathbf{y})$. Then, T is minimally sufficient for θ.

Following this, let's say we have $X_1, X_2, \cdots, X_n$, which are iid $N(\mu, \sigma^2)$. Then, we can deduce the following:

$$\frac{f_{\mathbf{X}}(\mathbf{x} \mid \mu, \sigma^2)}{f_{\mathbf{X}}(\mathbf{y} \mid \mu, \sigma^2)} = \frac{(2\pi\sigma^2)^{-\frac{n}{2}} e^{-\frac{1}{2\sigma^2}\sum_i(x_i - \mu)^2}}{(2\pi\sigma^2)^{-\frac{n}{2}} e^{-\frac{1}{2\sigma^2}\sum_i(y_i - \mu)^2}}$$

$$= e^{-\frac{1}{2\sigma^2}\left(\sum_i x_i^2 - \sum_i y_i^2\right) + \frac{\mu}{\sigma^2}\left(\sum_i x_i - \sum_i y_i\right)}$$

This is a constant function that tells us that $\displaystyle\sum_i x_i^2 = \sum_i y_i^2$ and $\displaystyle\sum_i x_i = \sum_i y_i$. Therefore,

$$T(\mathbf{X}) = \left(\sum_i X_i^2, \sum_i X_i\right)$$

is minimally sufficient.

The advantage of minimally sufficient statistics is that they give us the ability to store our experiments' results in the most efficient way and we can use them to improve our estimator.

This leads us to the Rao-Blackwell theorem, which states that if T is a sufficient statistic for θ, and if $\tilde{\theta}$ is an estimator of θ—where for all θ, $\mathbb{E}(\tilde{\theta}) < \infty$. Let $\check{\theta}(x) = \mathbb{E}[\tilde{\theta}(\mathbf{X}) \mid T(\mathbf{X}) = T(\mathbf{x})]$—then, for all cases of θ, we have $\mathbb{E}[(\check{\theta} - \theta)] \leq \mathbb{E}[(\tilde{\theta} - \theta)]$.

Likelihood

Generally, in practice, when we want to determine whether or not our estimator is good, we usually use the **maximum likelihood estimator (MLE)**.

Given n random variables (with $f_{\mathbf{X}}(\mathbf{x} \mid \theta)$ being the joint PDF), then if $X = x$, the likelihood of θ is defined as $\text{like}(\theta) = f_{\mathbf{X}}(\mathbf{x} \mid \theta)$. Therefore, the MLE of θ is an estimate of the value of θ that maximizes $\text{like}(\theta)$.

In practice, however, we maximize the log-likelihood instead of simply the likelihood.

Going back to the example of having n iid random variables with the $f_X(x \mid \theta)$ PDF, the likelihood and log-likelihood are as follows:

$$\text{like}(\theta) = \prod_{i=1}^{n} f_X(x_i \mid \theta)$$

$$\log \text{like}(\theta) = \prod_{i=1}^{n} \log f_X(x_i \mid \theta)$$

Suppose our n variables are Bernoulli (p). Then, $l(p) = \log \text{like}(p) = \left(\sum x_i\right) \log p + \left(n - \sum x_i\right) \log(1 - p)$.
Therefore, $\frac{dl}{dp} = \frac{\sum x_i}{p} - \frac{n - \sum x_i}{1 - p}$ when $p = \frac{\sum x_i}{n}$ is equal to 0 and is an unbiased MLE.

By now, you're probably wondering what exactly the MLE has to do with sufficiency. If T is sufficient for θ, then its likelihood is $g(T(\mathbf{x}), \theta) h(\mathbf{x})$ and to maximize our estimate, we have to maximize g. Therefore, the MLE is a function of the sufficient statistic—voila!

Confidence intervals

The confidence interval gives us the ability to determine the probability that certain intervals contain θ. We formally define it as follows.

A $100\gamma\%$ $(0 < \gamma < 1)$ confidence interval for θ is a random interval $(A(\mathbf{X}), B(\mathbf{X}))$, such that $\mathbb{P}(A(\mathbf{X}) < \theta < B(\mathbf{X})) = \gamma$, regardless of the true value of θ.

Suppose that we calculate $(A(\mathbf{X}), B(\mathbf{X}))$ for a number of samples, x. Then, $100\gamma\%$ of them will cover our true value of θ.

Say we have $X_1, X_2, \cdots, X_n$, which are iid $N(\theta, 1)$, and we want to find a 95% confidence interval for θ. We know that $\bar{X} \sim N\left(\theta, \frac{1}{n}\right)$ so that $\sqrt{n}(\bar{X} - \theta) \sim N(0, 1)$. Then, we choose z_1, z_2, such that $\phi(z_2) - \phi(z_1) = 0.95$, where Φ is the normal distribution. So, $\mathbb{P}\left[\bar{X} - \frac{z_2}{\sqrt{n}} < \theta < \bar{X} - \frac{z_1}{\sqrt{n}}\right] = 0.95$, from which we get the following confidence interval:

$$\left(\bar{X} - \frac{z_2}{\sqrt{n}}, \bar{X} - \frac{z_1}{\sqrt{n}}\right)$$

Here is a three-step approach that is commonly used to find confidence intervals:

1. Find $R(\mathbf{X}, \theta)$, such that the $\mathbb{P}_\theta-\text{distribution}$ of $R(\mathbf{X}, \theta)$ isn't dependent on θ. We call this a **pivot**.
2. Above $R(\mathbf{X}, \theta) = \sqrt{n}(\bar{X} - \theta)$, write the probability statement in the $\mathbb{P}_\theta(c_1 < R(\mathbf{X}, \theta) < c_2) = \gamma$ form.
3. Rearrange the inequalities to find the interval.

Usually, c_1 and c_2 are percentage points from a known distribution; for example, for a 95% confidence interval, we would have the 2.5% and 97.5% points.

Bayesian estimation

Throughout this section on statistics, we have dealt with what is known as the frequentist approach. Now, however, we will look at what is known as the Bayesian approach, where we treat θ as a random variable, we tend to have prior knowledge about the distribution, and, after collecting some additional data, we find the posterior distribution.

Formally, we define the prior distribution as a probability distribution of θ before collecting any additional data; we denote this as $\pi(\theta)$. The posterior distribution is the probability distribution of θ dependent on the outcome of our conducted experiment; we denote this as $\pi(\theta | x)$.

The relationship between the prior and posterior distributions are as follows:

$$\pi(\theta \mid \mathbf{x}) = \frac{f_{\mathbf{X}}(\mathbf{x} \mid \theta)\pi(\theta)}{f_{\mathbf{X}}(\mathbf{x})}$$

Generally, we avoid calculating $f_{\mathbf{X}}(\mathbf{x})$ and we only observe the relationship:

$$\pi(\theta \mid \mathbf{x}) \propto f_{\mathbf{X}}(\mathbf{x} \mid \theta)\pi(\theta)$$

We can read this as posterior $\propto$ likelihood $\times$ prior.

After conducting our experiments and coming up with the posterior, we need to determine an estimator, but to find the best estimator, we need a loss function, such as quadratic loss or absolute error loss, to see how far off the true value of θ is from our estimated value of a parameter.

Let's suppose the parameter we are estimating is b. Then, the Bayes estimator, $\hat{\theta}$, minimizes the expected posterior loss, as follows:

$$h(b) = \int L(\theta, b)\pi(\theta \mid \mathbf{x})\mathrm{d}\theta$$

If we choose our loss function to be a quadratic loss, then we have the following:

$$h(b) = \int (\theta - b)^2 \pi(\theta \mid \mathbf{x})\mathrm{d}\theta$$

However, if we choose an absolute error loss, then we have the following:

$$h(b) = \int |\theta - b| \pi(\theta \mid \mathbf{x})\mathrm{d}\theta$$

Since the posterior distribution is our true distribution, we know that by integrating over it, our result is as follows:

$$\int \pi(\theta \mid \mathbf{x})\mathrm{d}\theta = 1$$

If you're wondering how these two schools of statistics compare, think of frequentist versus Bayesian as absolute versus relative, respectively.

Hypothesis testing

In statistics, we usually have to test out hypotheses and most likely, we will compare two different hypotheses—the null hypothesis and the alternative hypothesis. The null hypothesis tells us that our experiment contains statistical significance; that is, that no relationship is observed between the variables. The alternative hypothesis tells us that there is a relationship between the variables.

In general, we start with the assumption that the null hypothesis is true, and to reject this, we need to find evidence through our experiments that contradict it.

Simple hypotheses

A simple hypothesis H is one in which the parameters of the distribution are completely specified, otherwise it is called a composite hypothesis.

When testing the null hypothesis (H_0) against the alternative hypothesis (H_1), we use our test to divide $\mathcal{X}^n$ into two regions C and $\tilde{C}$. If $\mathbf{x} \in C$, then we reject the null hypothesis, but if $\mathbf{x} \in \tilde{C}$ then we do not reject the null hypothesis. We call C the critical region.

When we perform tests, we hope to arrive at the correct conclusion, but we could make either of the following two errors:

- **Error 1**: rejecting H_0 when H_0 is true
- **Error 2**: not rejecting H_0 when H_0 is false

If H_0 and H_1 are both simple hypotheses, then we have the following:

$$\alpha = \mathbb{P}(\text{Type 1 error}) = \mathbb{P}(\mathbf{X} \in C \mid H_0 \text{ is true})$$
$$\beta = \mathbb{P}(\text{Type 2 error}) = \mathbb{P}(\mathbf{X} \notin C \mid H_1 \text{ is true})$$

Here, α is the size of our test and 1-β is the power of the test to find H_1.

If we have a simple hypothesis, $H : \theta = \theta^*$, then we also want to find its likelihood given x. We do this as follows:

$$L_{\mathbf{x}}(H) = f_{\mathbf{X}}(\mathbf{x} \mid \theta = \theta^*)$$

We can also find the likelihood ratio of H_0 and H_1 given x as follows:

$$\Lambda_{\mathbf{x}}(H_0; H_1) = \frac{L_{\mathbf{x}}(H_1)}{L_{\mathbf{x}}(H_0)}$$

A likelihood ratio test is where, given k, the critical region is as follows:

$$C = \{\mathbf{x} : \Lambda_{\mathbf{x}}(H_0; H_1) > k\}$$

Let's go through an example and develop a bit of intuition about this. Say we have $X_1, X_2, \cdots, X_n$, which are iid $N(\mu, \sigma_0^2)$, and σ_0^2 is a known quantity. Now, we want to find out what the best test size for our null hypothesis, $H_0 : \mu = \mu_0$, is versus the alternative hypothesis, $H_1 : \mu = \mu_1$. Let's assume that μ_0 and μ_1 are known to us as well, such that $\mu_1 > \mu_0$. Therefore, we have the following:

$$\Lambda_{\mathbf{x}}(H_0; H_1) = \frac{(2\pi\sigma_0^2)^{-\frac{n}{2}} e^{\left(-\frac{1}{2\sigma_0^2} \sum(x_i - \mu_1)^2\right)}}{(2\pi\sigma_0^2)^{-\frac{n}{2}} e^{\left(-\frac{1}{2\sigma_0^2} \sum(x_i - \mu_0)^2\right)}}$$

$$= e^{\left(\frac{\mu_1 - \mu_0}{\sigma_0^2} n\bar{x} + \frac{\mu_0^2 - \mu_1^2}{2\sigma_0^2} n\right)}$$

We know that this function is increasing, so $\Lambda_x > k$ for any case of k, which tells us that for some arbitrary values of c, $\bar{x} > c$.

We choose our value of c so that $\mathbb{P}(\bar{X} > c \mid H_0) = \alpha$, and if $\bar{x} > c$, we reject the null hypothesis.

Under the null hypothesis, $\bar{X} \sim N\left(\mu_0, \frac{\sigma_0^2}{n}\right)$; so, $Z = \frac{\sqrt{n}(\bar{X} - \mu_0)}{\sigma_0} \sim N(0, 1)$. Now, since $z > c'$, the test size rejects the null hypothesis if we have the following:

$$z = \frac{\sqrt{n}(\bar{x} - \mu_0)}{\sigma_0} > z_\alpha$$

This is known as the z-test and we use it to test a hypothesis, while the z-score tells us how many standard deviations away from the mean our data point is.

Here, the likelihood ratio rejects the null hypothesis if $z > k$. The test size is $\alpha = \mathbb{P}(Z > k \mid H_0) - 1 - \Phi(k)$, which decreases as k increases. The value of z is in the rejection region if $\alpha > p^* = \mathbb{P}(Z > z \mid H_0)$.

In the preceding equation, p^*, is known as the p-value of the data, x; it is, in other words, the probability of observing data (evidence) against the null hypothesis.

Composite hypothesis

Now, if we have a composite hypothesis, such as $H : \theta \geq 0$, the error probabilities are not singular-valued.

So, we define the power function, which is as follows:

$$W(\theta) = \mathbb{P}(\mathbf{X} \in C \mid \theta) = \mathbb{P}(\text{reject } H_0 \mid \theta).$$

Ideally, we would like $W(\theta)$ to be small on the null hypothesis and large on the alternative hypothesis.

The size of the test is $\alpha = \sup_{\theta \in \Theta_0} W(\theta)$, which is not an ideal size. Given $\theta \in \Theta_1$, $1 - W(\theta) = \mathbb{P}(\text{Type 2 error} \mid \theta).$

Previously, we saw that the best size of the test of H_0 versus H_1 is given by the following critical region:

$$C = \left\{ x : \frac{\sqrt{n}(\bar{x} - \mu_0)}{\sigma_0} > z_\alpha \right\}$$

This depends on $\mu_0, n, \sigma_0, \alpha$ and $\mu_1 > \mu_0$, but not the value of μ_1.

We call a test, which is specified by C, the uniformly most powerful size, α, of the $H_0 : \theta \in \Theta_0$ test versus $H_1 : \theta \in \Theta_1$, but only if the following is true:

- $\sup_{\theta \in \Theta_0} W(\theta) = \alpha$

- $W(\theta) \geq W^*(\theta)$ for all cases of $\theta \in \Theta_1$ if $C^* \leq \alpha$

Now, as before, we want to find the likelihood of a composite hypothesis, $H : \theta \in \Theta$, given some data, x. We do so as follows:

$$L_x(H) = \sup_{\theta \in \Theta} f(\mathbf{x} \mid \theta)$$

The multivariate normal theory

In this section, we have so far dealt with random variables or a vector of iid random variables. Now, let's suppose we have a random vector, $\mathbf{X} = (X_1, X_2, \cdots, X_n)$, where the X_i values are all correlated.

Now, if we want to find the mean of X, we do so as follows:

$$\mu = \mathbb{E}[\mathbf{X}] = (\mathbb{E}(X_1), \mathbb{E}(X_2), \cdots, \mathbb{E}(X_n)) = (\mu_1, \mu_2, \cdots, \mu_n)$$

If it exists, the covariance matrix is as follows:

$$\text{cov}(\mathbf{X}) = \mathbb{E}[(\mathbf{X} - \mu)(\mathbf{X} - \mu)^{\mathrm{T}}] = (\text{cov}(X_i, X_j))_{i,j}$$

Additionally, if we have $A \in \mathbb{R}^{m \times n}$, then $\mathbb{E}[A\mathbf{X}] = A\mu$ and $\text{cov}(A\mathbf{X}) = A\text{cov}(\mathbf{X})A^{\mathrm{T}}$.

If we're dealing with two random vectors, then we have the following:

- $\text{cov}(\mathbf{V}, \mathbf{W}) = (\text{cov}(V_i, W_j))_{i,j}$
- $\text{cov}(A\mathbf{X}, B\mathbf{X}) = A\text{cov}(\mathbf{X})B^{\mathrm{T}}$

Now, let's define what a multivariate normal distribution is.

Suppose we have a random vector, X. It has a multivariate normal distribution if for , $\mathbf{t}^{\mathrm{T}}\mathbf{X}$ has a normal distribution. $\mathbf{t} \in \mathbb{R}^n$

If $\mathbb{E}[\mathbf{X}] = \mu$ and $\text{cov}(\mathbf{X}) = \Sigma$, then $\mathbf{X} \sim N_n(\mu, \Sigma)$, where Σ is a symmetric and positive semi-definite matrix, because $\mathbf{t}^{\mathrm{T}}\Sigma\mathbf{t} = \text{var}(\mathbf{t}^{\mathrm{T}}\mathbf{X}) \geq 0$.

Some of you may be wondering what the PDF of a multivariate normal distribution looks like. We'll get there momentarily.

Now, suppose $\mathbf{X} \sim N_n(\mu, \Sigma)$ and we split $\mathbf{X} \in \mathbb{R}^n$ into two smaller random vectors, such that $\mathbf{X} = \begin{pmatrix} \mathbf{X}_1 \\ \mathbf{X}_2 \end{pmatrix}$, where $\mathbf{X}_i \in \mathbb{R}^{n_i}$ and $n_1 + n_2 = n$.

Similarly, $\mu = \begin{pmatrix} \mu_1 \\ \mu_2 \end{pmatrix}$ and $\Sigma = \begin{pmatrix} \Sigma_{1,1} & \Sigma_{1,2} \\ \Sigma_{2,1} & \Sigma_{2,2} \end{pmatrix}$.

Now, we have the following:

- $\mathbf{X}_i \sim N_{n_i}(\mu_i, \Sigma_{i,i})$
- $\mathbf{X}_1$ and $\mathbf{X}_2$ are independent if $\Sigma_{1,2} = 0$

When Σ is positive semi-definite, then X has the following PDF:

$$f_{\mathbf{X}}(\mathbf{x}; \mu, \Sigma) = \frac{1}{\sqrt{(2\pi)^n |\Sigma|^2}} e^{-\frac{1}{2}(\mathbf{x}-\mu)^{\mathrm{T}}\Sigma^{-1}(\mathbf{x}-\mu)}$$

Here, n is the dimension of x.

Suppose we have $X_1, X_2, \cdots, X_n$, which are iid $N(\mu, \sigma^2)$, and $\bar{X} = \frac{1}{n}\sum X_i$ and $S_{XX} = \sum(X_i - \bar{X})^2$. Then, we have the following:

- $\bar{X} \sim N(\mu, \frac{\sigma^2}{n})$

- $\frac{S_{XX}}{\sigma^2} \sim \chi^2_{n-1}$

- X and S_{xx} are independent

Linear models

In statistics, we use linear models to model the relationship between a dependent variable and one or more predictor variables.

As an example, let's suppose we have n observations Y_i and p predictors x_{j}, where $n > p$. We can write each observation as follows:

$$Y_i = \beta_1 x_{i,1} + \beta_2 x_{i,2} + \cdots + \beta_p x_{i,p} + \epsilon_i$$

For all cases of $i = 1, \cdots, n$, we can assume the following:

- $\beta_1, \beta_2, \cdots, \beta_p$ are the unknown, fixed parameters that we want to figure out
- $x_{i,1}, x_{i,2}, \cdots, x_{i,p}$ are the values of the p predictors for the ith response
- $\epsilon_1, \epsilon_2, \cdots, \epsilon_n$ are independent random variables with 0 mean and σ^2 variance

We generally consider $\beta_j x_{i,j}$ to be casual effects of x_{ij} and ε_i to be a random error term. Therefore, $\mathbb{E}(Y_i) = \beta_1 x_{i,1} + \beta_2 x_{i,2} + \cdots + \beta_p x_{i,p}$, $\mathrm{var}(Y_i) = \mathrm{var}(\epsilon_i) = \sigma^2$ and $Y_1, Y_2, \cdots, Y_n$ are independent.

Given all the data, we may want to plot a straight line on the data, so a possible model could be as follows:

$$Y_i = ax_i + \epsilon_i + b$$

Here, a and b are constants.

We can rewrite the preceding model as follows:

$$\mathbf{Y} = \mathbf{X}\beta + \epsilon$$

Here, the expanded form is as follows:

$$\mathbf{Y} = \begin{pmatrix} Y_1 \\ Y_2 \\ \vdots \\ Y_n \end{pmatrix}, \ \mathbf{X} = \begin{pmatrix} x_{1,1} & x_{1,2} & \cdots & x_{1,p} \\ x_{2,1} & x_{2,2} & \cdots & x_{2,p} \\ \vdots & \vdots & \ddots & \cdots \\ x_{n,1} & x_{n,2} & \cdots & x_{n,p} \end{pmatrix}, \ \beta = \begin{pmatrix} \beta_1 \\ \beta_2 \\ \vdots \\ \beta_p \end{pmatrix}, \ \epsilon = \begin{pmatrix} \epsilon_1 \\ \epsilon_2 \\ \vdots \\ \epsilon_n \end{pmatrix}$$

Also, $\mathbb{E}(\epsilon) = \mathbf{0}$ and $\text{cov}(\mathbf{Y}) = \sigma^2 I$.

The least-squares estimator, $\hat{\beta}$, of β minimizes our linear model by minimizing the square of the vertical distance between the line and the points, as follows:

$$\begin{aligned} S(\beta) &= \|\mathbf{Y} - \mathbf{X}\beta\|^2 \\ &= (\mathbf{Y} - \mathbf{X}\beta)^{\mathrm{T}}(\mathbf{Y} - \mathbf{X}\beta) \\ &= \sum_{i=1}^{n}(Y_i - x_{i,j}\beta_j)^2 \end{aligned}$$

To minimize it, we apply the following for all cases of k:

$$\left. \frac{\partial S}{\partial \beta_k} \right|_{\beta = \hat{\beta}} = 0$$

So, we have $-2x_{i,k}(Y_i - x_{i,j}\hat{\beta}_j) = 0$ and so, $x_{i,k}x_{i,j}\hat{\beta}_j = x_{i,k}Y_i$ for all cases of k.

By putting the preceding function into matrix form, as we did earlier, we get $\mathbf{X}^{\mathrm{T}}\mathbf{X}\hat{\beta} = \mathbf{X}^{\mathrm{T}}\mathbf{Y}$.

We know that $\mathbf{X}^{\mathrm{T}}\mathbf{X}$ is positive, semi-definite, and has an inverse. Therefore, $\hat{\beta} = (\mathbf{X}^{\mathrm{T}}\mathbf{X})^{-1}\mathbf{X}^{\mathrm{T}}\mathbf{Y}$.

TIP

Under normal assumptions, our least-squares estimator is the same as the MLE.

We now have the following:

$$\mathbb{E}(\hat{\beta}) = (\mathbf{X}^T\mathbf{X})^{-1}\mathbf{X}^T\mathbb{E}[\mathbf{Y}] = (\mathbf{X}^T\mathbf{X})^{-1}\mathbf{X}^T\mathbf{X}\beta = \beta$$

This tells us that our estimator is unbiased and
$$\text{cov}(\hat{\beta}) = (\mathbf{X}^T\mathbf{X})^{-1}\mathbf{X}^T\text{cov}(\mathbf{Y})\mathbf{X}(\mathbf{X}^T\mathbf{X})^{-1} = \sigma^2(\mathbf{X}^T\mathbf{X})^{-1} = \sigma^2 I.$$

I know what you're thinking—that was intense! Good job on making it this far; we are very close to finishing this chapter, so hang in there.

Hypothesis testing

In hypothesis testing, our goal is to ascertain whether certain variables influence the outcome.

Let's test a hypothesis of a general linear model. Suppose we have
$$\mathbf{X} \in \mathbb{R}^{n \times p} = \left(\mathbf{X}_0 \in \mathbb{R}^{n \times p} \quad \mathbf{X}_1 \in \mathbb{R}^{n \times (p - p_0)}\right) \text{ and } \mathbf{B} = \begin{pmatrix} \beta_0 \\ \beta_1 \end{pmatrix}.$$ We would like to test $H_0 : \beta_1 = 0$ against $H_1 : \beta_1 \neq 0$ and $\mathbf{Y} = \mathbf{X}_0\beta_0 + \epsilon$, since under H_0, $\mathbf{X}_1\beta_1$ vanishes.

Under the null hypothesis, the maximum likelihood of β_0 and σ^2 are $\hat{\hat{\beta}} = (\mathbf{X}_0^T\mathbf{X}_0)^{-1}\mathbf{X}_0^T\mathbf{Y}$ and $\hat{\hat{\sigma}}^2 = \frac{1}{n}(\mathbf{Y} - \mathbf{X}_0\hat{\hat{\beta}}_0)^T(\mathbf{Y} - \mathbf{X}_0\hat{\hat{\beta}}_0)$, which, as we know from earlier, are independent.

The estimators of the null hypothesis wear two hats instead of one and the alternative hypothesis has one.

Congratulations! You have officially completed this chapter and you have now developed a solid intuition for probability and statistics.

Summary

In this chapter, we learned a lot of concepts. I recommend going through the chapter again if needed because the topics in this chapter are very important to gaining a deep understanding of deep learning. Many of you may be wondering what the chapters you have learned so far have to do with neural networks; we will tie it all together in a couple more chapters.

The next chapter focuses on both convex and non-convex optimization methods and builds the foundation for understanding the optimization algorithms used in training neural networks.

4
Optimization

Optimization is a branch of applied mathematics that has applications in a multitude of fields, such as physics, engineering, economics, and so on, and is of vital importance in developing and training of deep neural networks. In this chapter, a lot of what we covered in previous chapters will be very relevant, particularly linear algebra and calculus.

As we know, deep neural networks are developed on computers and are, therefore, expressed mathematically. More often than not, training deep learning models comes down to finding the correct (or as close to the correct) set of parameters. We will learn more about this as we progress further through this book.

In this chapter, we'll mainly learn about two types of continuous optimization—constrained and unconstrained. However, we will also briefly touch on other forms of optimization, such as genetic algorithms, particle swarm optimization, and simulated annealing. Along the way, we will also learn when and how to use each of these techniques.

This chapter will cover the following topics:

- Understanding optimization and it's different types
- Exploring the various optimization methods
- Exploring population methods

Understanding optimization and it's different types

In optimization, our goal is to either minimize or maximize a function. For example, a business wants to minimize its costs while maximizing its profits or a shopper might want to get as much as possible while spending as little as possible. Therefore, the goal of optimization is to find the best case of $\mathbf{x} \in \mathbb{X}$, which is denoted by x^* (where x is a set of points), that satisfies certain criteria. These criteria are, for our purposes, mathematical functions known as **objective functions**.

For example, let's suppose we have the $f(x) = x^4 + 8x^3 + 10x^2 - 14x - 4$ equation. If we plot it, we get the following graph:

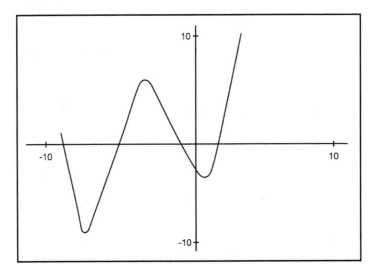

You will recall from Chapter 1, *Vector Calculus*, that we can find the gradient of a function by taking its derivative, equating it to 0, and solving for x. We can find the point(s) at which the function has a minimum or maximum, as follows:

$$\frac{\mathrm{d}f}{\mathrm{d}x} = 4x^3 + 24x^2 + 20x - 14$$

After solving this equation, we find that it has three distinct solutions (that is, three points where the minima and maxima occur).

To find which of these three solutions are the minima and maxima, we find the second derivative, $\frac{d^2 f}{dx^2} = 12x^2 + 48x + 20$, and check whether our stationary points are positive or negative.

Visually, when we see the graph, we can identify the local and global minima, but it isn't as simple as this when we calculate it computationally. So, instead, we start at a value and follow the gradient until we get to the minima (hopefully, the global minima).

Say we start from the right side at $x = 2$. The gradient is negative, which means we move to the left incrementally (these increments are called **step size**) and we get to the local minima, which isn't the one we want to find. However, if we start at $x = -2$, then we end up at the global minima.

Constrained optimization

Constrained optimization, in general, has certain rules or constraints attached that must be followed. In general, the problem is defined in the following form:

$$\text{minimize } f(x) \text{ subject to } h(x) = b \text{ given that } x \in X$$

In the preceding equation, $x \in \mathbb{R}^n$ contains the decision variables, $f : \mathbb{R}^n \to \mathbb{R}$ is our objective function, $h : \mathbb{R}^n \to \mathbb{R}^m$ and $b \in \mathbb{R}^m$ are the functional constraints, while $X \subseteq \mathbb{R}^n$ is the regional constraint.

 All of these variables are vectors; in fact, all of the variables in this chapter will be vectors, so for simplification, we will not be writing them in boldface as we did previously, in Chapter 1, *Vector Calculus*, and Chapter 2, *Linear Algebra*.

Sometimes, our constraints could be in the form of an inequality, such as $h(x) \geq b$, and we can add in a slack variable, z, which now makes our functional constraint $h(x) - z = b$ and the regional constraint $z \geq 0$.

We could simply write out all the constraints explicitly, but that's just too messy. We generally write them as follows:

$$\text{minimize } c^T x \text{ subject to } Ax \geq b, \text{ where } x \geq 0$$

This is the general form of a linear program. The standard form, however, is written as follows:

$$\text{minimize } c^{\mathrm{T}}x \text{ subject to } Ax = b, \text{ where } x \geq 0$$

I know this may all seem very unclear right now, but don't fear—we will make sense of all of it soon.

Unconstrained optimization

The goal of optimization problems is to minimize *f(x)*, and we will primarily be dealing with functions that are twice differentiable and where $f : \mathbb{R}^n \to \mathbb{R}$. A rather important property to be aware of is that since *f* is differentiable and convex, we have the following:

$$\nabla f(x^*) = 0$$

This should be apparent if you remember what we learned in Chapter 1, *Vector Calculus*.

Unconstrained optimization, as you can probably tell, is the case in which we do not have any constraints whatsoever and any point could be a minimum, maximum, or a saddle point, which doesn't make the problem easy.

Let's suppose we have a problem with *n* equations and *n* variables. Solving this and finding the optimal solution isn't simple, and we generally solve the problem iteratively. Think of this as computing a set sequence of points in the domain of *f*, which gradually gets us to the optima.

Now, say we have a function, $f : \mathbb{R}^n \to \mathbb{R}$, and $x^* \in \mathbb{R}^n$, such that $\nabla f(x^*) = 0$. The problem now looks as follows:

$$\nabla f = \left(\frac{\partial f}{\partial x_1}, \frac{\partial f}{\partial x_2}, \cdots, \frac{\partial f}{\partial x_n} \right)$$

Here, we have ∇f, which we know from previous chapters is the gradient of *f*.

Naturally, to start computing these points, we need a starting point, which we call the initial point, and it must lie within the domain of *f*. Then, we iterate and find better points from there until we find the optimal one.

Convex optimization

Convex optimization concerns minimizing a convex function over a convex set. In general, it takes the following form:

$$\text{minimize } f_0(x) \text{ subject to } f_i(x) \leq b_i, \ i = 1, \cdots, m$$

Here, $f_0, \cdots, f_m : \mathbb{R}^n \to \mathbb{R}$ are convex functions and so they satisfy the following:

$$f_i(\alpha x + \beta y) \leq \alpha f_i(x) + \beta f_i(y)$$

This is the case when $x, y \in \mathbb{R}^n$ and $\alpha, \beta \in \mathbb{R}_{\geq 0}$ are non-negative and $\alpha + \beta = 1$.

Convex sets

In optimization, we come across the terms convex and non-convex fairly often.

We define a convex set as one where if we were to take any two random points and draw a line to join them, the line would lie completely within the boundaries of the set.

We label our convex set $C \subseteq \mathbb{R}^n$ and if we have two points, $x, y \in C$ and some scalar $0 \leq \theta \leq 1$ value, then $\theta x + (1 - \theta)y \in C$.

Now, let's suppose we have the $f = \theta x + (1 - \theta)y$ function. Then, if $\theta = 0$, $f = y$; but if $\theta = 1$, then $f = x$. From this, we can tell that as θ increases, f moves gradually from y to x.

A function, $f : S \to \mathbb{R}$, is convex if S is convex for all cases of $x, y \in S$ and $\delta \in [0, 1]$. We then have $\delta f(x) + (1 - \delta)f(y) \geq f(\delta x + (1 - \delta)y)$.

Additionally, if we have $f : C \to \mathbb{R}$, where the domain of the function is the convex set for all cases of $x, y \in C$, then $f(\theta x + (1 - \theta)y) \leq \theta f(x) + (1 - \theta)f(y)$.

To aid us in visualizing a convex function, we have the following diagram, where we can see that it looks almost like a bowl and that all the points within the bowl are points in the convex set:

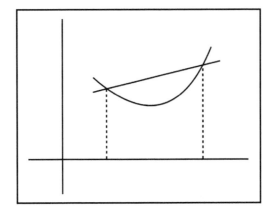

Now, let's suppose our function can be differentiated twice. Then, *f* is convex on a convex region and we can define our Hessian matrix as follows:

$$H f_{i,j} = \frac{\partial^2 f}{\partial x_i \partial x_j}$$

This is positive semi-definite for all cases of $x \in S$.

Affine sets

If we have a $\mathcal{C} \in \mathbb{R}^n$ set, it is affine if the line connecting our two points in $\mathcal{C}$ lies in $\mathcal{C}$; that is, this space contains a linear combination of the points in $\mathcal{C}$, but only if the sum of the coefficients is equal to 1 so that $x_1, x_2 \in \mathcal{C}$, $\theta \in \mathbb{R}$ and $\theta x_1 + (1 - \theta) x_2 \in \mathcal{C}$.

Additionally, if we have more than two points, then $\theta_1 x_1 + \theta_2 x_2 + \cdots + \theta_n x_n \in \mathcal{C}$ is an affine combination of *n* points, given the following:

$$\sum_{i=1}^{n} \theta_i = 1$$

Also, if $\mathcal{C}$ is an affine set and we have a $x_0 \in \mathcal{C}$ point, then we have the following:

$$\mathcal{V} = \mathcal{C} - x_0 = \{x - x_0 \mid x \in \mathcal{C}\}$$

This is a subspace of C.

Now, suppose we have some $v_1, v_2 \in V$ and $\alpha, \beta \in \mathbb{R}$ points. From earlier, we know that $v_1 + x_0 \in C$ and $v_2 + x_0 \in C$. Therefore, we can express C as follows:

$$C = V + x_0 = \{v + x_0 \mid v \in V\}$$

In general, we call the set of all combinations of points in C the affine hull of C.

Let's now assume that we have a unit sphere in $\mathbb{R}^2$ where x is its center, r is the radius, and $\{x \in \mathbb{R}^2 \mid x_1^2 + x_2^2 = 1\}$. The relative interior of C, where the dimension of $C \in \mathbb{R}^n$ is less than n, is defined as the $\{x \in C \mid B(x, r) \cap \text{aff } C \text{ where } r > 0\}$ set, where $B(x, r) = \{y \mid \|y - x\| \leq r\}$.

Then, the relative boundary of C is defined as the difference between the closure of C and the relative interior of C.

Convex functions

A convex function is defined as a $f : \mathbb{R}^n \to \mathbb{R}$ function if its domain is a convex set and if for $x, y \in \text{dom } f$ and $0 \leq \theta \leq 1$, which gives us the following:

$$f(\theta x + (1 - \theta)y) \leq \theta f(x) + (1 - \theta)f(y)$$

Let's visualize this inequality with the following graph:

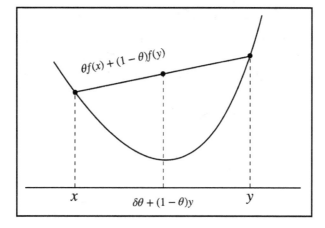

The line that connects the two points is above the function, which tells us that it is convex. However, the function is concave when it is *-f* and is convex otherwise.

Affine functions, on the other hand, have equality and are, therefore, concave and convex.

Optimization problems

We can recall from earlier in this chapter that the optimization problem can be defined as follows:

$$\text{minimize } f_0(x) \text{ subject to some constraints}$$

The optimal value of our problem is defined as follows:

$$p^* = \inf\{f_0(x) \mid \text{constraints}\}$$

We call x^* an optimal point (or solution to our problem) if $f_0(x^*) = p^*$. Therefore, the optimal set containing all the optimal points is as follows:

$$X_{\text{opt}} = \{x \mid \text{constraints and } f_0(x) = p^*\}$$

In convex optimization, there is a rather major property that states that any point that is locally optimal is also globally optimal.

Non-convex optimization

In convex optimization, we deal with having to find a local optimum, which also happens to be the global minimum. However, in non-convex optimization, we have to find the global minimum, which isn't the local minimum; in fact, there could be more than one local minimum, as well as saddle points.

This makes non-convex optimization far more challenging than convex optimization.

Exploring the various optimization methods

Now that you know what optimization is, it's time to explore some of the methods used in practice. We will not be covering the entire field of optimization because that would require an entire book to cover. We will only cover the essential optimization methods that are applicable to deep learning.

Least squares

Least squares is a subclass of convex optimization. It is classified as having no constraints and takes the following form:

$$\text{minimize } f_0(x) = \|Ax - b\|_2^2 = \sum_{i=1}^{k}(a_i^T x - b_i)^2$$

Here, $A \in \mathbb{R}^{k \times n}$, a_i^T are rows of A, and $x \in \mathbb{R}^n$ is our optimization variable.

We can also express this as a set of linear equations of the $(A^T A)x = A^T b$ form. Therefore, $x = (A^T A)^{-1} A^T b = A^T b$.

The problem of least squares is very similar to that of maximum likelihood estimation.

Lagrange multipliers

When solving constrained optimization problems, it is best to include the constraints in the objective function. This way, anything that is not included in the constraints is not considered a minimum.

Let's revisit our earlier problem:

$$\text{minimize } f(x) \text{ subject to } h(x) = b, \ x \in X$$

We'll call our constraint C.

So, we define the Lagrangian of C as follows:

$$L(x, \lambda) = f(x) - \lambda^T(h(x) - b)$$

Here, $\lambda \in \mathbb{R}^m$ and is known as the **Lagrange multiplier**.

When our constraint is satisfied, then $h(x) - b = 0$ and $L(x, \lambda) = f(x)$. By minimizing L over x and λ, we find the solution with respect to the constraints.

Suppose we have $x^* \in X$ and $\lambda* \in \mathbb{R}^m$, such that we have the following:

$$L(x^*, \lambda^*) = \inf_{x \in X} L(x, \lambda^*) \text{ and } h(x^*) = b$$

Then, x^* is optimal for C; that is, it minimizes f. This is called **Lagrangian sufficiency**.

To find λ^* and x^*, we must solve the following:

$$\nabla f = \lambda \nabla h \text{ and } h(x) = b.$$

For example, say we want to minimize $2x_1 + x_2 - x_3$ subject to $x_1 + x_2 + x_3 = 4$ and $x_1^2 + x_2^2 = 4$.

So, the equation for Lagrangian sufficiency is as follows:

$$L(x, \lambda) = 2x_1 + x_2 - x_3 - \lambda_1(x_1 + x_2 + x_3 - 4) - \lambda_2(x_1^2 + x_2^2 - 4)$$

We can rewrite this as follows:

$$L(x, \lambda) = ((2 - \lambda_1)x_1 - \lambda_2 x_1^2) + ((1 - \lambda_1)x_2 - \lambda_2 x_2^2) + (-1 - \lambda_1)x_3 + 4\lambda_1 + 4\lambda_2$$

We also need to pick a λ^* and x^* value so that $L(x^*, \lambda^*)$ is minimal. So, for λ^*, $L(x, \lambda^*)$ must have a finite minimum.

From the preceding equation, we know that $(-1 - \lambda_1)x_3$ has a finite minimum at $\lambda_1 = -1$ and the x_1 and x_2 terms only have a finite minimum when $\lambda_2 < 0$.

Now, to find a minimum, we take the first derivatives and make them equal to 0, as follows:

$$\frac{\partial L}{\partial x_1} = 2 - \lambda_1 - 2\lambda_2 x_1 = 3 - 2\lambda_2 x_1$$

$$\frac{\partial L}{\partial x_2} = 1 - \lambda_1 - 2\lambda_2 x_2 = 2 - 2\lambda_2 x_2$$

Since the first derivatives must be equal to 0, we have the following:

$$x_1 = \frac{3}{2\lambda_2}, \quad x_2 = \frac{2}{2\lambda_2}$$

To confirm that these are the minimum, we find the Hessian matrix:

$$HL = \begin{pmatrix} -2\lambda_2 & 0 \\ 0 & -2\lambda_2 \end{pmatrix}$$

As we would expect, this is positive semi-definite when $\lambda_2 < 0$.

The values of λ that we want are in the $Y = \{\lambda : \mathbb{R}^2 : \lambda_1 = -1, \lambda_2 < 0\}$ set, which tells us that the unique minimum of $L(x, \lambda)$ is as follows:

$$x(\lambda) = \left(\frac{3}{2\lambda_2}, \frac{2}{2\lambda_2}, x_3 \right)$$

All we have to do now is find the values of λ and x for $x(\lambda)$ that satisfy the constraints.

Newton's method

Newton's method is a second-order optimization method that rescales the gradients in all directions using the inverse of the corresponding eigenvalues of the Hessian.

As we know, we are trying to find the value of x^* that minimizes $f(x)$ and satisfies $\nabla f(x^*) = 0$. Imagine that we are currently at a point, x_k, and we move to x_{k+1}, which is closer to x^*. We can write this step as $\triangle x_k = x_{k+1} - x_k$ (or $x_{k+1} = x_k + \triangle x_k$).

The reason why Newton step works well is because it behaves well when x is near x^* since it takes the steepest descent direction at x. However, its performance is slow when we are at x_0 because the second derivative at x_0 does not give us reliable information about which direction we need to move in to reach x^*.

Now, let's suppose that $x \in \text{dom } f$. Then, we have the following:

$$\nabla f(x_{k+1}) = \nabla f(x_k) + Hf(x_k)(\triangle x_k)$$

Here, $Hf(x_k)(\triangle x_k) = -\nabla f(x_k)$.

We can rewrite this as follows:

$$\triangle x_k = -Hf(x_k)^{-1}\nabla f(x_k)$$

This is known as the Newton step. Therefore, at x_k, x_{k+1} minimizes the following quadratic function:

$$f(x_k) + \nabla f(x_k)^{\mathrm{T}}(x - x_k) + \frac{1}{2}(x - x_k)^{\mathrm{T}}Hf(x_k)(x - x_k)$$

We also know that $Hf(x)$ is positive definite, which tells us $\nabla f(x)^{\mathrm{T}}\triangle x_{nt} = \nabla f(x)^{\mathrm{T}}Hf(x)^{-1}\nabla f(x) < 0$, unless $\nabla f(x) = 0$.

When we receive our new value, x_{k+1}, we can expect an error in it. This error is proportional to the square of the error in x_k. We can see this as follows:

$$\|x_{k+1} - x^*\| \le c\|x_k - x^*\|$$

This leads to this method converging quadratically (speedily, but only as long as x_k is close to the optimal value).

The secant method

In Newton's method, we calculated the first and second derivatives, but calculating the Hessian in a large problem is not ideal.

Suppose we have a function, $f(x_1, x_2, \cdots, x_n)$, and $n = 50$. If we take the first derivative of f, with respect to each case of x_i, we get 50 equations. Now, if we calculate the second derivative, we have 2,500 equations, with respect to x_i and x_j, in a matrix. However, because Hessians are symmetric, we only really have to calculate 1,275 second derivatives. This is still a considerably large amount.

The secant method uses the Newton method, but instead of computing the second derivative, it estimates them using the first derivative, which makes it better suited to practice.

It approximates the second derivative as follows:

$$\nabla^2 f(x_k) \approx \frac{\nabla f(x_k) - \nabla f(x_{k-1})}{x_k - x_{k-1}}$$

We take this approximation and plug it into the Newton method, which gives us the following:

$$x_{k+1} = x_k - \left(\frac{\nabla f(x_k) - \nabla f(x_{k-1})}{x_k - x_{k-1}} \right)^{-1} \nabla f(x_k)$$

While this does reduce the computational complexity, it suffers the same fate as Newton's method because it requires additional iterations to converge.

The quasi-Newton method

The secant method approximated the second derivative, but the quasi-Newton method approximates the inverse of the Hessian. The steps are computed as follows:

$$x_{k+1} = x_k - c_k Q_k \nabla f(x_k)$$

Here, Q_k is the approximated inverse of the Hessian at x_k.

We start by letting $Q_1 = 1$ and use two terms, α and β, to update the matrix at each iteration to aid in improving our estimation. They are defined as follows:

$$\beta_{k+1} = \nabla f(x_{k+1}) - \nabla f(x_k) \text{ and } \triangle x_{k+1} = x_{k+1} - x_k$$

To update the matrix at each iteration, we make use of the **Broyden-Fletcher-Goldfarb-Shanno (BFGS)** method, which works as follows:

$$Q_{k+1} = Q_k - \left(\frac{\triangle x_k \beta_k^T Q_k + Q_k \beta_k \triangle x_k^T}{\triangle x_k^T} \right) + \left(1 + \frac{\beta_k^T Q_k \beta_k}{\triangle x_k^T} \right) \frac{\triangle x_k \triangle x_k^T}{\triangle x_k^T \beta_k}$$

For minimization to work, Q must be positive definite.

Game theory

Let's diverge to game theory for a bit. Games that consist of three or more players tend to be very challenging to solve, but two-player games are much simpler and are what we will focus on here.

Let's suppose we have two players that are represented by $X, Y \in \mathbb{R}^{m \times n}$, respectively, and they are playing rock paper scissors. As we know, in this game we tend to make decisions without any information about what the other player will choose. Each player naturally wants to win, so each player has the following payoff matrices:

$$X_{i,j} = \begin{bmatrix} 0 & -1 & 1 \\ 1 & 0 & -1 \\ -1 & 1 & 0 \end{bmatrix}, \quad Y_{i,j} = \begin{bmatrix} 0 & 1 & -1 \\ -1 & 0 & 1 \\ 1 & -1 & 0 \end{bmatrix}$$

Personally, I am not the biggest fan of showing the payoff in this way because you have to write two matrices and look up the individual payoff each time. I prefer to write it in the following way:

	R	P	S
R	(0, 0)	(-1, 1)	(1, -1)
P	(1, -1)	(0, 0)	(-1, 1)
S	(-1, 1)	(1, -1)	(0, 0)

In the preceding table, player 1 chooses a row, $i \in \{1, \cdots, m\}$, and player 2 chooses a column, $j \in \{1, \cdots, n\}$. So, if we look at the preceding table, (-1, 1) tells us that player 1 lost and player 2 won.

In game theory, players have strategies that determine how they act or what actions they can take.

Player X, in our case, has the following set of strategies:

$$X = \{x \in \mathbb{R}^m : x \geq 0, \sum x_i = 1\}$$

Player Y has the following set of strategies:

$$Y = \{y \in \mathbb{R}^n : y \geq 0, \sum y_i = 1\}$$

Here, each vector represents the probability of choosing each column or row.

Each case of $(x, y) \in X \times Y$ represents a strategy profile, and we calculate the expected payoff for player X as $p(x, y) = x^T X y$. If, for some case of i, $x_i = 1$, then we always choose i and call x a **pure strategy**.

Let's move on to another well-known example—the **prisoner's dilemma**. Here, we have two people who commit a crime and are caught. They each have two choices that they can make—testify (T) or stay quiet (Q).

The following are the outcomes of the choices they can make:

- If they both keep quiet, they both end up in jail serving a 2-year sentence.
- If one testifies and the other stays quiet, then the one who stays quiet ends up serving a 3-year sentence and the testifier is freed for cooperating with the police.
- If they both testify, then they both serve a 5-year sentence.

Our payoff table looks as follows:

	S	T
S	(2, 2)	(0, 3)
T	(3, 0)	(1, 1)

Naturally, each person wants to maximize their own payoff; note that neither of the two has the opportunity to know or discuss what the other is going to do, so colluding is not an option. Therefore, each person would prefer to testify since this option is strictly better. We call T a dominant strategy and (1, 1) is Pareto, dominated by (2, 2).

Let's suppose we have a game and a strategy profile (x, y), such that they are in equilibrium (where x is the best response to y and vice versa). Then, we define $x \in X$ as having the best response to $y \in Y$, if for all cases of $x' \in X$ we have the following:

$$p(x, y) \geq p(x', y)$$

Many of you will likely have heard the term zero-sum before, but for those of you haven't, it is a special game where the total payoff is 0, such that $x_{i,j} = -y_{i,j}$. The earlier example of rock-paper-scissor is a good demonstration of this.

A very important solution to the two-player matrix game is the minimax theorem. Suppose we have a $P \in \mathbb{R}^{m \times n}$ payoff matrix. Then, we have the following:

$$\max_{x \in X} \min_{y \in Y} p(x, y) = \max_{y \in Y} \min_{x \in X} p(x, y)$$

This states that if both players use the minimax strategy, then they are in equilibrium since this results in both player 1 and player 2 getting the worst payoff, which satisfies the criteria. This is quite similar to finding the optimal value of $\max \min p(x, y)$, subject to constraints, as in a linear program.

Descent methods

Generally, descent methods take the following form:

$$x_{k+1} = x_k + c_k \triangle x_k$$

Here, $k = 0, 1, \cdots, m$, and $c_k > 0$. In the preceding algorithm, k is a sequence of steps, x_k is the optimal point, and $\triangle x$ is a step. The scalar value, c_k, is the size of the step at the kth iteration.

In descent methods, $f(x_{k+1}) < f(x_k)$, except in the case where x_k is the optimal value, which tells us that $x_k \in \text{dom } f$ for all cases of k.

Gradient descent

Gradient descent is a widely used first-order optimization problem, and it takes steps in the direction of the negative of the gradient of the function from the point it is currently at until it eventually terminates at the optimal solution.

Imagine you're at a skateboarding park and you have a tennis ball in your hand. You bend down and place the ball on the surface of a ramp and let it go; gravity does its thing and the ball follows the ramp's curvature, finding its way to the bottom. This is the concept behind gradient descent.

In this case, the natural choice for the step is the negative gradient; that is, $\triangle x = -\nabla f(x)$. This is known as **gradient descent**, which takes the following form:

$$x_{k+1} = x_k - c_k \nabla f(x_k)$$

In optimization, we generally define the stopping criteria as a condition that, when satisfied, should stop our algorithm from continuing to optimize. It usually takes the following form:

$$\|\nabla f(x)\|_2 \leq \eta$$

Here, η is a small positive number.

We should remember, from the previous chapter, that if we have a function, $f(x, y)$, then its gradient is $\nabla f = \left(\frac{\partial f}{\partial x}, \frac{\partial f}{\partial y} \right)$. Therefore, we can compute the magnitude (or steepness) of the function at (x, y) as follows:

$$\|\nabla f\| = \sqrt{\left(\frac{\partial f}{\partial x}\right)^2 + \left(\frac{\partial f}{\partial y}\right)^2}$$

This acts as a guide and tells us the direction that we should move at each step (since the curvature changes as we move downwards) to get to the minima.

However, gradient descent isn't perfect. It can be quite slow if the step size, $c^{(k)}$, is too small, and if the step size is too large, we may not reach the optimal point due to overshooting, which would result in our algorithm failing to converge, thus diverging instead.

To understand this better, let's take a look at the following two diagrams. The first diagram has a small step size and looks as follows:

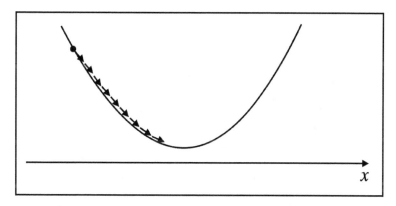

The second diagram shows a large step size:

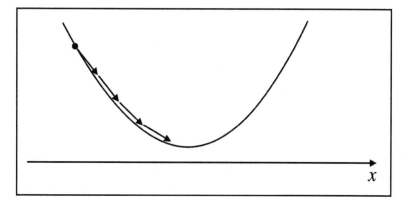

As you can see, a good step size is important, and picking it isn't always an easy task. Luckily, there is a method known as **adaptive step size** that adjusts the step size after each iteration. It follows two rules:

- If the value of the function increases after a step—which means the step size was too large—then undo the step and decrease the step size.
- If the value of the function decreases the size of the step, then increase the step size.

Still, this isn't perfect either. As you can tell from the diagram, the optimization is somewhat erratic, and when we encounter more flat surfaces, our algorithm tends to slow down.

Stochastic gradient descent

By now, you should be able to tell that computing the gradient and getting to the optima isn't easy and is time-consuming.

This is why computing an approximation that points us in the same general direction instead is useful. We call this method **stochastic Gradient Descent (SGD)**, and it is a very important algorithm that theoretically guarantees convergence. The word **stochastic** comes from the fact that we do not know the precise value of the gradient, only an approximation of it.

Let's suppose we have M points $(v_1, v_2, \cdots, v_m)$, where M is very large. This becomes a big optimization problem. So, we take an objective function, $L(x)$, which is a sum of the losses over the points. We write this as follows:

$$L(x) = \sum_1^M L_m(x, v_i)$$

Here, our goal is to minimize the loss as much as possible so that our model best fits the true function, y, as in regression. By minimizing the loss, we reduce the distance between our model's calculated point and the true point.

The reason we use this method is that when we have a lot of points or a large optimization problem, it can be very computationally infeasible to calculate the gradient at each point, even more so if we were to calculate the Hessian. This method is, on the other hand, a lot more computationally feasible.

Loss functions

We know that we are trying to approximate a function and we are trying to get as close as possible to the true function. To do this, we need to define a loss function—we have many to choose from. The following are the main ones that are used in practice:

- $L(x) = \dfrac{\sum_{i=1}^{n}(y_i - \hat{y}_i)^2}{n}$, known as **mean squared error**

- $L(x) = \dfrac{\sum_{i=1}^{n}|y_i - \hat{y}_i|}{n}$, known as **mean absolute error**

- $L(x) = \sum_{i=1}^{n} \|L(x, v_i) - y\|^2$, known as **square loss**

- $L(x) = \sum_{i=1}^{n} \max(0, 1 - cF(x))$, known as **hinge loss**

- $L(x) = -(y_i \log \hat{y}_i + (1 - y_i) \log(1 - \hat{y}_i))$, known as **cross-entropy loss**

- $L(x)_\delta = \begin{cases} \frac{1}{2}(y - F(x))^2, \text{if } |y - F(x)| \le \delta \\ \delta |y - F(x)| - \frac{1}{2}\delta^2 \end{cases}$, known as **Huber loss**

We will revisit them later on and understand when it is best to use each one.

Gradient descent with momentum

As we have seen, gradient descent takes some time to find its way to a relatively flat surface. An improvement to the preceding example is gradient descent with momentum, which smoothes the gradient updates so that it is less erratic. Consider a tennis ball and a boulder both rolling down a mountain. The tennis ball would bounce around more and likely get stuck, but the boulder would gain momentum as it goes and maintain a relatively straight path toward the bottom. That is the key idea behind this improvement. It does so by remembering the previous updates and each update is a combination of the previous and current gradients, as follows:

$$x_{k+1} = x_k - c_k \nabla f(x_k) + \alpha \triangle x_k$$

Here, $\triangle x_k = x_k - x_{k+1}$ and $\alpha \in [0, 1]$.

In this method, as you will notice, we not only have to choose the step size, c_k, but also the momentum coefficient, α.

The Nesterov's accelerated gradient

While momentum dampens the oscillations of gradient descent, Nesterov's method allows the ball traveling down the slope to look ahead and calculate the gradient with respect to the future position.

In essence, instead of calculating the gradient at x_k, we use $x_k + \gamma_k \triangle x_k$ (where $\triangle x_k = x_k - x_{k-1}$), which is close to where we would be after the next step. So, we have the following:

$$x_{k+1} = x_k + \alpha \triangle x_k - c_k \nabla f(x_k + \gamma \triangle x_k)$$

We could also combine the momentum update with Nesterov's accelerated gradient by making $\gamma = \alpha$, which would give us $x_{k+1} = y_k - c_k \nabla f(y_k)$ and $y_{k+1} = x_{k+1} + \alpha(x_{k+1} - x_k)$.

Here, as you will notice, we now have three parameters (c, α, and γ) instead of the two that we had in momentum.

Adaptive gradient descent

We briefly touched on adaptive step sizes earlier. These methods generally use the gradients from previous steps to guide the search direction and the step size to get us to convergence faster. The two main ones that we will look at are **adaptive gradient** (**Adagrad**) and **adaptive moment estimation** (**Adam**).

As before, our goal is to find x^*, which minimizes the loss function.

These gradient descent methods take the form of $x_{k+1} = x_k - c_k G_k$, where G_k is the gradient at the kth step.

In the case of Adagrad, we have $G_k = \nabla L(x_k)$ and $c_k = c_k \left(\sum_{i=1}^{k} \|\nabla L_i(x)\|^2 \right)^{\frac{1}{2}}$, which, if we plug into the preceding equation, gives us the following:

$$x_{k+1} = x_k + c_k \left(\sum_{i=1}^{k} \|\nabla L(x_i)\|^2 \right)^{\frac{1}{2}} \nabla L(x_k)$$

As you can see, we use the square root of the sum of the squares of the losses to update the step size at each step, which eliminates the need to do this ourselves.

Adam also keeps a history of the previous gradients, but it differs from Adagrad in that it stores an exponentially moving average of both the squared gradients and the gradients.

We write this as $G_k = \beta G_k + (1 - \beta)\nabla L(x_k)$ and $c_k = c_k\left((1 - \gamma)\sum_{i=1}^{k}\gamma^{k-i}\|\nabla L_i(x)\|^2\right)^{\frac{1}{2}}$.

Simulated annealing

Simulated annealing is inspired by the field of metallurgy, where we use heat to alter the properties of a material. The applied heat increases the energy of ions and moves more freely. As the material starts to cool, it takes on a different shape upon reaching its equilibrium state. The heat needs to be slowly and gradually reduced to avoid the material getting stuck in a metastable state, which represents a local minimum.

In our case, to optimize a problem, we use temperature to control stochasticity. When the temperature is high, this means the process is freely and randomly exploring the space with the hope that it comes across a good convex region with a more favorable minimum. By reducing the temperature, we reduce the stochasticity and make the algorithm converge to a minimum.

Simulated annealing is a non-convex optimization algorithm and is effective because of its ability to escape local minima.

At each iteration, we sample a possible step from a transition distribution, T, which is accepted according to the following probability:

$$\begin{cases} 1 \text{ if } \triangle y \leq 0 \\ \min(e^{\frac{\triangle y}{t}}, 1) \text{ if } \triangle y > 0 \end{cases}$$

Here, $\triangle y = f(x_{k+1}) - f(x_k)$ and t is the temperature. This probability is known as the **Metropolis criterion** and is what gives simulated annealing the ability to escape local minima when we have a high temperature.

To gradually bring the temperature down, we use a decay factor, $\gamma \in [0, 1]$, which looks as follows:

$$t_{k+1} = \gamma t_k$$

The process continues until it meets the stopping criteria; that is, the temperature drops to the point where we see no improvements from n_k to n_{k+1}.

Natural evolution

Natural evolution is a method that makes use of gradient descent, and our goal is to minimize $\mathbb{E}_{x \sim p(\bullet|\theta)}[f(x)]$. We estimate the gradient from the samples, as follows:

$$
\begin{aligned}
\nabla_\theta \mathbb{E}_{x \sim p(\bullet|\theta)}[f(x)] &= \int \nabla_\theta p(x \mid \theta) f(x) \mathrm{d}x \\
&= \mathbb{E}_{x \sim p(\bullet|\theta)}[f(x) \nabla_\theta \log p(x \mid \theta)] \\
&\approx \frac{1}{n} \sum_{i=1}^{n} f(x_i) \nabla_\theta \log p(x_i \mid \theta)
\end{aligned}
$$

Earlier, when looking at gradient descent, we needed to calculate the gradient of the objective function; but here, we work with the log likelihood, $\log p(x \mid \theta)$, and we can use this estimation of the gradient in any of the gradient descent methods we covered earlier to improve θ.

Exploring population methods

So far, we have dealt with optimization problems where we have a *ball* or *particle* that we edge along the curved space gradually and move toward the minima using gradient descent or Newton's method. Now, however, we will take a look at another class of optimization, where we use a population of individuals.

We spread these individuals across the optimization space, which prevents the optimization algorithm from getting stuck at local minima or a saddle point. These individuals can share information with each other about the local area they're in and use this to find an optimal solution that minimizes our function.

With these algorithms, we have an initial population and we would like to distribute them so that we cover as much ground as we can to give us the best chance of finding a globally optimal region.

We can sample our population from a multivariate normal distribution that is entered over a region that we are interested in, or uniformly distribute the population under some constraints; however, these two distributions are only recommended if you want to limit the space your population covers. Alternatively, we can use **Cauchy distribution**, which allows us to cover a larger space.

Genetic algorithms

Genetic algorithms are inspired by Darwinism, where a fitter individual passes on certain heritable characteristics to the next generation. The objective function, in this case, has an inverse relationship with the individual's fitness or ability to reproduce. The chromosomes from the fitter individuals in each generation are passed on to the subsequent generation after having been subjected to crossover and mutation.

The simplest way for us to represent a chromosome is by using a binary string, similar to how DNA is encoded. However, a better method is writing each chromosome as a vector in $\mathbb{R}^n$ that represents a point in the optimization space. This allows us to express crossover and mutation with greater ease.

We start with a random population, and from it, we choose a set of chromosomes that will be the parents for the subsequent generation. If we have a population of n chromosomes, then we will select n parental pairs that will produce n children in the subsequent generation.

Our goal is to minimize the objective function. So, we sample k random individuals from the population and pick the top-performing individuals from each of the samples or with the probability of their performance relative to the population. The fitness, then, of each individual has an inverse relation to $y^{(i)} = f(x^{(i)})$, and we can calculate it using $\max\{y^{(i)} \mid i = 1, 2, \cdots, n\} - y^{(i)}$.

Crossover, on the other hand, is a combination of the chromosomes of the parents, which results in the children. There are a number of ways that this combination can occur, such as single-point crossover, two-point crossover, or uniform crossover, or we can use one of our own making.

In fitness and crossover, there are only so many traits that can be passed on from the initial population to subsequent generations. However, if only the best traits are passed on, we will end up with a saturated population, which isn't what we want. This is where mutations are useful. They allow new traits to be created and passed on, which enables individuals to explore more of the optimization space. After each crossover, each child in the population experiences some mutation, subject to a probability.

Particle swarm optimization

This algorithm uses the concept of swarm intelligence, where you have a school of fish or a flock of birds. Let's suppose they are trying to find some food. They arrive at an area and spread out a bit, starting to look for food individually. When one of them finds food, it lets the others know so that they can join in.

Each individual in the population knows its current position and velocity and only keeps track of the previous best positions it has visited. The velocity vector determines the direction of the search, and if the individual has a high velocity, then it has a more explorative character, whereas if it has a low velocity, it has a more exploitative character.

At the start of each iteration, the whole population is accelerated to the best position that any individual has come across so far. The updates are computed as follows:

$$x^{(i)} = x^{(i)} + v^{(i)}$$
$$v^{(i)} = w v^{(i)} + \alpha_1 c_1 (x^{(i)}_{best} - x^{(i)}) + \alpha_2 c_2 (x_{best} - x^{(i)})$$

Here, x_{best} is the best position found by the group as a whole, $x^{(i)}_{best}$ is the best position that an individual has found, w, α_1, and α_2 are parameters, and $c_1, c_2 \sim U(0, 1)$.

The values of c_1 and c_2 heavily influence the rate at which they converge.

Summary

In this chapter, we covered a number of different kinds of optimization, such as convex and non-convex optimization, as well as what makes optimization such a challenging problem. We also had a look at how to define an optimization problem and explored a variety of methods, including population methods, simulated annealing, and gradient descent-based methods. In later chapters, we'll come to understand how optimization is used in deep learning and why it is such an important field for us to understand.

In the next chapter, we will learn about graph theory and its uses in the field to solve various problems.

5
Graph Theory

Now that we have got a taste of linear algebra, calculus, statistics, and optimization, it is time to move on to a very fascinating topic, known as graph theory. This involves, as the name suggests, the study of graphs, which we use to model relationships between objects. We use these graphs to help visualize and analyze problems, which in turn helps us solve them.

Graph theory is a very important field and is used for a variety of problems, including page ranking in search engines, social network analysis, and in a GPS to find the best route home. It is also important for us to further our understanding of deep neural networks since the majority of them are based on a type of graph known as a **directed acyclic graph** (**DAG**).

Covering everything in graph theory goes beyond the scope of this chapter (and this book), but we will cover everything that is important for developing a deeper understanding of neural networks.

The topics that are covered in this chapter are as follows:

- Understanding the basic concepts and terminology
- Adjacency matrix
- Types of graphs
- Graph Laplacian

Understanding the basic concepts and terminology

Graph theory was first introduced in the 18th century by Leonhard Euler to solve a famous problem known as the **Königsberg bridge problem**, which asks whether it is possible to walk around the Königsberg bridge while crossing over each of the seven bridges exactly once. The bridge looks as follows:

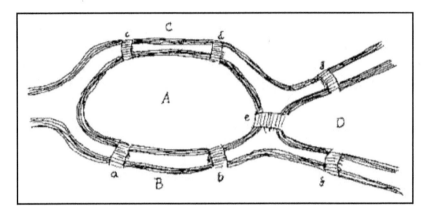

Before we move on, try it out for yourself by using your finger to trace along the path or draw it and trace it with a pencil. Did you manage to find a solution? It's alright if you didn't!

Let's stop for a moment and ask ourselves what exactly a graph is. A graph (G) is a mathematical structure made up of two sets—vertices (V(G)) and edges (E(G)). Two vertices (v_1 and v_2) are connected if there is an edge (e or (v_1, v_2)) between them. Now that that's settled, there are some rules associated with graphs that are important to our understanding of them. They are as follows:

- If $\{v_1, v_2\} \in E(G)$, then v_1 and v_2 are adjacent (connected/neighbors); but if $\{v_1, v_2\} \notin E(G)$, then v_1 and v_2 are non-adjacent (not connected/not neighbors).
- If v_1 is adjacent to v_2, then we can say that the neighborhood of v_1 (denoted as $N(v_1)$) is the set of vertices that are connected to v_1. We write this as $N(v_1) = \{v_1 \in V(G) \mid (v_1, v_2) \in E(G)\}$.
- If $e = (v_1, v_2) \in E(G)$, then e is incident to v_1 and v_2 (that is, v_1 and v_2 are e's endpoints).

- If G has n vertices, then v_1 can have, at most, *n-1* neighbors.
- If v_1 has neighbors, then the degree of v_1 is the number of neighbors (or incidences) it has. We can write this as $\deg(v_1) = |N(v_1)|$. The minimum degree of a vertex in the graph is denoted as $\delta(G)$ and the maximum degree of a vertex in the graph is denoted as $\triangle(G)$.
- If $\deg(v_1) = 0$, then it is an isolated vertex.

Now that we know what the fundamental rules of graphs are, let's revisit the preceding problem we introduced and see if we can work out its solution. We can redraw the bridge problem as a graph, as in the following diagram (refer to the color version provided in the graphics bundle):

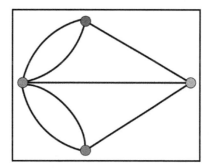

Here, we have the following:

- The green vertex is A
- The red vertex is B
- The blue vertex is C
- The orange vertex is D
- The curved edge connecting A and B is bridge a
- The straight edge connecting A and B is bridge b
- The curved edge connecting A and C is bridge c
- The straight edge connecting A and B is bridge d
- The straight edge connecting A and D is bridge e
- The straight edge connecting B and D is bridge f
- The straight edge connecting C and D is bridge g

If we look at the graph and traverse over the edges, we can easily observe that there is no solution to the Königsberg bridge problem, regardless of what path we take. However, if we were to add an extra path from D to A, D to B, or D to C, then we do in fact have a solution to this problem.

Now, let's suppose we have a bunch of polyhedrons. In geometry, polyhedra are three-dimensional objects, such as tetrahedrons (pyramids), cubes, dipiramids, deltoidals, dodecahedrons, pentagonal hexacontahedrons, and so on (don't worry, you don't need to know what all of them are). In the following diagram, we have two different polyhedrons, along with their corresponding graphs:

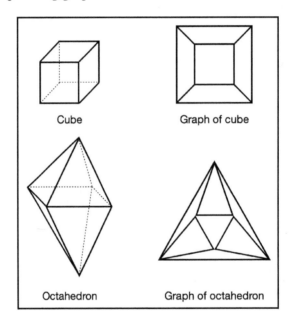

Let's observe the shapes and their graphs for a moment. As you can see, the graph looks a bit different from the actual structure but still captures the properties of the shape. Each graph here has vertices (V) and edges (E), which we already know. But there is one additional property—faces (F). Using the preceding diagrams, we can deduce a general rule that captures the relationships between the vertices, edges, and faces. It is as follows:

$$V - E + F = 2$$

Here, $|V| = n$, $|E| = m$, and $|F| = r$. To verify this, let's take a look at the preceding graphs.

In the case of the cube, there are 8 vertices, 12 edges, and 6 faces, so we have the following:

$$n - m + r = 2 \rightarrow 8 - 12 + 6 = 2$$

In the case of the octahedron, there are 6 vertices, 12 edges, and 8 faces, so we have the following:

$$n - m + r = 2 \rightarrow 6 - 12 + 8 = 2$$

Now that we understand the basics, it is time for us to learn about what is often referred to as the first theorem in graph theory. Suppose we have a graph that has n vertices and m edges. Then, we can observe the following:

$$\deg(v_1) + \deg(v_2) + \cdots + \deg(v_n) = 2m$$

This tells us that the sum of the degrees of each vertex of the graph is twice the number of edges in the graph. Alternatively, we can write this as follows:

$$m = \frac{n(n-1)}{2}$$

Adjacency matrix

As you can imagine, writing down all the pairs of connected nodes (that is, those that have edges between them) to keep track of the relationships in a graph can get tedious, especially as graphs can get very large. For this reason, we use what is known as the adjacency matrix, which is the fundamental mathematical representation of a graph.

Let's suppose we have a graph with n nodes, each of which has a unique integer label ($1, \cdots, n$) so that we can refer to it easily and without any ambiguity whatsoever. For the sake of simplicity, in this example, $n = 6$. Then, this graph's corresponding adjacency matrix is as follows:

$$A = \begin{bmatrix} 0 & 1 & 0 & 0 & 1 & 0 \\ 1 & 0 & 1 & 1 & 0 & 0 \\ 0 & 1 & 0 & 1 & 1 & 1 \\ 0 & 1 & 1 & 0 & 0 & 0 \\ 1 & 0 & 1 & 0 & 0 & 0 \\ 0 & 0 & 1 & 0 & 0 & 0 \end{bmatrix}$$

Let's take a look at the matrix for a moment and see why it is the way it is. The first thing that immediately pops out is that the matrix has a size of 6 × 6 (or $n \times n$) because size is important to us. Next, we notice that it is symmetric and there are only zeros along the diagonal. But why? What is the significance of it being written this way?

If we look at the diagram of the graph in the preceding section, we can see that the edges are as follows:

$$(1, 2), (1, 5), (2, 3), (2, 4), (3, 4), (3, 5), (3, 6)$$

Looking back at the matrix at either the upper triangle or lower triangle, we can see that there are seven 1s at specific (i, j) locations. Each 1 represents an edge between two numbered nodes, and there is a 0 if there is no edge between the two nodes. We can generalize this and write the following:

$$A_{i,j} = \begin{cases} 1 \text{ if there is an edge between nodes } i \text{ and } j \\ 0 \text{ otherwise} \end{cases}$$

The reason for there only being zeros along the diagonal is that there are no self-edges; that is, no node has a connection back to itself. This is referred to as a simple graph. However, there are also more complex graphs, such as those with self-edges and multi-edges.

The difference between graphs with multi-edges and simple graphs is that there can be one or more edges between a pair of nodes in a multi-edge graph. To get a clearer understanding of this, let's consider the following adjacency matrix, where we can see that there are now self-edges and multiple edges between pairs of nodes:

$$A = \begin{bmatrix} 0 & 1 & 0 & 0 & 3 & 0 \\ 1 & 2 & 2 & 1 & 0 & 0 \\ 0 & 2 & 0 & 1 & 1 & 1 \\ 0 & 1 & 1 & 0 & 0 & 0 \\ 3 & 0 & 1 & 0 & 0 & 0 \\ 0 & 0 & 1 & 0 & 0 & 2 \end{bmatrix}$$

There are some notable differences in this adjacency matrix compared with that of the simple graph. The first thing we notice is that the matrix no longer consists of just ones (1) and zeroes (0). What do you think the numbers represent? In this adjacency matrix, a double-edge between two nodes is written as $A_{i,j} = A_{j,i} = 2$. Self-edges, on the other hand, are those that go from i to i; that is, we can write this as $A_{i,i}$ and it is equal to 2. The reason for it being equal to 2 and not 1 is that the edge is connected to i at both ends (and it also makes things easier when doing calculations).

Types of graphs

In the previous section, we learned about the basics of graph theory, and as you saw, this is a very powerful mathematical tool that can be used for a plethora of tasks in various fields. However, there is no one-size-fits-all solution and so we need additional tools to help us because each problem is unique. In this section, we will learn about the various types of graphs and their use cases and strengths. This includes weighted graphs, directed graphs, multilayer graphs, dynamic graphs, and tree graphs.

Weighted graphs

So far, we have seen graphs that have a sort of binary representation, where 1 represents the existence of an edge between two nodes and 0 signifies that there is no connection between two edges. We have also seen graphs that have self-edges and multiple edges. However, sometimes we may want to represent the strength between the two nodes instead, which we represent as a weight. The greater the weight, the greater the strength.

These sorts of graphs can be used in a variety of settings, such as in social networks where the weight represents how frequently two people communicate with each other, which we can use to determine their closeness. In the adjacency matrix for a weighted graph, each $A_{i,j}$ instance represents the weight between nodes i and j.

Let's suppose we have the following adjacency matrix:

$$A = \begin{bmatrix} 0 & 2 & 1 \\ 2 & 0 & 4 \\ 1 & 4 & 0 \end{bmatrix}$$

We can see that the weight (or strength) between nodes 1 and 2 is twice that of the weight between nodes 1 and 3, and the weight between nodes 2 and 3 is four times that between nodes 1 and 3.

The weight on these edges doesn't necessarily have to represent how strong the connection between two nodes is; it could also represent the time it takes to travel from one node to another or the distance between two nodes.

Directed graphs

The difference between regular graphs and directed graphs is that the edges in regular graphs could go in either direction, which is why the adjacency matrix was symmetric. So, if there is an edge between node i and node j, then we can go from i to j or from j to i. However, in the case of directed graphs, the edges have a direction. These edges are directed edges and can only go in one direction.

The adjacency matrix for this type of graph is as follows:

$$A_{i,j} = \begin{cases} 1 \text{ if there is an edge from } j \text{ to } i \\ 0 \qquad\qquad\qquad\qquad \text{otherwise} \end{cases}$$

Now, suppose we have the following graph:

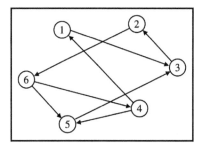

Then, its corresponding adjacency matrix is as follows:

$$A = \begin{bmatrix} 0 & 0 & 0 & 1 & 0 & 0 \\ 0 & 0 & 1 & 0 & 0 & 0 \\ 1 & 0 & 0 & 0 & 1 & 0 \\ 0 & 0 & 0 & 0 & 0 & 1 \\ 0 & 0 & 0 & 1 & 0 & 1 \\ 0 & 1 & 0 & 0 & 0 & 0 \end{bmatrix}$$

As you can see, this matrix is asymmetric (not symmetric). For example, node 3 goes to node 2 and node 6 goes to node 4, but they don't ever go in the opposite direction.

As in the case of undirected networks, directed networks, too, can have multiple edges and self-edges. However, in this case, if there is a self-edge, then the element along the diagonal will hold a value of 1 instead of 2.

Directed acyclic graphs

A DAG is a type of directed graph that doesn't have cycles in it. What this means is that there are no closed loops; that is, three or more nodes in a similar direction. So, suppose we have the following adjacency matrix:

$$A = \begin{bmatrix} 0 & 0 & 0 & 1 \\ 0 & 0 & 0 & 0 \\ 1 & 0 & 0 & 0 \\ 0 & 0 & 1 & 0 \end{bmatrix}$$

We can see, in the preceding adjacency matrix, that we have an edge from node 1 to node 3, an edge from node 3 to node 4, and an edge from node 4 to node 1. This creates a cycle within the graph.

Visually, you can think of a DAG as having a hierarchy where nodes can flow downward or upward through subsequent levels. So, if our edges are all directed upwards, none of the nodes will ever point from a higher level back to a lower level. But if this is the case, our network could go on forever, so where does this graph end? Surely there must be at least one node that has incoming edges, but none outgoing.

To determine whether our network is acyclic, we can use a simple procedure:

1. Find a node that does not have any outgoing edges.
2. If a node such as this does not exist, then the graph is acyclic. However, if there is a node like this, then remove it and its incoming edges from the graph.
3. If all of these nodes have been removed, then the graph is acyclic. Else start from *Step 1* again.

Now, the adjacency matrix for this type of graph is rather interesting. Suppose we number all our nodes so that the edges point from higher-numbered nodes to lower-numbered nodes. Then, its adjacency matrix will be strictly triangular with zeros along the diagonal. If we have the following adjacency matrix, we can clearly observe that there are no self edges and this will always be true for acyclic graphs:

$$A = \begin{bmatrix} 0 & 0 & 1 & 0 & 1 & 0 & 0 & 0 & 0 \\ 0 & 0 & 1 & 0 & 0 & 1 & 0 & 0 & 0 \\ 0 & 0 & 0 & 0 & 0 & 1 & 0 & 0 & 0 \\ 0 & 0 & 0 & 0 & 1 & 0 & 0 & 1 & 0 \\ 0 & 0 & 0 & 0 & 0 & 0 & 1 & 0 & 1 \\ 0 & 0 & 0 & 0 & 0 & 0 & 1 & 0 & 0 \\ 0 & 0 & 0 & 0 & 0 & 0 & 0 & 1 & 1 \\ 0 & 0 & 0 & 0 & 0 & 0 & 0 & 0 & 0 \\ 0 & 0 & 0 & 0 & 0 & 0 & 0 & 0 & 0 \end{bmatrix}$$

It is very important that we notice why this adjacency matrix is strictly triangular. It is because of the ordering (numbering) of the nodes. If this is not done properly, we will not have a triangular matrix. Curiously, there is always at least one ordering of nodes that results in an upper-triangular matrix, and it can be found using the preceding three-step procedure.

Multilayer and dynamic graphs

Often, we use graphs to map very complex relationships. So, suppose we wanted to create a graph for all the modes of transportation and the routes, similar to how Google Maps give us routes that involve buses, trains, cars, planes, or even combinations of them. We could create something like this using a multilayer graph, where nodes represent airports, bus stops, train stations, and other transportation modes, whereas edges represent flights, routes, and so on.

We could just label the edges and nodes to describe what each one represents, but that could turn out quite messy. So, instead, we can use a multilayer graph, where each layer is its own network representing a particular type or class of nodes. These layers are then stacked on top of each other and there are interlinking edges connecting nodes in different layers. These multilayer edges could be used to represent nodes that are within a certain radius of each other:

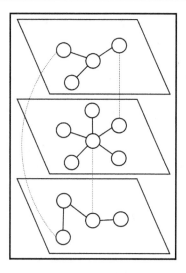

A particularly important subclass of multilayer networks is the multiplex graph where each layer has the same nodes, which could represent people, objects, places, and so on, but it has various types of edges representing different relationships. This is very useful in social networks where different people are related in different ways:

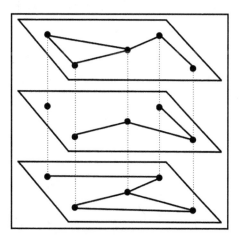

Another subclass of multilayer graphs is the dynamic (or temporal) graph. The significance of these graphs is that their structure changes over time. These could either be a fixed number of nodes, where the edges keep changing or nodes can be added to or removed from the graph over time.

We can represent a multiplex graph mathematically using a set of $n \times n$ adjacency matrices, A^α, where α represents the layer number or a time step (if it is a dynamic or temporal graph). We can write the elements of the matrices as $A^\alpha_{i,j}$. These elements form a three-dimensional tensor. In comparison, multilayer graphs are a lot more complicated because the number of nodes at each layer can differ and they have both intralayer and interlayer edges. We can represent the intralayer edges using adjacency matrices, A^α, where each layer, α, has an adjacency matrix with a size of $n_\alpha \times n_\alpha$. The adjacency matrix for the interlayer edges, on the other hand, can be represented as $B^{\alpha\beta}$ (which is of size $n_\alpha \times n_\beta$), where the matrices element is $B^{\alpha\beta}_{i,j} = 1$ if there is an edge between node i in layer α and node j and layer β.

Tree graphs

Tree graphs are types of graphs that, as the name suggests, have a tree-like structure. They are undirected and do not have any loops. They also have a rather interesting property, referred to as **connectedness**, where we can find a path to any node on the graph from any other node.

In the following diagram, we can see what a tree graph looks like:

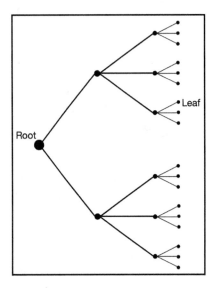

As you can see, the graph starts at one node (the root node) and ends with leaf nodes. In between, they branch out to form smaller sub-trees. An interesting property is that a tree graph with n nodes has $n-1$ edges.

Graph Laplacian

Earlier in this chapter, in the *Adjacency matrix* section, we learned about the adjacency matrix and how we can use it to tell what the structure of a graph is. However, there are other ways of representing graphs in matrix form.

Now, let's suppose we have an undirected, unweighted graph. Then, its Laplacian matrix will be a symmetric $n \times n$ matrix, L, whose elements are as follows:

$$L_{i,j} = \begin{cases} k_i \text{ if } i = j \\ -1 \text{ if } i = j \text{ and there is an edge between nodes } i \text{ and } j \\ 0 \text{ otherwise} \end{cases}$$

Here, $k_i = \deg(v_i)$. We can also write this as follows:

$$L_{i,j} = k_i \delta_{i,j} - A_{i,j}$$

Here, $A_{i,j}$ is the adjacency matrix and $\delta_{i,j}$ is the Kronecker delta. We can rewrite this in matrix form, as follows:

$$L = D - A$$

Here, we have the following:

$$D = \begin{bmatrix} k_1 & 0 & 0 & 0 \\ 0 & k_2 & 0 & 0 \\ \vdots & \vdots & \ddots & \vdots \\ 0 & 0 & 0 & k_n \end{bmatrix}$$

Similarly, we can also write the graph Laplacian matrix for a weighted graph by replacing the adjacency matrix here with the one we defined previously for weighted graphs.

Summary

In this chapter, we learned about a very fascinating topic in mathematics that has applications in nearly every field, from social sciences, to social networking, to the World Wide Web, to artificial intelligence—but particularly, in our case of neural networks.

In the next chapter, we will learn about linear neural networks, which are the simplest type of neural networks and are used most frequently in statistical learning.

Section 2: Essential Neural Networks

2

Having built a sound understanding of the fundamental ideas behind deep learning in the previous section, in this section, you will learn about the key neural networks that are in use today.

This section is comprised of the following chapters:

- Chapter 6, *Linear Neural Networks*
- Chapter 7, *Feedforward Neural Networks*
- Chapter 8, *Regularization*
- Chapter 9, *Convolutional Neural Networks*
- Chapter 10, *Recurrent Neural Networks*

6
Linear Neural Networks

In this chapter, we will go over some of the concepts in machine learning. It is expected that you have previously studied and have an understanding of machine learning. So this chapter will serve as a refresher for some of the concepts that will be needed throughout this book, rather than a comprehensive study of all the machine learning approaches.

In this chapter, we will focus on linear neural networks, which are the simplest type of neural networks and are used for tasks such as linear regression, polynomial regression, logistic regression, and softmax regression, which are used most frequently in statistical learning.

We use regression to explain the relationship between one or more independent variables and a dependent variable. The concepts we will learn in this chapter are crucial for furthering our understanding of how machine learning works before we dive into deep neural networks in the next chapter.

The following topics will be covered in this chapter:

- Linear regression
- Polynomial regression
- Logistic regression

Linear regression

The purpose of regression is to find the relationship that exists between data (denoted by x) and its corresponding output (denoted by y) and predict it. The output of all regression problems is a real number ($y \in \mathbb{R}$). This can be applied to a range of problems, such as predicting the price of a house or what rating a movie will have.

In order for us to make use of regression, we need to use the following:

- Input data, which could be either scalar values or vectors. This is sometimes referred to as **features**.
- Training examples, which include a good number of (x_i, y_i) pairs; that is, the output for each input.
- A function that captures the relationship between the input and output—the model.
- A loss or an objective function, which tells us how accurate our model is.
- Optimization, to minimize the loss or the objective function.

Before we go further, let's look back to `Chapter 1`, *Vector Calculus*, where we noted that the equation of a straight line is as follows:

$$y = mx + b$$

Here, m is the gradient (or slope) and b is a correction term. We found the slope using two pairs of points on the line using the following equation:

$$m = \frac{y_2 - y_1}{x_2 - x_1}$$

As we know, this is easy to do. In linear regression, however, we are given many (x_i, y_i) points, and our goal is to find the line of best fit that best captures the relationship. This line is what our model learns. We can represent this as follows:

$$y \approx \hat{y} = f(x) + \epsilon$$

Here, ϵ represents an error, which we assume to be Gaussian, y is the true label, and $\hat{y}$ is the prediction that our model provides.

Let's now consider a case where we have multiple independent variables and we want to find the relationship between one dependent variable. This type of regression is known as **multiple regression**. In this case, each of the independent variables has an impact on the predicted output.

Our inputs, in this case, will take the following form:

$$\mathbf{x} = [x_1, \cdots, x_n]$$

Here, n is the number of independent variables.

To find $\hat{y}$, we could just average over all the dependent variables or sum them together, but this is not likely to give us the desired result. Suppose we want to predict the price of a house; our inputs could be the square footage of the lot, the number of bedrooms, the number of bathrooms, and whether or not it has a swimming pool.

Each of the inputs will have a corresponding weight, which the model will learn from the data points, that best describes the importance of each of the inputs. This then becomes the following:

$$\hat{y} = w_1 x_1 + w_2 x_2 + \cdots + w_n x_n + b$$

Or, we have the following:

$$\hat{y} = b + \sum_{i=1}^{n} w_i x_i$$

We can also rewrite this in matrix form:

$$\hat{y} = \begin{bmatrix} w_1 & w_2 & \cdots & w_n \end{bmatrix} \begin{bmatrix} x_1 \\ x_2 \\ \vdots \\ x_n \end{bmatrix} + b = \mathbf{w}^{\mathsf{T}} \mathbf{x} + b$$

But now, the obvious question arises—*how does our model learn these weights and this relationship?* This is easy for us to do because our brains instantly spot patterns and we can analytically spot relationships. However, if our machine is to learn this relationship, it needs a guide. This guide is the loss function, which tells the model how off its prediction is and which direction it needs to move in to improve.

The loss is generally the distance between the prediction ($\hat{y}_i$) and the true value (y_i), which we can write as follows:

$$l_i(\mathbf{w}, b) = \frac{1}{2}(\hat{y}_i - y_i)^2$$

But that still doesn't give us the full picture. Our goal is to minimize the loss over all the data samples that the model is trained on, so we average the sum of the losses over all the data samples. This looks as follows:

$$L(\mathbf{w}, b) = \frac{1}{2n} \sum_{i=1}^{n} (\mathbf{w}^{\mathsf{T}} \mathbf{x}_i + b - y_i)^2$$

The goal of training is to find the optimal parameters:

$$\mathbf{w}^*, b^* = \arg\min_{\mathbf{w},b} L(\mathbf{w}, b)$$

Having learned what linear regression is, let's now see what polynomial regression is all about in the following section.

Polynomial regression

Linear regression, as you might imagine, isn't a one-size-fits-all solution that we can use for any problem. A lot of the relationships that exist between variables in the real world are not linear; that is, a straight line isn't able to capture the relationship. For these problems, we use a variant of the preceding linear regression known as **polynomial regression**, which can capture more complexities, such as curves. This method makes use of applying different powers to the explanatory variable to discover non-linear problems. This looks as follows:

$$y = w_1 x^1 + w_2 x^2 + \cdots + w_n x^n + b$$

Or, we could have the following:

$$y = b + \sum_{i=1}^{n} w_i x^i$$

This is the case for $i = 1, 2, \cdots, n$.

As you can see from the preceding equation, a model such as this is not only able to capture a straight line (if needed) but can also generate a second-order, third-order, or n^{th}-order equation that fits the data points.

Let's suppose we have the following data points:

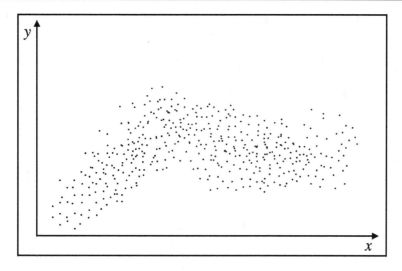

We can immediately tell that a straight line will not do the job, but after we apply polynomial regression to it, we can see that our model learns to fit the curve, which resembles a sinusoidal wave. We can observe this in the following graph:

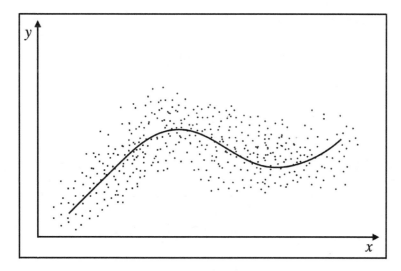

Let's now take a look at a case where we are trying to learn a surface and we have two inputs, $\mathbf{x} = [x_1, x_2]$, and one output, y. Again, as we can see in the following diagram, the surface is not flat; in fact, it is quite bumpy:

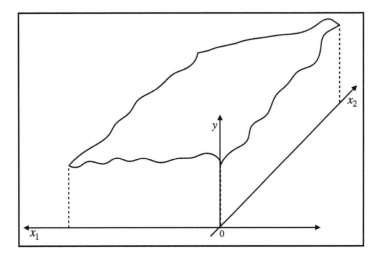

We could approximate model this using the following third-order polynomial:

$$y = b + w_1 x_1 + w_2 x_2 + w_3 x_1^2 + w_4 x_1 x_2 + w_5 x_2^2 + w_6 x_1^3 + w_7 x_1^2 x_2 + w_8 x_1 x_2^2 + w_9 x_2^3$$

If this gives us a satisfactory result, we can add another higher-degree polynomial (and so on) until there is one that models the surface.

Logistic regression

There is another kind of regression that we often use in practice—**logistic regression**. Suppose we want to determine whether or not an email is spam. In this case, our $x(s)$ value could be occurrences of $!(s)$ or the total number of spelling errors in the email. Then, y can take on the value of 1 (for spam) and 0 (for not spam).

In this kind of case, linear regression will simply not work since we are not predicting a real value—we are trying to predict which class the email belongs to.

This will usually end up looking as follows:

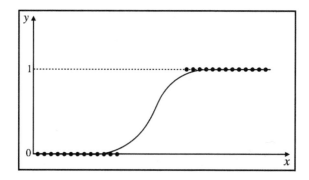

As you can see, the data is grouped into two areas—one that represents non-spam and another that represents spam.

We can calculate this as follows:

$$y = \frac{1}{1 + e^z}$$

Here, $z = b + \sum_{i=1}^{n} w_i x^i$.

However, this only works for binary classification. What if we want to classify multiple classes? Then, we can use softmax regression, which is an extension of logistic regression. This will look as follows:

$$y = \frac{e^{z_i}}{\sum_{j=1}^{K} e^{z_j}}$$

This is the case for $i = 1, \cdots, K$ and $z = z_1, \cdots, z_K$.

Summary

In this chapter, we learned about various forms of regression, such as (multiple) linear regression, polynomial regression, logistic regression, and softmax regression. Each of these models has aided us in figuring out the relationship that exists between one or more independent variable(s) and a dependent variable. For some of you, these concepts may seem very rudimentary, but they will serve us well on our journey throughout this book and in gaining a deeper understanding of the concepts to come.

In the next chapter, we will learn about feedforward neural networks.

Feedforward Neural Networks 7

In the previous chapter, we covered linear neural networks, which have proven to be effective for problems such as regression and so are widely used in the industry. However, we also saw that they have their limitations and are unable to work effectively on higher-dimensional problems.

In this chapter, we will take an in-depth look at the **multilayer perceptron** (**MLP**), a type of **feedforward neural network** (**FNN**). We will start by taking a look at how biological neurons process information, then we will move onto mathematical models of biological neurons. The **artificial neural networks** (**ANNs**) we will study in this book are made up of mathematical models of biological neurons (we will learn more about this shortly). Once we have built a foundation, we will move on to understanding how MLPs—which are the FNNs—work and their involvement with deep learning.

What FNNs allow us to do is approximate a function that maps input to output and this can be used in a variety of tasks, such as predicting the price of a house or a stock or determining whether or not an event will occur.

The following topics are covered in this chapter:

- Understanding biological neural networks
- Comparing the perceptron and the McCulloch-Pitts neuron
- MLPs
- Training neural networks
- Deep neural networks

Understanding biological neural networks

The human brain is capable of some remarkable feats—it performs very complex information processing. The neurons that make up our brains are very densely connected and perform in parallel with others. These biological neurons receive and pass signals to other neurons through the connections (synapses) between them. These synapses have strengths associated with them and increasing or weakening the strength of the connections between neurons is what facilitates our learning and allows us to continuously learn and adapt to the dynamic environments we live in.

As we know, the brain consists of neurons—in fact, according to recent studies, it is estimated that the human brain contains roughly 86 billion neurons. That is a lot of neurons and a whole lot more connections. A very large number of these neurons are used simultaneously every day to allow us to carry out a variety of tasks and be functional members of society. Neurons by themselves are said to be quite slow, but it is this large-scale parallel operation that gives our brains its extraordinary capability.

The following is a diagram of a biological neuron:

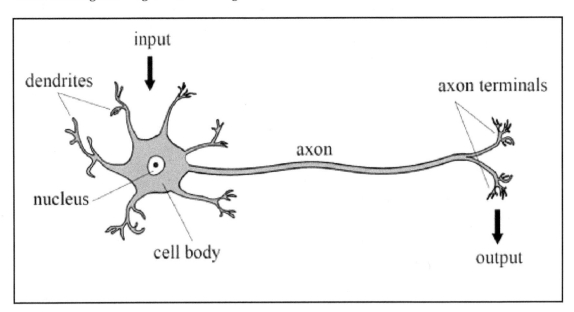

As you can see from the preceding diagram, each neuron has three main components—the body, an axon, and many dendrites. The synapses connect the axon of one neuron to the dendrites of other neurons and determine the weight of the information that is received from other neurons. Only when the sum of the weighted inputs to the neuron exceeds a certain threshold does the neuron fire (activate); otherwise, it is at rest. This communication between neurons is done through electrochemical reactions, involving potassium, sodium, and chlorine (which we will not go into as it is beyond the scope of this book; however, if this interests you, there is a lot of literature you can find on it).

The reason we are looking at biological neurons is that the neurons and neural networks we will be learning about and developing in this book are largely biologically inspired. If we are trying to develop artificial intelligence, where better to learn than from actual intelligence?

Since the goal of this book is to teach you how to develop ANNs on computers, it is relatively important that we take a look at the differences between the computational power of our brains as opposed to computers.

Computers have a significant advantage over our brains as they can perform roughly 10 billion operations per second, whereas the human brain can only perform around 800 operations per second. However, the brain requires roughly 10 watts to operate, which is 10 times less than what a computer requires. Another advantage that computers have is their precision; they can perform operations millions of times more accurately. Lastly, computers perform operations sequentially and cannot deal with data they have not been programmed to deal with, but the brain performs operations in parallel and is well equipped to deal with new data.

Comparing the perceptron and the McCulloch-Pitts neuron

In this section, we will cover two mathematical models of biological neurons—the **McCulloch-Pitts (MP)** neuron and Rosenblatt's perceptron—which create the foundation for neural networks.

The MP neuron

The MP neuron was created in 1943 by Warren McCulloch and Walter Pitts. It was modeled after the biological neuron and is the first mathematical model of a biological neuron. It was created primarily for classification tasks. The MP neuron takes as input binary values and outputs a binary value based on a threshold value. If the sum of the inputs is greater than the threshold, then the neuron outputs 1 (if it is under the threshold, it outputs 0). In the following diagram, we can see what a basic neuron with three inputs and one output looks like:

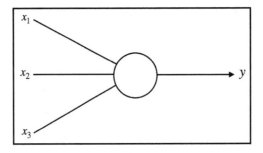

As you can see, this isn't entirely dissimilar to the biological neuron we saw earlier.

Mathematically, we can write this as follows:

$$y = \begin{cases} 1 \text{ if } \sum_{i=1}^{n} x_i \geq b \\ 0 \qquad \text{otherwise} \end{cases}$$

Here, $x_i = 0$ or 1.

We can think of this as outputting Boolean answers; that is, `true` or `false` (or yes or no).

While the MP neuron may look simple, it has the ability to model any logic function, such as OR, AND, and NOT; but it is unable to classify the XOR function. Additionally, it does not have the ability to learn, so the threshold (b) needs to be adjusted analytically to fit our data.

Perceptron

The perceptron model, created by Frank Rosenblatt in 1958, is an improved version of the MP neuron and can take any real value as input. Each input is then multiplied by a real-valued weight. If the sum of the weighted inputs is greater than the threshold, then the output is 1, and if it is below the threshold, then the output is 0. The following diagram illustrates a basic perceptron model:

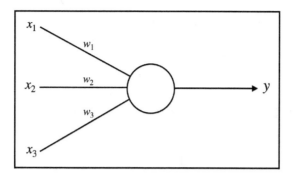

This model shares a lot of similarities with the MP neuron, but it is more similar to the biological neuron.

Mathematically, we can write this as follows:

$$y = \begin{cases} 1 \text{ if } \sum_{i=1}^{n} x_i w_i \geq b \\ 0 \qquad\qquad \text{otherwise} \end{cases}$$

Here, $x_i \in \mathbb{R}$.

Sometimes, we rewrite the perceptron equation in the following form:

$$y = \begin{cases} 1 \text{ if } \sum_{i=0}^{n} x_i w_i \geq 0 \\ 0 \qquad\qquad \text{otherwise} \end{cases}$$

The following diagram shows how the perceptron equation will look like:

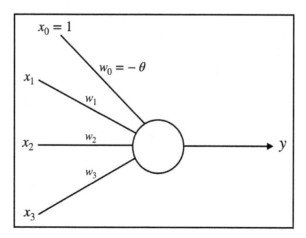

Here, $x_0 = 1$ and $w_0 = -\theta$. This prevents us from having to hardcode the threshold, which makes the threshold a learnable parameter instead of something we have to manually adjust (as is the case with the MP neuron).

Pros and cons of the MP neuron and perceptron

The advantage the perceptron model has over the MP neuron is that it is able to learn through error correction and it linearly separates the problem using a hyperplane, so anything that falls below the hyperplane is 0 and anything above it is 1. This error correction allows the perceptron to adjust the weights and move the position of the hyperplane so that it can properly classify the data.

Earlier, we mentioned that the perceptron learns to linearly classify a problem—but what exactly does it learn? Does it learn the nature of the question that is asked? No. It learns the effect of the input on the output. *So, the greater the weight associated with a certain input, the greater its impact on the prediction (classification).*

The update for the weights (learning) happens as follows:

$$w_{new} = w_{old} + \delta x$$

Here, δ = expected value – predicted value.

We could also add a learning rate ($0 < \eta \leq 1$) if we want to speed up the learning; so, the update will be as follows:

$$w_{new} = w_{old} + \eta \delta x$$

During these updates, the perceptron calculates the distance of the hyperplane from the points to be classified and adjusts itself to find the best position that it can perfectly linearly classify the two target classes. So, it maximally separates both points on either side, which we can see in the following plot:

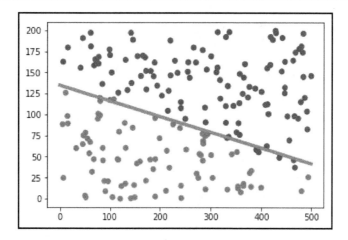

What is even more fascinating about this is that because of the aforementioned learning rule, the perceptron is guaranteed to converge when given a finite number of updates and so will work on any binary classification task.

But alas, the perceptron is not perfect either and it also has limitations. As it is a linear classifier, it is unable to deal with nonlinear problems, which makes up the majority of the problems we usually wish to develop solutions for.

MLPs

As mentioned, both the MP neuron and perceptron models are unable to deal with nonlinear problems. To combat this issue, modern-day perceptrons use an activation function that introduces nonlinearity to the output.

The perceptrons (neurons, but we will mostly refer to them as **nodes** going forward) we will use are of the following form:

$$y = \phi \left(\sum_i w_i x_i + b \right)$$

Here, y is the output, φ is a nonlinear activation function, x_i is the inputs to the unit, w_i is the weights, and b is the bias. This improved version of the perceptron looks as follows:

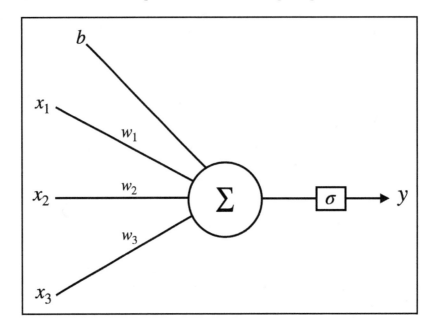

In the preceding diagram, the activation function is generally the sigmoid function:

$$\phi = \frac{1}{1 + e^{\sum_{i=1}^{n} w_i x_i + b}}$$

What the sigmoid activation function does is squash all the output values into the (0, 1) range. The sigmoid activation function is largely used for historical purposes since the developers of the earlier neurons focused on thresholding. When gradient-based learning was introduced, the sigmoid function turned out to be the best choice.

An MLP is the simplest type of FNN. It is basically a lot of nodes combined together and the computation is carried out sequentially. The network looks as follows:

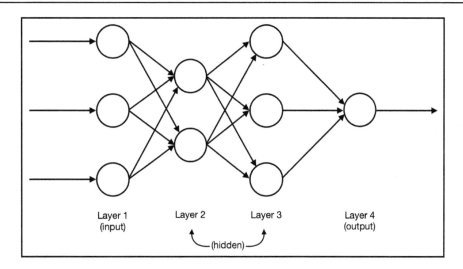

Layer 1 (input) Layer 2 Layer 3 Layer 4 (output)

(hidden)

An FNN is essentially a directed acyclic graph; that is, the connections are always moving in one direction. There are no connections that feed the outputs back into the network.

As you can see from the preceding diagram, the nodes are arranged in layers and the nodes in each layer are connected to each of the neurons in the next layer. However, there aren't any connections between nodes in the same layer. We refer to networks such as this as being fully connected.

The first layer is referred to as the input layer, the last layer is referred to as the output layer, and all the layers in between are called hidden layers. The number of nodes in the output layer depends on the type of problem we build our MLP for. It is important that you remember that the inputs to and outputs from layers are not the same as the inputs to and outputs from the network.

You may also notice that in the preceding architecture, there is only one unit in the output layer. This is generally the case when we have a regression or binary classification task. So, if we want our network to be able to detect multiple classes, then our output layer will have K nodes, where K is the number of classes.

Note that the depth of the network is the number of layers it has and the width is the number of nodes in a layer.

However, what makes neural networks so powerfully effective, and the reason we are studying them, is that they are universal function approximators. The universal approximation theorem states that "*a feedforward neural network with a single hidden layer containing a finite number of neurons can approximate continuous functions on compact subsets of* $\mathbb{R}^n$, *under mild assumptions on the activation function.*" What this means is that if the hidden layer contains a specific number of neurons, then our neural network can reasonably approximate any known function.

 You will notice that it is unclear exactly how many neurons are needed in the hidden layer for it to be able to approximate any function. This could vary greatly, depending on the function we want it to learn.

By now, you might be thinking that if MLPs have been around since the late 1960s, why has it taken nearly 50 years for them to take off and be used as widely as they are today? This is because the computing power that was available 50 years ago was nowhere near as powerful as what is available today, nor was the same amount of data that is available now available back then. So, because of the lack of results that MLPs were able to achieve back then, they faded into obscurity. Because of this, as well as the universal approximation theorem, researchers at the time hadn't looked deeper than into a couple of layers.

Let's break the model down and see how it works.

Layers

We know now that MLPs (and so FNNs) are made of three different kinds of layers—input, hidden, and output. We also know what a single neuron looks like. Let's now mathematically explore MLPs and how they work.

Suppose we have an MLP with $\mathbf{x} \in \mathbb{R}^d$ input (where $d \in \mathbb{N}$), L layers, N neurons in each layer, an activation function $\phi : \mathbb{R} \to \mathbb{R}$, and the network output, y. The MLP looks as follows:

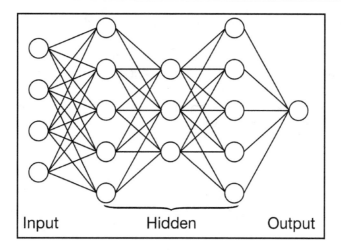

Input   Hidden   Output

As you can see, this network has four inputs—the first hidden layer has five nodes, the second hidden layer has three nodes, the third hidden layer has five nodes, and there is one node for the output. Mathematically, we can write this as follows:

$$h_i^{[1]} = \phi^{[1]}\left(\sum_j w_{i,j}^{[1]} x_j + b_i^{[1]}\right)$$

$$h_i^{[2]} = \phi^{[2]}\left(\sum_j w_{i,j}^{[2]} h_j^{[1]} + b_i^{[2]}\right)$$

$$h_i^{[3]} = \phi^{[3]}\left(\sum_j w_{i,j}^{[3]} h_j^{[2]} + b_i^{[3]}\right)$$

$$y_i = \phi^{[4]}\left(\sum_j w_{i,j}^{[4]} h_j^{[3]} + b_i^{[4]}\right)$$

Here, $h_i^{[l]}$ is the ith node in the lth layer, $\phi^{[l]}$ is an activation function for the lth layer, x_j is the jth input to the network, $b_i^{[l]}$ is the bias for the ith node in the lth layer, and $w_{i,j}^{[l]}$ is the directed weight that connects the jth node in the $l-1^{st}$ layer to the ith node in the lth layer.

Before we move forward, let's take a look at the preceding equations. From them, we can easily observe that each hidden node depends on the weights from the previous layer. If you take a pencil and draw out the network (or use your fingers to trace the connections), you will notice that the deeper we get into the network, the more complex the relationship nodes in the later hidden layers have with those in the earlier layers.

Now that you have an idea of how each neuron is computed in an MLP, you might have realized that explicitly writing out the computation on each node in each layer can be a daunting task. So, let's rewrite the preceding equation in a cleaner and simpler manner. We generally do not express neural networks in terms of the computation that happens on each node. We instead express them in terms of layers and because each layer has multiple nodes, we can write the previous equations in terms of vectors and matrices. The previous equations can now be written as follows:

$$\mathbf{h}^{[1]} = \phi^{[1]} \left(\mathbf{W}^{[1]} \mathbf{x} + \mathbf{b}^{[1]} \right)$$
$$\mathbf{h}^{[2]} = \phi^{[2]} \left(\mathbf{W}^{[2]} \mathbf{h}^{[1]} + \mathbf{b}^{[2]} \right)$$
$$\mathbf{h}^{[3]} = \phi^{[3]} \left(\mathbf{W}^{[3]} \mathbf{h}^{[2]} + \mathbf{b}^{[3]} \right)$$
$$\mathbf{y} = \phi^{[4]} \left(\mathbf{W}^{[4]} \mathbf{h}^{[3]} + \mathbf{b}^{[4]} \right)$$

This is a whole lot simpler to follow.

 Remember from Chapter 2, *Linear Algebra*, that when you multiply a vector or matrix with a scalar value, the scalar value is applied to all the entries.

For the networks we want to build, the input more than likely will not be a vector, as it is in the preceding examples; it will be a matrix, so we can then rewrite it as follows:

$$\mathbf{H}^{[1]} = \phi^{[1]} \left(\mathbf{X} \mathbf{W}^{[1]\top} + \mathbf{1} \mathbf{b}^{[1]\top} \right)$$
$$\mathbf{H}^{[2]} = \phi^{[2]} \left(\mathbf{H}^{[1]} \mathbf{W}^{[2]\top} + \mathbf{1} \mathbf{b}^{[2]\top} \right)$$
$$\mathbf{H}^{[3]} = \phi^{[3]} \left(\mathbf{H}^{[2]} \mathbf{W}^{[3]\top} + \mathbf{1} \mathbf{b}^{[3]\top} \right)$$
$$\mathbf{Y} = \phi^{[4]} \left(\mathbf{H}^{[3]} \mathbf{W}^{[4]\top} + \mathbf{1} \mathbf{b}^{[4]\top} \right)$$

Here, $\mathbf{X}$ is the matrix containing all the data we want to train our model on, $\mathbf{H}^{[l]}$ contains the hidden nodes at each layer for all the data samples, and everything else is the same as it was earlier.

If you have been paying attention, you will have noticed that the order of the multiplication taking place in the matrix is different than what took place earlier. Why do you think that is? (I'll give you a hint—transpose.)

You should now have a decent, high-level understanding of how neural networks are constructed. Let's now lift up the hood and take a look at what is going on underneath. We know from the previous equations that neural networks are comprised of a series of matrix multiplications and matrix additions and scalar multiplications. Since we are now dealing with vectors and matrices, their dimensions are important because if they don't line up properly, we can't multiply and add them.

Let's view the preceding MLP in its full matrix form. (To keep things simple, we will go through it layer by layer and we will use the second form since our input is in vector form.) To simplify the view and to properly understand what is happening, we will now denote

$$\mathbf{z}^{[1]} = \mathbf{W}^{[1]}\mathbf{x} + \mathbf{b}^{[1]} \text{ and } \mathbf{h}^{[1]} = \phi^{[1]}\left(\mathbf{z}^{[1]}\right).$$

Calculate $z^{[1]}$ as follows:

$$\underbrace{\begin{bmatrix} z_1^{[1]} \\ z_2^{[1]} \\ z_3^{[1]} \\ z_4^{[1]} \\ z_5^{[1]} \end{bmatrix}}_{\mathbb{R}^{5\times1}} = \underbrace{\begin{bmatrix} w_{1,1}^{[1]} & w_{1,2}^{[1]} & w_{1,3}^{[1]} & w_{1,4}^{[1]} \\ w_{2,1}^{[1]} & w_{2,2}^{[1]} & w_{2,3}^{[1]} & w_{2,4}^{[1]} \\ w_{3,1}^{[1]} & w_{3,2}^{[1]} & w_{3,3}^{[1]} & w_{3,4}^{[1]} \\ w_{4,1}^{[1]} & w_{4,2}^{[1]} & w_{4,3}^{[1]} & w_{4,4}^{[1]} \\ w_{5,1}^{[1]} & w_{5,2}^{[1]} & w_{5,3}^{[1]} & w_{5,4}^{[1]} \end{bmatrix}}_{\mathbb{R}^{5\times4}} \underbrace{\begin{bmatrix} x_1 \\ x_2 \\ x_3 \\ x_4 \end{bmatrix}}_{\mathbb{R}^{4\times1}} + \underbrace{\begin{bmatrix} b_1^{[1]} \\ b_2^{[1]} \\ b_3^{[1]} \\ b_4^{[1]} \\ b_5^{[1]} \end{bmatrix}}_{\mathbb{R}^{5\times1}}$$

Calculate $h^{[1]}$ as follows:

$$\underbrace{\begin{bmatrix} h_1^{[1]} \\ h_2^{[1]} \\ h_3^{[1]} \\ h_4^{[1]} \\ h_5^{[1]} \end{bmatrix}}_{\mathbb{R}^{5\times1}} = \phi^{[1]} \underbrace{\begin{bmatrix} z_1^{[1]} \\ z_2^{[1]} \\ z_3^{[1]} \\ z_4^{[1]} \\ z_5^{[1]} \end{bmatrix}}_{\mathbb{R}^{5\times1}} = \underbrace{\begin{bmatrix} \phi^{[1]}\left(z_1^{[1]}\right) \\ \phi^{[1]}\left(z_2^{[1]}\right) \\ \phi^{[1]}\left(z_3^{[1]}\right) \\ \phi^{[1]}\left(z_4^{[1]}\right) \\ \phi^{[1]}\left(z_5^{[1]}\right) \end{bmatrix}}_{\mathbb{R}^{5\times1}}$$

Calculate $z^{[2]}$ as follows:

$$
\underbrace{\begin{bmatrix} z_1^{[2]} \\ z_2^{[2]} \\ z_3^{[2]} \end{bmatrix}}_{\mathbb{R}^{3\times1}} = \underbrace{\begin{bmatrix} w_{1,1}^{[2]} & w_{1,2}^{[2]} & w_{1,3}^{[2]} & w_{1,4}^{[2]} & w_{1,5}^{[2]} \\ w_{2,1}^{[2]} & w_{2,2}^{[2]} & w_{2,3}^{[2]} & w_{2,4}^{[2]} & w_{2,5}^{[2]} \\ w_{3,1}^{[2]} & w_{3,2}^{[2]} & w_{3,3}^{[2]} & w_{3,4}^{[2]} & w_{3,5}^{[2]} \end{bmatrix}}_{\mathbb{R}^{3\times5}} \underbrace{\begin{bmatrix} h_1^{[1]} \\ h_2^{[1]} \\ h_3^{[1]} \\ h_4^{[1]} \\ h_5^{[1]} \end{bmatrix}}_{\mathbb{R}^{5\times1}} + \underbrace{\begin{bmatrix} b_1^{[2]} \\ b_2^{[2]} \\ b_3^{[2]} \end{bmatrix}}_{\mathbb{R}^{3\times1}}
$$

Calculate $h^{[2]}$ as follows:

$$
\underbrace{\begin{bmatrix} h_1^{[2]} \\ h_2^{[2]} \\ h_3^{[2]} \end{bmatrix}}_{\mathbb{R}^{3\times1}} = \phi^{[2]} \underbrace{\begin{bmatrix} z_1^{[2]} \\ z_2^{[2]} \\ z_3^{[2]} \end{bmatrix}}_{\mathbb{R}^{3\times1}}
$$

Calculate $z^{[3]}$ as follows:

$$
\underbrace{\begin{bmatrix} z_1^{[3]} \\ z_2^{[3]} \\ z_3^{[3]} \\ z_4^{[3]} \\ z_5^{[3]} \end{bmatrix}}_{\mathbb{R}^{5\times1}} = \underbrace{\begin{bmatrix} w_{1,1}^{[3]} & w_{1,2}^{[3]} & w_{1,3}^{[3]} \\ w_{2,1}^{[3]} & w_{2,2}^{[3]} & w_{2,3}^{[3]} \\ w_{3,1}^{[3]} & w_{3,2}^{[3]} & w_{3,3}^{[3]} \\ w_{4,1}^{[3]} & w_{4,2}^{[3]} & w_{4,3}^{[3]} \\ w_{5,1}^{[3]} & w_{5,2}^{[3]} & w_{5,3}^{[3]} \end{bmatrix}}_{\mathbb{R}^{5\times3}} \underbrace{\begin{bmatrix} h_1^{[2]} \\ h_2^{[2]} \\ h_3^{[3]} \end{bmatrix}}_{\mathbb{R}^{3\times1}} + \underbrace{\begin{bmatrix} b_1^{[3]} \\ b_2^{[3]} \\ b_3^{[3]} \\ b_4^{[3]} \\ b_5^{[3]} \end{bmatrix}}_{\mathbb{R}^{5\times1}}
$$

Calculate $h^{[3]}$ as follows:

$$
\underbrace{\begin{bmatrix} h_1^{[3]} \\ h_2^{[3]} \\ h_3^{[3]} \\ h_4^{[3]} \\ h_5^{[3]} \end{bmatrix}}_{\mathbb{R}^{5\times1}} = \phi^{[3]} \underbrace{\begin{bmatrix} z_1^{[3]} \\ z_2^{[3]} \\ z_3^{[3]} \\ z_4^{[3]} \\ z_5^{[3]} \end{bmatrix}}_{\mathbb{R}^{5\times1}}
$$

Calculate $z^{[4]}$ as follows:

$$
\underbrace{\begin{bmatrix} z_1^{[4]} \end{bmatrix}}_{\mathbb{R}^{1\times1}} = \underbrace{\begin{bmatrix} w_1^{[4]} & w_2^{[4]} & w_3^{[4]} & w_4^{[4]} & w_5^{[4]} \end{bmatrix}}_{\mathbb{R}^{1\times5}} \underbrace{\begin{bmatrix} h_1^{[3]} \\ h_1^{[3]} \\ h_1^{[3]} \\ h_1^{[3]} \\ h_1^{[3]} \end{bmatrix}}_{\mathbb{R}^{5\times1}} + \underbrace{\begin{bmatrix} b_1^{[4]} \end{bmatrix}}_{\mathbb{R}^{1\times1}}
$$

Calculate y as follows:

$$
\underbrace{\mathbf{y}}_{\mathbb{R}^{1\times1}} = \phi^{[4]} \underbrace{\begin{bmatrix} z_1^{[4]} \end{bmatrix}}_{\mathbb{R}^{1\times1}}
$$

There we have it. Those are all the operations that take place in our MLP.

I have slightly tweaked the preceding notation by putting $z_1^{[4]}$ in brackets and writing y as a vector, even though it is clearly a scalar. This was only done to keep the flow and to avoid changing the notation. y is a vector if we use the k-class classification (giving us multiple output neurons).

Now, if you think back to Chapter 2, *Linear Algebra*, where we did matrix multiplication, we learned that when a matrix or vector is multiplied by another matrix with differing dimensions, then the resulting matrix or vector is of a different shape (except, of course, when we multiply by the identity matrix). We call this mapping because our matrix maps points in one space to points in another space. Keeping this in mind, let's take a look again at the operations that were carried out in our MLP. From this, we can deduce that our neural network maps our input vector from one Euclidean space to our output vector in another Euclidean space.

Using this observation, we can generalize and write the following:

$$\mathcal{N} : \mathbb{R}^{n_1} \to \mathbb{R}^{n_L}$$

Here, $\mathcal{N}$ is our MLP, $\mathbb{R}^{n_1}$ is the number of nodes in the dimension of the input layer, $\mathbb{R}^{n_L}$ is the number of nodes in the output layer, and L is the total number of layers.

However, there are a number of matrix multiplications that take place in the preceding network and each has different dimensions, which tells us that a sequence of mappings takes place (from one layer to the next).

We can then write the mappings individually, as follows:

$$f_1 : \mathbb{R}^{n_1} \to \mathbb{R}^{n_2}, f_2 : \mathbb{R}^{n_2} \to \mathbb{R}^{n_3}, \cdots, f_{L-1} : \mathbb{R}^{n_{L-1}} \to \mathbb{R}^{n_L}$$

Here, each f value maps the lth layer to the $l+1^{st}$ layer. To make sure we have covered all of our bases, $\mathbf{W}^{[l]} \in \mathbb{R}^{n_l \times n_{l-1}}$ and $\mathbf{b}^{[l]} \in \mathbb{R}^{n_l}$.

Now, we can summarize our MLP in the following equation:

$$\mathcal{N}(\mathbf{x}) = \phi^{[4]}(\mathbf{W}^{[4]}(\phi^{[3]}(\mathbf{W}^{[3]}(\phi^{[2]}(\mathbf{W}^{[2]}(\underbrace{\phi^{[1]}(\mathbf{W}^{[1]}(\mathbf{x}) + \mathbf{b}^{[1]})}_{\mathbf{h}^{[1]}}) + \mathbf{b}^{[2]})) + \mathbf{b}^{[3]})) + \mathbf{b}^{[4]})$$

With that done, we can now move on to the next subsection where we will understand activation functions.

Activation functions

We have mentioned activation functions a few times so far and we introduced one of them as well—the sigmoid activation function. However, this isn't the only activation function that we use in neural networks. In fact, it is an active area of research, and today, there are many different types of activation functions. They can be classified into two types—linear and non-linear. We will focus on the latter because they are differentiable and this property is very important for us when we train neural networks.

Sigmoid

To start, we will take a look at sigmoid since we've already encountered it. The sigmoid function is written as follows:

$$f(x) = \frac{1}{1 + e^x}$$

The function looks as follows:

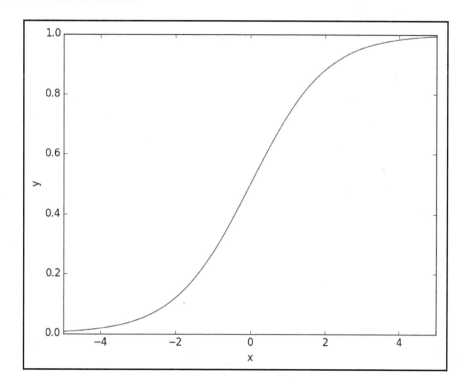

The sigmoid activation function takes the sum of the weighted inputs and bias as input and compresses the value into the (0, 1) range.

Its derivative is as follows:

$$\frac{d}{dx}f(x) = \frac{e^{-x}}{(1+e^{-x})^2} = f(x)(1 - f(x))$$

The derivative will look as follows:

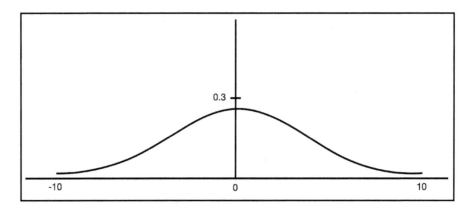

This activation function is usually used in the output layer for predicting a probability-based output. We avoid using it in the hidden layers of deep neural networks because it leads to what is known as the vanishing gradient problem. When the value of x is either greater than 2 or less than –2, then the output of the sigmoid function is very close to 1 or 0, respectively. This hinders the network's ability to learn or slows it down drastically.

Hyperbolic tangent

Another activation function used instead of the sigmoid is the hyperbolic tangent (*tanh*). It is written as follows:

$$f(x) = \frac{e^x - e^{-x}}{e^x + e^{-x}}$$

The function looks as follows:

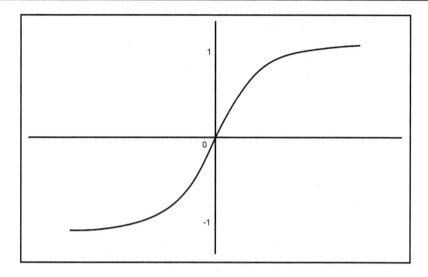

The tanh function squashes all the output values into the (-1, 1) range. Its derivative is as follows:

$$\frac{d}{dx}f = 1 - f(x)^2$$

The derivative looks as follows:

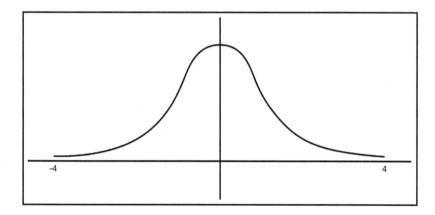

From the preceding graph you can tell that the tanh function is zero-centered, which allows us to model values that are very positive, very negative, or neutral.

Softmax

The softmax activation function normalizes a vector containing K elements into a probability distribution over the K elements. For this reason, it is generally used in the output layer to predict the probability of it being one of the classes.

The softmax function is as follows:

$$f(x) = \frac{e^{x_i}}{\sum_{k=1}^{K} e^{x_k}}$$

Its derivative can be found using the following:

$$f'(x) = \frac{e^{x_i}}{\sum_{k=1}^{K} e^{x_k}} - \frac{(e^{x_i})^2}{(\sum_{k=1}^{K} e^{x_k})^2}$$

Rectified linear unit

Rectified linear unit (ReLU) is one of the most widely used activation functions because it is more computationally efficient than the activation functions we have already seen; therefore, it allows the network to train a lot faster and so converge more quickly.

The ReLU function is as follows:

$$f(x) = \max(0, x) = \begin{cases} 0 \text{ if } x < 0 \\ x \text{ if } x \geq 0 \end{cases}$$

The function looks as follows:

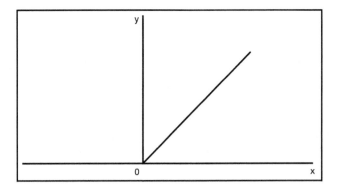

As you can see, all the negative values for x are clipped off and turn into 0. It may surprise you to know that even though this looks like a linear function, it has a derivative that is as follows:

$$\frac{d}{dx}f = \begin{cases} 1 \text{ if } x \geq 0 \\ 0 \text{ otherwise} \end{cases}$$

The derivative looks as follows:

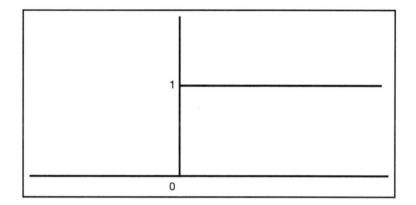

This, too, faces some problems in training—particularly, the dying ReLU problem. This occurs when the input values are negative and this hinders learning because we cannot differentiate 0.

Leaky ReLU

Leaky ReLU is a modification of the ReLU function that we saw in the previous section and it not only enables the network to learn faster but it is also more balanced as it helps deal with vanishing gradients.

The leaky ReLU function is as follows:

$$f(x) = \max(0.01x, x) = \begin{cases} 0.01x \text{ if } x < 0 \\ x \quad\ \text{ if } x \geq 0 \end{cases}$$

The function looks as follows:

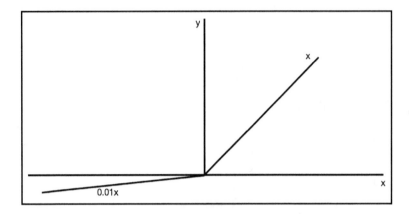

As you can see, the difference here is that the negative values of x that were clipped off before are now rescaled to $0.01x$, which overcomes the dying ReLU problem. The derivative of this activation function is as follows:

$$\frac{d}{dx} f = \begin{cases} 1 & \text{if } x \geq 0 \\ 0.01 & \text{otherwise} \end{cases}$$

The derivative looks as follows:

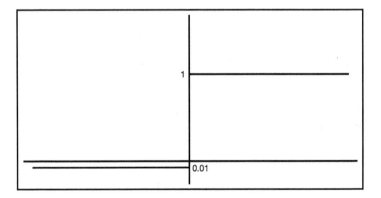

Parametric ReLU

Parametric ReLU (PReLU) is a variation of the leaky ReLU activation function and has similar performance improvements to it, except that here, the parameters are learnable whereas before they were not.

The PReLU function is as follows:

$$f(x) = \begin{cases} \alpha x \text{ if } x < 0 \\ x \quad \text{if } x \geq 0 \end{cases}$$

The function looks as follows:

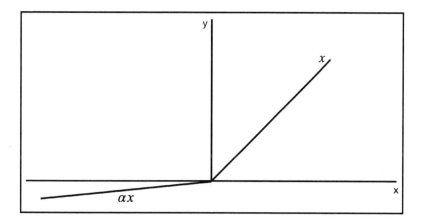

The derivative is as follows:

$$\frac{\mathrm{d}}{\mathrm{d}x}f = \begin{cases} \alpha \quad \text{if } x < 0 \\ 1 \quad \text{otherwise} \end{cases}$$

The derivative looks as follows:

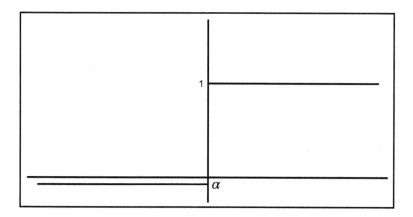

Exponential linear unit

Exponential linear unit (**ELU**) is another variation of the leaky ReLU activation function, where instead of having a straight line for all cases of $x < 0$, it is a log curve.

The ELU activation function is as follows:

$$f(x) = \begin{cases} \alpha(e^x - 1) & \text{if } x < 0 \\ x & \text{if } x \geq 0 \end{cases}$$

The function looks as follows:

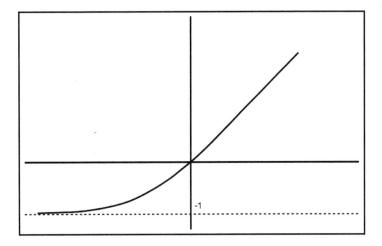

The derivative of this activation function is as follows:

$$\frac{\mathrm{d}}{\mathrm{d}x} f = \begin{cases} f(x) + \alpha & \text{if } x < 0 \\ 1 & \text{otherwise} \end{cases}$$

The loss function

The loss function is a very critical part of neural networks and their training. They give us a means of calculating the error of a network after a forward pass has been computed. This error compares the neural network output with the target output that was specified in the training data.

There are two errors in particular that are of concern to us—the local error and the global error. The local error is the difference between the output expected of a neuron and its actual output. The global error, however, is the total error (the sum of all the local errors) and it tells us how well our network is performing on the training data.

There are a number of methods that we use in practice and each has its own use cases, advantages, and disadvantages. Conventionally, the loss function is referred to as the cost function and is denoted as $J(\theta)$ (or, equivalently, $J(W,b)$).

Mean absolute error

Mean absolute error (**MAE**) is the same as the L1 loss we saw in `Chapter 3`, *Probability and Statistics*, and it looks as follows:

$$\text{MAE} = \frac{\sum_{i=1}^{N} |\hat{y}_i - y_i|}{N}$$

Here, N is the number of samples in our training dataset.

What we are doing here is calculating the absolute distance between the prediction and the true value and averaging over the sum of the errors.

Mean squared error

Mean squared error (**MSE**) is one of the most commonly used loss functions, especially for regression tasks (it takes in a vector and outputs a scalar). It calculates the square of the difference between the output and the expected output. It looks as follows:

$$\text{MSE} = \frac{1}{N} \sum_{i} \|\hat{y}_i - y_i\|_2^2$$

Here, N is the number of samples in our training dataset.

In the preceding equation, we calculate the square of the L2 norm. Intuitively, we should be able to tell that when $\hat{y} = y$, the error is 0, and the larger the distance between the points, the larger the error. The reason we use this is that it always outputs a positive value and by squaring the distance between the output and expected output, it allows us to differentiate between small and large errors with greater ease and correct them.

Root mean squared error

Root mean squared error (**RMSE**) is simply the square root of the preceding MSE function and it looks as follows:

$$\text{RMSE} = \sqrt{\frac{\sum_{i=1}^{N} \|\hat{y}_i - y_i\|_2^2}{N}}$$

The reason we use this is that it scales back the MSE function to the scale it was originally at before we squared the errors, which gives us a better idea of the error with respect to the target(s).

The Huber loss

The Huber loss looks as follows:

$$\text{Huber loss} = \begin{cases} \frac{1}{2}(y - \hat{y})^2 & \text{when } |y - \hat{y}| \leq \epsilon \\ \epsilon |y - \hat{y}| - \frac{\epsilon^2}{2} & \text{otherwise} \end{cases}$$

Here, ε is a constant term that we can configure. The smaller it is, the more insensitive the loss is to large errors and outliers, and the larger it is, the more sensitive the loss is to large errors and outliers.

Now, if you look closely, you should notice that when ε is very small, the Huber loss is similar to MAE, but when it is very large, it is similar to MSE.

Cross entropy

Cross entropy loss is used mostly when we have a binary classification problem; that is, where the network outputs either 1 or 0.

Suppose we are given a training dataset, $\mathbb{D} = \{(x_i, y_i), \cdots, (x_N, y_N)\}$ and $y_i \in \{0, 1\}$. We can then write this in the following form:

$$\hat{y}_i = f(x_i; \theta)$$

Here, θ is the parameters of the network (weights and biases). We can express this in terms of a Bernoulli distribution, as follows:

$$P(x_i \rightarrow y_i \mid \theta) = \hat{y}_i^{y_i}(1 - \hat{y}_i)^{1-y_i}$$

The probability, given the entire dataset, is then as follows:

$$P(x_1, \cdots, x_N, y_1, \cdots, y_N) = \prod_{i=1}^{N} P(x_i \rightarrow y_i \mid \theta) = \prod_{i=1}^{N} \hat{y}_i^{y_i}(1 - \hat{y}_i)^{1-y_i}$$

If we take its negative-log likelihood, we get the following:

$$-\log P(x_1, \cdots, x_N, y_1, \cdots, y_N) = -\log \prod_{i=1}^{N} \hat{y}_i^{y_i}(1 - \hat{y}_i)^{1-y_i}$$

So, we have the following:

$$L(\hat{y}, y) = -\sum_{i=1}^{N} y_i \log \hat{y}_i + (1 - y_i) \log(1 - \hat{y}_i)$$

Cross entropy is also used when we have more than two classes. This is known as **multiclass cross entropy**. Suppose we have K output units, then, we would calculate the loss for each class and then sum them together, as follows:

$$-\sum_{k=1}^{K} y_{i,k} \log \hat{y}_{i,k}$$

Here, $\hat{y}_{i,k}$ is the probability that observation (i) belongs to class k.

Kullback-Leibler divergence

Kullback-Leibler (KL) **divergence** measures the divergence of two probability distributions, p and q. It looks as follows:

$$D_{KL}(p\|q) = \int_x p(x) \log \frac{p(x)}{q(x)} \mathrm{d}x$$

So, when $p(x)=q(x)$, the KL divergence value is 0 at all points. This is usually used in generative models.

Jensen-Shannon divergence

Like the KL divergence, the **Jensen-Shannon** (JS) divergence measures how similar two probability distributions are; however, it is smoother. The following equation represents the JS divergence:

$$D_{JS}(p\|q) = \frac{1}{2}D_{KL}\left(p\|\frac{p+q}{2}\right) + \frac{1}{2}D_{KL}\left(q\|\frac{p+q}{2}\right)$$

This behaves a lot better than KL divergence when $p(x)$ and $q(x)$ are both small.

Backpropagation

Now that we know how the forward passes are computed in MLPs, as well as how to best initialize them and calculate the loss of the network, it is time for us to learn about backpropagation—a method that allows us to calculate the gradient of the network using the information from the loss function. This is where our knowledge of multivariable calculus and partial derivatives comes in handy.

If you recall, this network is fully connected, which means all the nodes in each layer are connected to—and so have an impact on—the next layer. It is for this reason that in backpropagation we take the derivative of the loss with respect to the weights of the layer closest to the output, then the one before that, and so on, until we reach the first layer. If you don't yet understand this, don't worry. We will go through backpropagation in detail and use the network from earlier as an example. We will assume that the activation function is sigmoid and our loss function is cross entropy. We will first calculate the derivative of the loss ($\mathcal{J}$) with respect to $W^{[4]}$, which looks as follows:

$$\frac{\partial J}{\partial W^{[4]}} = -\frac{\partial}{\partial W^{[4]}}[y\log\hat{y} + (1-y)\log(1-\hat{y})]$$

$$\frac{\partial J}{\partial W^{[4]}} = -y\frac{\partial}{\partial W^{[4]}}\log\left[\phi^{[4]}\left(W^{[4]}h^{[3]} + b^{[4]}\right)\right] - (1-y)\frac{\partial}{\partial W^{[4]}}\log\left[1 - \phi^{[4]}\left(W^{[4]}h^{[3]} + b^{[4]}\right)\right]$$

$$\frac{\partial J}{\partial W^{[4]}} = -y\frac{1}{\phi^{[4]}\left(W^{[4]}h^{[3]} + b^{[4]}\right)}\left[\phi^{[4]'}\left(W^{[4]}h^{[3]} + b^{[4]}\right)h^{[3]}\right] - (1-y)\frac{1}{1 - \phi^{[4]}\left(W^{[4]}h^{[3]} + b^{[4]}\right)}\left[-\phi^{[4]'}\left(W^{[4]}h^{[3]} + b^{[4]}\right)h^{[3]}\right]$$

$$\frac{\partial J}{\partial W^{[4]}} = -y(1 - \sigma(W^{[4]}h^{[3]} + b^{[4]}))h^{[3]} + (1-y)\sigma(W^{[4]}h^{[3]} + b^{[4]})h^{[3]}$$

$$\frac{\partial J}{\partial W^{[4]}} = -y(1-\hat{y})h^{[3]} + (1-y)\hat{y}h^{[3]}$$

$$(\hat{y}-y)h^{[3]}$$

With that, we have finished computing the first derivative. As you can see, it takes quite a bit of work, and calculating the derivative for each layer can be a very time-consuming process. So, instead, we can make use of the chain rule from calculus.

For simplicity, let's say $z^{[l]} = W^{[l]}h^{[l-1]} + b^{[l]}$ and $h^{[l]} = \phi^{[l]}(z^{[l]})$ and assume that $b^{[l]} = 0$. Now, if we want to calculate the gradient of the loss with respect to $W^{[2]}$, we get the following:

$$\frac{\partial J}{\partial W^{[2]}} = \frac{\partial J}{\partial \hat{y}} \frac{\partial \hat{y}}{\partial z^{[4]}} \frac{\partial z^{[4]}}{\partial h^{[3]}} \frac{\partial h^{[3]}}{\partial z^{[3]}} \frac{\partial z^{[3]}}{\partial h^{[2]}} \frac{\partial h^{[2]}}{\partial z^{[2]}} \frac{\partial z^{[2]}}{\partial W^{[2]}}$$

We can rewrite this as follows:

$$\frac{\partial J}{\partial W^{[2]}} = (\hat{y}-y)W^{[4]}\phi^{[3]'}(z^{[3]})W^{[3]}\phi^{[2]}(z^{[2]})h^{[1]}$$

Suppose we do want to find the partial of the loss with respect to $b^{[4]}$; this looks as follows:

$$\frac{\partial J}{\partial b^{[4]}} = \frac{\partial J}{\partial \hat{y}} \frac{\partial \hat{y}}{\partial z^{[4]}} \frac{\partial z^{[4]}}{\partial b^{[4]}}$$

Before we move on to the next section, pay close attention to the preceding derivative, $\frac{\partial J}{\partial W^{[2]}}$. If you look back to earlier on in the *Layers* section, $W^{[l]}, h^{[l]}, z^{[l]}, b^{[l]}$ were all vectors and matrices. This is still true. Because we are again dealing with vectors and matrices, it is important that their dimensions line up.

We know that $\frac{\partial J}{\partial W^{[2]}} \in \mathbb{R}^{3 \times 5}$, but what about the others? I will leave this to you as an exercise to determine whether or not the other is correct and if it is not, how would you change the order to ensure it is?

If you're feeling very confident in your math abilities and are up for a challenge, I encourage you to try finding the derivative, $\frac{\partial J}{\partial w^{[2]}_{3,4}}$.

Training neural networks

Now that we have an understanding of backpropagation and how gradients are computed, you might be wondering what purpose it serves and what it has to do with training our MLP. If you will recall from `Chapter 1`, *Vector Calculus*, when we covered partial derivatives, we learned that we can use partial derivatives to check the impact that changing one parameter can have on the output of a function. When we use the first and second derivatives to plot our graphs, we can analytically tell what the local and global minima and maxima are. However, it isn't as straightforward as that in our case as our model doesn't know where the optima is or how to get there; so, instead, we use backpropagation with the gradient descent as a guide to help us get to the (hopefully global) minima.

In `Chapter 4`, *Optimization*, we learned about gradient descent and how we iteratively move from one point on the function to a lower point on the function that is in the direction of the local/global minima by taking a step in the direction of the negative of the gradient. We expressed it in the following form:

$$x_{k+1} = x_k - c_k \nabla f(x)$$

However, for neural networks, the update rule for the weights, in this case, is written as follows:

$$\theta^{[l]} = \theta^{[l]} - \alpha \frac{\partial J}{\partial \theta^{[l]}}$$

Here, $\theta = (W, b)$.

As you can see, while this does look similar, it isn't the optimization we have learned. Our goal here is to minimize the total loss of the network and update our weights accordingly.

Parameter initialization

In `Chapter 4`, *Optimization*, we mentioned that before we start optimizing, we need an initial (starting) point, which is the purpose of initialization. This is an extremely important part of training neural networks because as mentioned earlier on in this chapter, neural networks have a lot of parameters—often, well over tens of millions—which means that finding the point in the weight space that minimizes our loss can be very time consuming and challenging (because the weight space is non-convex; that is, there are lots of local minima and saddle points).

For this reason, finding a good initial point is important because it makes it easier to get to the optima and reduce the training time, as well as reducing the chances of our weights either vanishing or exploding. Let's now explore the various ways that we can initialize our weights and biases.

All zeros

As the name suggests, here we set the initial weights and biases of our model to be zeros. I don't recommend doing this because, as you may have guessed, this means that all the neurons in our model are dead. In fact, this is the very problem we want to avoid when training our network.

Let's see what happens anyway. For the sake of simplicity, let's suppose we have the following linear classifier:

$$\hat{y} = \mathbf{w} \cdot \mathbf{x} + b = \sum_{i=1}^{n} w_i x_i + b$$

If the weights are initialized as 0, then our output is always 0, which means we lost all the information that was part of our training data and the network that we put so much effort into building learns nothing.

Random initialization

One way of initializing our weights to be non-zero is to use random initialization and for this, we could use one of two distributions—the normal distribution or the uniform distribution.

To initialize our parameters using the normal distribution, we have to specify the mean and the standard deviation. Usually, we choose a mean of 0 and a standard deviation of 1. To initialize using the uniform distribution, we usually use the [-1, 1] range (where there is an equal probability of any value in the range being picked).

While this gives us weights that we can use in training, it is very slow and has previously resulted in vanishing and exploding gradients in deep networks, resulting in mediocre performance.

Xavier initialization

As we have seen, if our weights are too small, then they vanish, which results in dead neurons and, conversely, if our weights are too big, we get exploding gradients. We want to avoid both scenarios, which means we need the weights to be initialized just right so that our network can learn what it needs to.

To tackle this problem, Xavier Glorot and Yoshua Bengio created a normalized initialization method (generally referred to as Xavier initialization). It is as follows:

$$W_{i,j}^{[k]} \sim U\left[-\frac{\sqrt{6}}{n_k + n_{k-1}}, \frac{\sqrt{6}}{n_k + n_{k-1}}\right]$$

Here, n_k is the number of neurons in layer k.

But why does this work better than randomly initializing our network? The idea is that we want to maintain the variance as we propagate through subsequent layers.

The data

As you will know by now, what we are trying to build here are networks that can learn to map an input to an output. For our network to be able to do this, it needs to be fed data—and lots of it. Therefore, it is important for us to know what the data should look like.

Let's suppose we have a classification or regression task. Our data will then take the following form:

$$\mathbb{D} = \{(\mathbf{x}_i, y_i), \cdots, (\mathbf{x}_N, y_N)\}_{i=1}^{N}$$

Here, we assume the following:

$$\mathbf{x}_i, y_i \sim p(\mathbf{x}, y)$$

As you can see, each sample in the dataset has the input (x_i) and a corresponding output/target (y_i). However, depending on the task, our output will look a bit different. In regression, our output can take on any real value, whereas in classification, it must be one of the classes we can predict.

Our data (x), as you may expect, contains all the various information we want to use to predict our target variables (y) and this, of course, depends on the problem. As an example, let's take the Boston Housing dataset, which is a regression task. It contains the following features:

- The per-capita crime rate by town
- The proportion of residential land zoned for lots over 25,000 square feet
- The proportion of non-retail business acres per town
- The Charles River dummy variable (1 if tract bounds river and 0 if not)
- The nitric oxide concentration value (parts per 10 million)
- The average number of rooms per dwelling
- The proportion of owner-occupied units built before 1940
- The weighted distances to five Boston employment centers
- The index of accessibility to radial highways
- The full-value property tax rate per $10,000
- The pupil-to-teacher ratio by town
- The proportion of African Americans by town
- The percentage of the population that is of a lower status

The target variable is the median value of owner-occupied homes in $1,000.

All the data is numerical (since the machines don't really read or know what those labels mean, but they do know how to parse numbers).

Now, let's look at a classification problem—since we are trying to predict which class our data belongs to, the target will become a vector instead of a scalar (as it is in the preceding dataset), where the dimension of the target vector will be the number of categories. But how do we represent this target vector?

Suppose we have a dataset of images with the corresponding target labels:

$$\text{classes} = \{0 : \text{cat}, 1 : \text{dog}, 2 : \text{horse}, 3 : \text{turtle}\}$$

As you can see, each label has a digit assigned to it and during training, our network could mistake these for trainable parameters, which we obviously would want to avoid. Instead, we can one-hot encode this, thereby turning the label vector into the following:

$$\text{cat} : \begin{bmatrix} 1 & 0 & 0 & 0 \end{bmatrix}^T$$
$$\text{dog} : \begin{bmatrix} 0 & 1 & 0 & 0 \end{bmatrix}^T$$
$$\text{horse} : \begin{bmatrix} 0 & 0 & 1 & 0 \end{bmatrix}^T$$
$$\text{turtle} : \begin{bmatrix} 0 & 0 & 0 & 1 \end{bmatrix}^T$$

Great! Now we know what is in a dataset and how datasets are structured. But what now? We split the dataset into training, testing, and validation sets. How we split the data into the three respective sets depends largely on how much data we have. In the case of deep learning, we will, more often than not, be dealing with very large datasets; that is, millions to tens of millions of samples.

As a rule of thumb, we generally select 80-90% of the dataset to train our network, and the remaining 10-20% is split into two portions—the validation and test sets. The validation set is used during training to determine whether our network has overfit or underfit to the data and the test set is used at the end to check how well our model generalizes to unseen data.

Deep neural networks

Now, it's time to get into the really fun stuff (and what you picked up this book for)—deep neural networks. The depth comes from the number of layers in the neural network and for an FNN to be considered deep, it must have more than 10 hidden layers. A number of today's state-of-the-art FNNs have well over 40 layers. Let's now explore some of the properties of deep FNNs and get an understanding of why they are so powerful.

If you recall, earlier on we came across the universal approximation theorem, which stated that an MLP with a single hidden layer could approximate any function. But if that is the case, why do we need deep neural networks? Simply put, the capacity of a neural network increases with each hidden layer (and the brain has a deep structure). What this means is that deeper networks have far greater expressiveness than shallower networks. This is something we came across earlier when learning about MLPs. We saw that by adding hidden layers, we were able to create a network that was able to learn to solve a problem that a linear neural network was not able to.

Additionally, deeper networks are preferred over wider networks, not because they improve the overall performance, but because networks with more hidden layers (but less width) have much fewer parameters than wider networks with fewer hidden layers.

Let's suppose we have two networks—one that is wide and one that is deep. Both networks have 20 inputs and 6 output nodes. Let's calculate the total number of parameters for both layers; that is, the number of connections between all the layers and biases.

Our wide neural network has two hidden layers, each with 1,024 neurons. The total number of parameters is as follows:

$$(20 \times 1024) + (2014 \times 1024) + (1024 \times 8) + (1024 + 1024 + 8) = 1,079,304$$

Our deep neural network has 12 hidden layers, each with 150 neurons. The total number of parameters is as follows:

$$(20 \times 200) + (200 \times 200) \times 11 + (200 \times 8) + (200 \times 12 + 8) = 484,008$$

As you can see, the deeper network has less than half the parameters that the wider network does.

Summary

In this chapter, we first learned about a simple FNN, known as the MLP, and broke it down into its individual components to get a deeper understanding of how they work and are constructed. We then extended these concepts to further our understanding of deep neural networks. You should now have intimate knowledge of how FNNs work and understand how various models are constructed, as well as understand how to build and possibly improve them for yourself.

Let's now move on to the next chapter, where we will learn how to improve our neural networks so that they generalize better on unseen data.

8
Regularization

In the previous chapter, we learned about (deep) feedforward neural networks and how they are structured. We learned how these architectures can leverage their hidden layers and non-linear activations to learn to perform well on some very challenging tasks, which linear models aren't able to do. We also saw that neural networks tend to overfit to the training data by learning noise in the dataset, which leads to errors in the testing data. Naturally, since our goal is to create models that generalize well, we want to close the gap so that our models perform just as well on both datasets. This is the goal of regularization—to reduce test error, sometimes at the expense of greater training error.

In this chapter, we will cover a variety of methods used in regularization, how they work, and why certain techniques are preferred over others. This includes limiting the capacity of a neural network, applying norm penalties and dataset augmentation, and more.

We will cover the following topics in this chapter:

- The need for regularization
- Norm penalties
- Early stopping
- Parameter typing and sharing
- Dataset augmentation
- Dropout
- Adversarial training

The need for regularization

In previous chapters, we learned how feedforward neural networks are basically a complex function that maps an input to a corresponding target/label by learning the underlying distribution using the training data. We can recall that during training, after an error has been calculated during the forward pass, backpropagation is used to update the parameters in order to reduce the loss and better approximate the data distribution. We also learned about the capacity of neural networks, the bias-variance trade-off, and how neural networks can underfit or overfit to the training data, which prevents it from being able to perform well on unseen data or test data (that is, a generalization error occurs).

Before we get into what exactly regularization is, let's revisit overfitting and underfitting. Neural networks, as we know, are universal function approximators. Deep neural networks have many hidden layers, which means there are a lot of parameters that need to be trained. As a general rule, the more parameters a model has, the more complex it is, which means there's a greater risk of it overfitting to the training data.

This means that our model has perfectly learned all the patterns that exist in the data, including the noise, and has zero loss on the training data, but has a high loss on the test data. Additionally, overfitted models, in general, have a lower bias and a very high variance. Conversely, models with fewer parameters tend to be simpler, which means they are more likely to underfit to the training data because they observe a small portion of the data that doesn't differ much. Therefore, they tend to have a much greater bias, which also leads to high variance. The following diagram illustrates the preceding explanation:

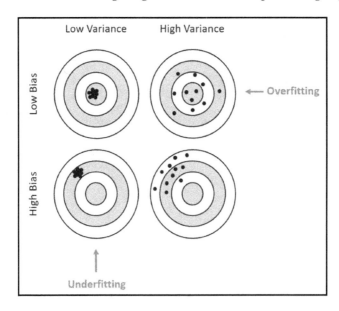

Somewhere in between overfitting and underfitting is a sweet spot where we have the optimal capacity; that is, the model hyperparameters that are perfectly suited to the task and data at hand—this is what we are aiming for. This tells us that the goal of regularization is to prevent our model from overfitting and that we prefer simpler models over vastly complex ones. However, the best model is one that is large and properly regularized.

Now that we know the purpose of regularization, let's explore some of the many ways that we can regularize our deep neural networks.

Norm penalties

Adding a parameter norm penalty to the objective function is the most classic of the regularization methods. What this does is limit the capacity of the model. This method has been around for several decades and predates the advent of deep learning. We can write this as follows:

$$\tilde{J}(\theta; X, y) = J(\theta; X, y) + \alpha \Omega(\theta)$$

Here, $\alpha \in [0, \infty]$. The α value, in the preceding equation, is a hyperparameter that determines how large a regularizing effect the regularizer will have on the regularized cost function. The greater the value of α is, the more regularization is applied, and the smaller it is, the less of an effect regularization has on the cost function.

In the case of neural networks, we only apply the parameter norm penalties to the weights since they control the interaction or relationship between two nodes in successive layers, and we leave the biases as they are since they need less data in comparison to the weights.

There are a few different choices we can make when it comes to what kind of parameter norm to use, and each has a different effect on the solution.

L2 regularization

The L2 regularization method is often referred to as **ridge regression** (but more commonly known as **weight decay**). It forces the weights of the network in the direction of the origin through the following regularization term to the objective function:

$$\Omega(\theta) = \frac{1}{2}\|\theta\|_2^2$$

 For simplicity, we will assume that $\theta = w$ and that all the letters are matrices.

The regularized objective function, in this case, will be as follows:

$$\tilde{J}(w; X, y) = J(w; X, y) + \frac{\alpha}{2}w^\mathrm{T}w$$

If we take its gradient, then it becomes the following:

$$\nabla_w \tilde{J}(w; X, y) = \nabla_w J(w; X, y) + \alpha w$$

Using the preceding gradient, we can calculate the update for the weights at each gradient step, as follows:

$$w \leftarrow w - \epsilon(\alpha w + \nabla_w J(w; X, y))$$

We can expand and rewrite the right-hand side of the preceding update as follows:

$$w \leftarrow (1 - \epsilon\alpha)w - \epsilon\nabla_w J(w; X, y)$$

From this equation, we can clearly see that the modified learning rule causes our weight to shrink by $(1 - \epsilon\alpha)$ at every step, as in the following diagram:

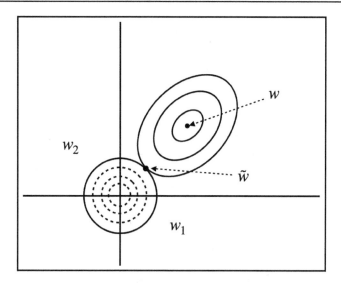

In the preceding diagram, we can see the effect that L2 regularization has on our weights. The solid circles toward the top-right side represent contours of equal value of the original object function, $J(w; X, y)$, which we have not yet applied our regularizer to. The dotted circles, on the other hand, represent the contours of the regularizer term, $\alpha w^T w$. Finally, $\tilde{w}$, the point where both the contours meet, represents when competing objectives reach equilibrium.

L1 regularization

Another form of norm penalty is to use L1 regularization, which is sometimes referred to as **least absolute shrinkage and selection operator (lasso)** regression. In this case, the regularization term is as follows:

$$\Omega(\theta) = \|w\|_1 = \sum_i |w_i|$$

What this does is it sums together the absolute values of the parameters. The effect that this has is that it introduces sparsity to our model by zeroing out some of the values, telling us that they aren't very important. This can be thought of as a form of feature selection.

Similar to the preceding L2 regularization, in L1 regularization, the α hyperparameter controls how much of an effect the regularization has on the objective function:

$$\tilde{J}\left(w; X, y\right) = J(w; X, y) + \alpha\|w\|_1$$

This is illustrated as follows:

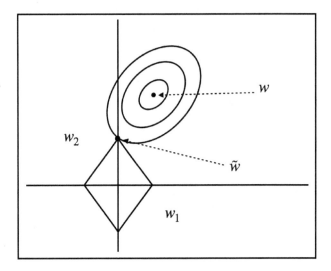

As you can see in the preceding diagram, the contours of the objective function now meet at the axes instead of at a point away from it, as was the case in L2 regularization, which is where the sparsity in this method comes from.

Now that we have learned how we can regularize our deep neural networks, let's have a look at what early stopping is in the following section.

Early stopping

During training, we know that our neural networks (which have sufficient capacity to learn the training data) have a tendency to overfit to the training data over many iterations, and then they are unable to generalize what they have learned to perform well on the test set. One way of overcoming this problem is to plot the error on the training and test sets at each iteration and analytically look for the iteration where the error from the training and test sets is the closest. Then, we choose those parameters for our model.

Another advantage of this method is that this in no way alters the objective function in the way that parameter norms do, which makes it easy to use and means it doesn't interfere with the network's learning dynamics, which is shown in the following diagram:

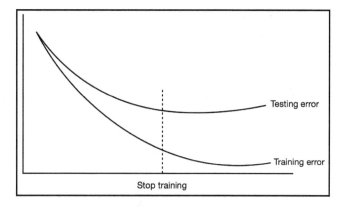

However, this approach isn't perfect—it does have a downside. It is computationally expensive because we have to train the network longer than is needed and collect more data for it, and then observe the point where the performance started to degrade.

Parameter tying and sharing

The preceding parameter norm penalties work by penalizing the model parameters when they deviate from 0 (a fixed value). But sometimes, we may want to express prior knowledge about which parameters would be better suited to the model. Although we may not know what those parameters are, thanks to domain knowledge and the architecture of the model, we know that there are likely to be some dependencies between the parameters of the model.

These dependencies could be some specific parameters that are closer to some than to others. Let's suppose we have two different models for a classification task and detect the same number of classes. Their input distributions, however, are not the same. Let's name the first model A with $\theta^{(A)}$ parameters and the second model B with $\theta^{(B)}$ parameters. Both of these models map their respective inputs to the outputs:

$$\hat{y}^{(A)} = f(\theta^{(A)}, x) \text{ and } \hat{y}^{(B)} = g(\theta^{(B)}, x)$$

Naturally, since both of these models are working on relatively similar (maybe even the same) task(s) and so likely have similar (or the same) input distributions, both model A and model B's parameters should be close to each other.

We can use a parameter norm penalty, such as the L2 penalty, to determine the closeness of the $\theta^{(A)}$ and $\theta^{(B)}$ parameters, as follows:

$$\Omega(\theta^{(A)}, \theta^{(B)}) = \|\theta^{(A)} - \theta^{(B)}\|_2^2$$

 We can use other metrics besides the L2 norm to measure the distance.

This method of forcing parameters to be close to each other is referred to as **parameter sharing**. The reason for this is that this can be interpreted as the different models sharing a set of parameters. This approach is preferred to parameter norm penalties because it requires less memory since we only have to store a unique set of shared parameters.

Dataset augmentation

Deep feedforward networks, as we have learned, are very data-hungry and they use all this data to learn the underlying data distribution so that they can use their gained knowledge to make predictions on unseen data. This is because the more data they see, the more likely it is that what they encounter in the test set will be an interpolation of the distribution they have already learned. But getting a large enough dataset with good-quality labeled data is by no means a simple task (especially for certain problems where gathering data could end up being very costly). A method to circumvent this issue is using data augmentation; that is, generating synthetic data and using it to train our deep neural network.

The way synthetic data generation works is that we use a generative model (more on this in Chapter 12, *Generative Models*) to learn the underlying distribution of the dataset that we will use to train our network for the task at hand, and then use the generative model to create synthetic data that is similar to the ground-truth data so that it appears to have come from the same dataset. We can also add small variations to the synthetic data to make the model more robust to noise.

This method has proven to be very effective in the case of computer vision—particularly object detection/classification—which we make use of in convolutional neural networks (which we will learn about in Chapter 9, *Convolutional Neural Networks*).

Another type of data augmentation that is often used in image recognition is image cropping and image rotation, where we either crop a large segment of the input image or rotate it by some angle. These methods have also been proven to increase robustness and improve generalization on unseen data. We could also corrupt, blur, or add in some Gaussian noise to the images to make the network more robust since a lot of real-world data tends to be noisy.

However, there are limitations to this. For example, in the case of optical character recognition (where we want to recognize letters and numbers), horizontal flips and 180-degree rotations can affect the class. After a transformation, a *b* can turn into a *d* and a *6* can turn into a *9*. There are also some problems where data augmentation simply isn't an option; an example of this is in the medical domain where we could be trying to work with MRI and CT scans. However, what we could do, in this case, is apply affine transformations, such as rotations and translations.

Let's focus for a moment on noise injection. There are two ways we can do this—the first is to inject noise to the input data and the second is to inject noise into the hidden units. In fact, it has been found that the addition of noise to hidden units can be a much better regularizer than parameter shrinking because it encourages stability.

Dropout

In the preceding section, we learned about applying penalties to the norm of the weights to regularize them, as well as other approaches, such as dataset augmentation and early stopping. However, there is another effective approach that is widely used in practice, known as dropout.

So far, when training neural networks, all the weights have been learned together. However, dropout alters this idea by having the network only learn a fraction of the weights during each iteration. The reason for this is to avoid co-adaptation. This occurs when we train the entire network over all the training data and some connections end up stronger than others, thereby contributing more toward the network's predictive capabilities because the stronger connections overpower the weaker connections, effectively ignoring them. As we train the network with more iterations, some of the weaker connections essentially die out and are no longer trainable, so only a subnetwork ends up being trained, putting part of the network to waste. This is something that the preceding norm penalties are unable to address.

The way that dropout overcomes overfitting is by randomly (according to some predefined probability) removing (dropping out) neurons from a hidden layer; that is, we temporarily zero out some of the incoming and outgoing edges of a node so that it does not have an impact on the network during that training iteration. For example, if we have a **multilayer perceptron (MLP)** with one hidden layer that consists of 10 neurons and we have dropout with $p = 0.5$, then half the neurons are set to 0. If $p = 0.2$, then 20 percent of the neurons are dropped:

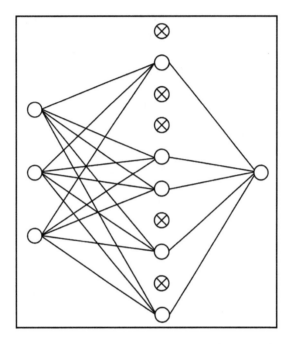

Let's consider an MLP with L hidden layers, such that $l = \{1, 2, \cdots, L\}$, where the vector input to each layer is $z^{(l)}$ and the output vector of each layer is $y^{(l)}$ (for the sake of simplicity, $y^{(0)} = x$). The weights and biases of each layer are denoted by $W^{(l)}$ and $b^{(l)}$, respectively. Then, we get the following:

$$z_i^{(l+1)} = w_i^{(l+1)} y^{(l)} + b_i^{(l+1)}$$
$$\text{and}$$
$$y_i^{(l+1)} = f(z_i^{(l+1)})$$

Here, f is any activation function.

Now, with dropout, the feedforward operations become the following:

$$r_j^{(l)} \sim \text{Bernoulli}(p)$$
$$\tilde{y}^{(l)} = r^{(l)} y^{(l)}$$
$$z_i^{(l+1)} = w_i^{(l+1)} \tilde{y}^{(l)} + b_i^{(l+1)}$$
$$y_i^{(l+1)} = f(z_i^{(l+1)})$$

So, we find that $p = 0.5$ has the best regularizing effect during training.

Adversarial training

Nowadays, neural networks have started to reach human-level accuracy on a number of tasks, and in some, they can be seen to have even surpassed humans. But have they really surpassed humans or does it just seem this way? In production environments, we often have to deal with noisy data, which can cause our model to make incorrect predictions. So, we will now learn about another very important method of regularization—**adversarial training**.

Before we get into the what and the how of adversarial training, let's take a look at the following diagram:

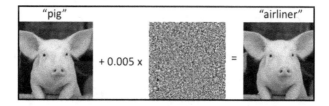

What we have done, in the preceding diagram, is added in negligible Gaussian noise to the pixels of the original image. To us, the image looks exactly the same, but to a convolutional neural network, it looks entirely different. This is a problem, and it occurs even when our models are perfectly trained and have almost no error.

What we do is find a data point, x', which is near to x, but the model predicts x' to be part of a different class. Now, to add noise to our image, we can do so as follows:

$$x' = x + \epsilon \, \text{sign}(\nabla_x J(\theta, x, y))$$

The reason this interests us is that adding adversarially perturbed data samples to our training dataset can help reduce the error on our test set.

Summary

In this chapter, we covered a variety of methods that are used to regularize the parameters of a neural network. These methods are very important when it comes to training our models because they help ensure that they can generalize to unseen data by preventing overfitting, thereby performing well on the tasks we want to use them for. In the following chapters, we will learn about different types of neural networks and how each one is best suited for certain types of problems. Each neural network has a form of regularization that it can use to help improve performance.

In the next chapter, we will learn about convolutional neural networks, which are used for computer vision.

Convolutional Neural Networks

9

In this chapter, we will cover one of the most popular and widely used deep neural networks—the **convolutional neural network** (**CNN**, also known as **ConvNet**).

It is this class of neural networks that is largely responsible for the incredible feats that have been accomplished in computer vision over the last few years, starting with AlexNet, created by Alex Krizhevsky, Geoffrey Hinton, and Ilya Sutskever, which outperformed all the other models in the 2012 **ImageNet Large Scale Visual Recognition Challenge** (**ILSVRC**), thus beginning the deep learning revolution.

ConvNets are a very powerful type of neural network for processing data. They have a grid-like topology (that is, there is a spatial correlation between neighboring points) and are tremendously useful in a variety of applications, such as facial recognition, self-driving cars, surveillance, natural language processing, time-series forecasting, and much more.

We will start by introducing the basic building blocks of ConvNets and introduce some of the architectures used in practice, such as AlexNet, VGGNet, and Inception-v1, as well as exploring what makes them so powerful.

The following topics will be covered in this chapter:

- The inspiration behind ConvNets
- Types of data used in ConvNets
- Convolutions and pooling
- Working with the ConvNet architecture
- Training and optimization
- Exploring popular ConvNet architectures

The inspiration behind ConvNets

CNNs are a type of **artificial neural network** (ANN); they are loosely inspired by the concept that the human visual cortex processes images and allows our brains to recognize objects in the world and interact with them, which allows us to do a number of things, such as drive, play sports, read, watch movies, and so on.

It has been found that computations that somewhat resemble convolutions take place in our brains. Additionally, our brains possess both simple and complex cells. The simple cells pick up basic features, such as edges and curves, while the complex cells show spatial invariance, while also responding to the same cues as the simple cells.

Types of data used in ConvNets

CNNs work exceptionally well on visual tasks, such as object classification and object recognition in images and videos and pattern recognition in music, sound clips, and so on. They work effectively in these areas because they are able to exploit the structure of the data to learn about it. This means that we cannot alter the properties of the data. For example, images have a fixed structure and if we were to alter this, the image would no longer make sense. This differs from ANNs, where the ordering of feature vectors does not matter. Therefore, the data for CNNs is stored in multidimensional arrays.

In computers, images are in grayscale (black and white) or are colored (RGB), and videos (RGB-D) are made of up pixels. A pixel is the smallest unit of a digitized image that can be shown on a computer and holds values in the form of [0, 255]. The pixel value represents its intensity.

If the pixel value is 0, then it is black, if it is 128, then it is gray, and if it is 255, then it is white. We can see this in the following screenshot:

As we can see, grayscale images only require 1 byte of data, but colored images, on the other hand, are made up of three different values—red, blue, and green—since any color can be shown using a combination of these three colors. We can see the colorspace in the following diagram (refer to the color diagram from the graphic bundle):

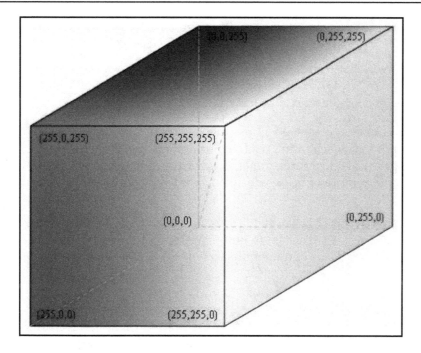

Depending on where in the cube we are, we clearly get a different color.

Instead of looking at it as a cube or varying color intensities, we can look at it as having three separate channels—red, blue, and green. Then, each pixel requires 3 bytes of storage.

Normally, we cannot see the individual pixels in the images and videos that we see on our monitors because they have a very high resolution. This can vary greatly, but the pixels are usually between several hundred to several thousands of **dots** (pixels) **per inch** (**dpi**).

 A bit (binary unit) is the fundamental unit of a computer and each bit can take on one of two values—0 or 1. A single byte consists of 8 bits. In case you're wondering, the [0, 255] range comes from the pixel value being stored in 8 bits, ($2^8 - 1 = 255$). However, we could also have a 16-bit data value. In colored images, we can have either 8-bit, 16-bit, 24-bit, or 30-bit values, but we usually use 24-bit values since we have three colored pixels, RGB, and each has an 8-bit data value.

Suppose we have a grayscale image with a size of 512 × 512 × 1 (height × width × channel). We can store it in a two-dimensional tensor (matrix), $\mathbb{R}^{h \times w \times 1}$, where each i and j value is a pixel with some intensity. To store this image on our disk, we need 512 × 512 = 262,144 bytes.

Now, suppose we have a colored image with a size of $512 \times 512 \times 3$ (height × width × channel). We can store it in a three-dimensional tensor, $\mathbb{R}^{h \times w \times 3}$, where each i, j, and k value is a colored pixel with some intensity. To store this image on our disk, we would need $512 \times 512 \times 3 = 786{,}432$ bytes, which tells us that storing a colored image requires a lot more space and so a longer time to process.

A colored video can be represented as a sequence of frames (images). We start by making the time discrete so that each frame is a fixed time step apart from the other. We can store a regular video (grayscale) in a three-dimensional array, where one axis represents the height of the frame, another represents the width, and the third represents the length of time.

We will learn, later in this chapter, that CNNs also work quite well for audio and time-series data because they are resistant to noise. We represent time-series data as a one-dimensional array, where the length of the array is time, which is what we convolve over.

Convolutions and pooling

In Chapter 7, *Feedforward Neural Networks*, we saw how deep neural networks are built and how weights connect neurons in one layer to neurons in the previous or following layer. The layers in CNNs, however, are connected through a linear operation known as **convolution**, which is where their name comes from and what makes it such a powerful architecture for images.

Here, we will go over the various kinds of convolution and pooling operations used in practice and what the effect of each is. But first, let's see what convolution actually is.

Two-dimensional convolutions

In mathematics, we write convolutions as follows:

$$(f * g)(x) = \int f(t)g(t - x)\mathrm{d}t$$

What this means is that we have a function, *f*, which is our input and a function, *g*, which is our kernel. By convolving them, we receive an output (sometimes referred to as a feature map).

However, in CNNs, we usually use discrete convolutions, which are written as follows:

$$(f * g)(x) = \sum_t f(t)g(t - x)$$

Let's suppose we have a two-dimensional array with a height of 5 and a width of 5, and a two-dimensional kernel with a height of 3 and a width of 3. Then, the convolution and its output will look as follows:

$$\begin{bmatrix} 2 & 4 & 3 & 7 & 2 \\ 6 & 1 & 4 & 3 & 1 \\ 7 & 2 & 3 & 5 & 5 \\ 1 & 7 & 3 & 9 & 1 \\ 4 & 2 & 9 & 1 & 5 \end{bmatrix} * \begin{bmatrix} 1 & 0 & -1 \\ 1 & 0 & -1 \\ 1 & 0 & -1 \end{bmatrix} = \begin{bmatrix} 5 & ? & ? \\ ? & -7 & ? \\ ? & -4 & ? \end{bmatrix}$$

Some of the values in the output matrix are left empty as an exercise for us to try the convolution by hand and get a better idea of how this operation works.

As you can see, the kernel slides over the input and produces a feature map with a height of 3 and a width of 3. This feature map tells us the degree to which the functions f and g overlap as one passes over the other. We can think of this as scanning the input for a certain pattern; in other words, the feature map is looking for the same pattern in different places of the input.

To get a better understanding of how the kernel moves over the input, think of a typewriter. The convolution starts at the top left, applies element-wise multiplication and addition, then moves a step to the right and repeats until it reaches the rightmost position without going beyond the bounds of the input. It then moves down one row and repeats this process until it reaches the bottom-right position.

Suppose that we now have a 3×3 two-dimensional tensor as input and apply to it a 2×2 kernel. It will look as follows:

$$\begin{bmatrix} I_{1,1} & I_{1,2} & I_{1,3} \\ I_{2,1} & I_{2,2} & I_{2,3} \\ I_{3,1} & I_{3,2} & I_{3,3} \end{bmatrix} * \begin{bmatrix} K_{1,1} & K_{1,2} \\ K_{2,1} & K_{2,2} \end{bmatrix} = \begin{bmatrix} O_{1,1} & O_{1,2} \\ O_{2,1} & O_{2,2} \end{bmatrix}$$

We can mathematically write the individual outputs in the feature map as follows:

$$O_{1,1} = I_{1,1}K_{1,1} + I_{1,2}K_{1,2} + I_{2,1}K_{2,1} + I_{2,2}K_{2,2}$$
$$O_{1,2} = I_{1,2}K_{1,1} + I_{1,3}K_{1,2} + I_{2,2}K_{2,1} + I_{2,3}K_{2,2}$$
$$O_{2,1} = I_{2,1}K_{1,1} + I_{2,2}K_{1,2} + I_{3,1}K_{2,1} + I_{3,2}K_{2,2}$$
$$O_{2,2} = I_{2,2}K_{1,1} + I_{2,3}K_{1,2} + I_{3,2}K_{2,1} + I_{3,3}K_{2,2}$$

Now, we can rewrite the preceding discrete convolution equation as follows:

$$(I * K)(i, j) = \sum_m \sum_n I(m, n)K(i - m, j - n)$$

This gives us a much clearer idea of what is happening.

From the preceding operation, we can tell that if we keep applying convolutions to feature maps, the height and width of each layer will decrease subsequently. So, sometimes, we may want to preserve the size of I after the convolution operation (especially if we are building a very deep CNN), in which case, we pad the outside of the matrix with zeros. What this does is it increases the size of the matrix before applying the convolution operation.

So, if I is an n × n array and our kernel is a k × k array and we want our feature map to be n × n as well, then we pad I once, turning it into an (n+2) × (n+2) array. Now, after we convolve the two, the resulting feature map will have an n × n size.

The padding operation looks as follows:

$$\begin{bmatrix} 3 & 1 & 5 \\ 4 & 9 & 3 \\ 2 & 1 & 8 \end{bmatrix} \xrightarrow{padding=1} \begin{bmatrix} 0 & 0 & 0 & 0 & 0 \\ 0 & 3 & 1 & 5 & 0 \\ 0 & 4 & 9 & 3 & 0 \\ 0 & 2 & 1 & 8 & 0 \\ 0 & 0 & 0 & 0 & 0 \end{bmatrix}$$

In practice, this is referred to as full padding. When we do not pad, we refer to it as zero padding.

Should we want to reduce the size of the feature map, we can use a larger kernel or we can increase the stride size—each will give a different result. When the stride is 1, we slide our kernel as normal, one at a time. However, when we increase the stride to 2, the kernel hops two positions each time.

Let's use the preceding matrix we convolved and see what happens when we change the stride to 2:

$$\begin{bmatrix} 2 & 4 & 3 & 7 & 2 \\ 6 & 1 & 4 & 3 & 1 \\ 7 & 2 & 3 & 5 & 5 \\ 1 & 7 & 3 & 9 & 1 \\ 4 & 2 & 9 & 1 & 5 \end{bmatrix} * \begin{bmatrix} 1 & 0 & -1 \\ 1 & 0 & -1 \\ 1 & 0 & -1 \end{bmatrix} = \begin{bmatrix} 5 & 2 \\ -3 & 4 \end{bmatrix}$$

Armed with this knowledge, we can calculate the resulting shape of the feature map using the following formula:

$$(n \times n) * (k \times k) = \left(\left(\frac{n + 2p - k}{s} + 1 \right) \times \left(\frac{n + 2p - k}{s} + 1 \right) \right)$$

Here, *I* is an n × n array, *K* is a k × k array, *p* is the padding, and *s* is the stride.

Additionally, we can repeat this process as many times as we like, using different kernels and producing multiple feature maps. We then stack these outputs together and form a three-dimensional array of feature maps, which we call a layer.

For example, say we have an image with a size of 52 × 52 and a kernel with a size of 12 × 12 and a stride of 2. We apply this to our input 15 times and stack the outputs together. We get a three-dimensional tensor with a size of $\mathbb{R}^{21 \times 21 \times 15}$.

When we are building CNNs for real-world applications, it is more than likely that we will want to work with colored images. We saw previously that grayscale images can be expressed as two-dimensional tensors (matrices) and so the convolutions were two-dimensional as well. However, colored images, as we know, are made up of three channels stacked on top of each other—red, blue, and green. The image then has the $\mathbb{R}^{h \times w \times 3}$ shape and so the associated convolution will also have the same shape. But interestingly, convolving a colored image with a three-dimensional convolution gives us a two-dimensional feature map.

In the preceding example, we went over how to perform a convolution on a two-dimensional tensor, but colored images have three channels. So, what we are going to do is split the three channels and convolve over them individually, then sum their respective outputs together using an element-wise addition to produce a two-dimensional tensor. To get a better understanding of this, let's assume we have an input with a size of $3 \times 3 \times 3$, which we can split into three channels, as so:

$$
\begin{bmatrix} I_{1,1} & I_{1,2} & I_{1,3} \\ I_{2,1} & I_{2,2} & I_{2,3} \\ I_{3,1} & I_{3,2} & I_{3,3} \end{bmatrix} = \begin{bmatrix} R_{1,1} & R_{1,2} & R_{1,3} \\ R_{2,1} & R_{2,2} & R_{2,3} \\ R_{3,1} & R_{3,2} & R_{3,3} \end{bmatrix} + \begin{bmatrix} B_{1,1} & B_{1,2} & B_{1,3} \\ B_{2,1} & B_{2,2} & B_{2,3} \\ B_{3,1} & B_{3,2} & B_{3,3} \end{bmatrix} + \begin{bmatrix} G_{1,1} & G_{1,2} & G_{1,3} \\ G_{2,1} & G_{2,2} & G_{2,3} \\ G_{3,1} & G_{3,2} & G_{3,3} \end{bmatrix}
$$

This tells us that $I_{i,j} = R_{i,j} + B_{i,j} + G_{i,j}$. Now that we have the channels separated, let's convolve them with our 2×2 kernel. After convolving each channel with our kernel, we get the following outputs:

- The result after convolving the red channel is as follows:

$$
\begin{bmatrix} R_{1,1} & R_{1,2} & R_{1,3} \\ R_{2,1} & R_{2,2} & R_{2,3} \\ R_{3,1} & R_{3,2} & R_{3,3} \end{bmatrix} * \begin{bmatrix} K_{1,1} & K_{1,2} \\ K_{2,1} & K_{2,2} \end{bmatrix} = \begin{bmatrix} O^R_{1,1} & O^R_{1,2} \\ O^R_{2,1} & O^R_{2,2} \end{bmatrix}
$$

- The result after convolving the blue channel is as follows:

$$
\begin{bmatrix} B_{1,1} & B_{1,2} & B_{1,3} \\ B_{2,1} & B_{2,2} & B_{2,3} \\ B_{3,1} & B_{3,2} & B_{3,3} \end{bmatrix} * \begin{bmatrix} K_{1,1} & K_{1,2} \\ K_{2,1} & K_{2,2} \end{bmatrix} = \begin{bmatrix} O^B_{1,1} & O^B_{1,2} \\ O^B_{2,1} & O^B_{2,2} \end{bmatrix}
$$

- The result after convolving the green channel is as follows:

$$
\begin{bmatrix} G_{1,1} & G_{1,2} & G_{1,3} \\ G_{2,1} & G_{2,2} & G_{2,3} \\ G_{3,1} & G_{3,2} & G_{3,3} \end{bmatrix} * \begin{bmatrix} K_{1,1} & K_{1,2} \\ K_{2,1} & K_{2,2} \end{bmatrix} = \begin{bmatrix} O^G_{1,1} & O^G_{1,2} \\ O^G_{2,1} & O^G_{2,2} \end{bmatrix}
$$

Should we want to go deeper, we can mathematically write out how each element of the output was calculated. This looks as follows:

$$O_{1,1} = (R_{1,1} + B_{1,1} + G_{1,1})K_{1,1} + (R_{1,2} + B_{1,2} + G_{1,2})K_{1,2} + (R_{2,1} + B_{2,1} + G_{2,1})K_{2,1} + (R_{2,2} + B_{2,2} + G_{2,2})K_{2,2}$$
$$O_{1,2} = (R_{1,2} + B_{1,2} + G_{1,2})K_{1,1} + (R_{1,3} + B_{1,3} + G_{1,3})K_{1,2} + (R_{2,2} + B_{2,2} + G_{2,2})K_{2,1} + (R_{2,3} + B_{2,3} + G_{2,3})K_{2,2}$$
$$O_{2,1} = (R_{2,1} + B_{2,1} + G_{2,1})K_{1,1} + (R_{2,2} + B_{2,2} + G_{2,2})K_{1,2} + (R_{3,1} + B_{3,1} + G_{3,1})K_{2,1} + (R_{3,2} + B_{3,2} + G_{3,2})K_{2,2}$$
$$O_{2,2} = (R_{2,2} + B_{2,2} + G_{2,2})K_{1,1} + (R_{2,3} + B_{2,3} + G_{2,3})K_{1,2} + (R_{3,2} + B_{3,2} + G_{3,2})K_{2,1} + (R_{3,3} + B_{3,3} + G_{3,3})K_{2,2}$$

We can think of this as applying a three-dimensional convolution to the input. It is important to make a note here that the depth of the kernel is the same as that of the image and so it moves just as the two-dimensional convolution operation does.

Instead of applying a kernel separately to each channel, we apply a single three-dimensional kernel to the input at once and use element-wise multiplication and addition. We do so because this allows us to convolve over volumetric data.

Here, we applied 15 kernels with a size of 12×12 and a stride of 2 to an input with a size of 52×52, and the resulting output had a size of $21 \times 21 \times 15$. Now, to this output, we can apply a convolution with a size of $8 \times 8 \times 15$. So, the output from this operation will have a size of 14×14. Of course, as before, we can stack multiple outputs together to form a layer.

One-dimensional convolutions

Now that we know how convolutions work in two dimensions, it is time for us to see how they work in one dimension. We use these for time-series data, such as those associated with stock prices or audio data. In the preceding section, the kernel moved from the top left along the axis to the top right, then dropped one or more rows (depending on the stride). This process was repeated until it reached the bottom right of the grid.

Here, we only convolve along the time axis—that is, the temporal dimension (from left to right). However, the effects of padding and stride still apply here as well.

Let's suppose we have the following data:

$$[2 \quad 1 \quad 4 \quad 1 \quad 1 \quad 0 \quad 3 \quad 2 \quad 2]$$

We also have the following kernel with a size of 1×3 that we want to apply to it:

$$[2 \quad 0 \quad -1]$$

Then, after convolving it with a stride of 2, we get the following output:

$$\begin{bmatrix} 0 & 7 & -1 & 4 \end{bmatrix}$$

Interestingly, we can also apply one-dimensional convolutions to matrices (images). Let's see how this works. Say we have a 4 × 4 input matrix and a 4 × 1 kernel. Then, the convolution will be carried out as follows:

$$\begin{bmatrix} I_{1,1} & I_{1,2} & I_{1,3} & I_{1,4} \\ I_{2,1} & I_{2,2} & I_{2,3} & I_{2,4} \\ I_{3,1} & I_{3,2} & I_{3,3} & I_{3,4} \\ I_{4,1} & I_{4,2} & I_{4,3} & I_{4,4} \end{bmatrix} * \begin{bmatrix} K_1 \\ K_2 \\ K_3 \\ K_4 \end{bmatrix} = \begin{bmatrix} O_1 & O_2 & O_3 & O_4 \end{bmatrix}$$

Let's take a look under the hood and see how each of the outputs is calculated:

$$O_1 = I_{1,1} K_1 + I_{2,1} K_2 + I_{3,1} K_3 + I_{4,1} K_4$$
$$O_2 = I_{1,2} K_1 + I_{2,2} K_2 + I_{3,2} K_3 + I_{4,2} K_4$$
$$O_3 = I_{1,3} K_1 + I_{2,3} K_2 + I_{3,3} K_3 + I_{4,3} K_4$$
$$O_4 = I_{1,4} K_1 + I_{2,4} K_2 + I_{3,4} K_3 + I_{4,4} K_4$$

However, our kernel size could be larger as well, just as in the earlier case of two-dimensional convolutions.

1 × 1 convolutions

In the previous section, we covered two-dimensional convolutions on volumetric data and these convolutions were performed depth-wise (the depth of each convolution is the same as the depth of the input). This is essentially the same as multiplying the values along the depth of the channel with those of the kernel and then summing them together to get a single value.

If we take the same input as previously with a shape of 21 × 21 × 15 and apply our 1 × 1 kernel, which has a 1 × 1 × 15 shape, our output will have a shape of 21. If we apply this operation 12 times, our output will then be 21 × 21 × 12. We use these shapes because they can reduce the dimensionality of our data because applying kernels of a larger size is computationally more expensive.

Three-dimensional convolutions

Now that we have a good idea of how two-dimensional convolutions work, it is time to move on to three-dimensional convolutions. But wait—didn't we just learn about three-dimensional convolutions? Kind of, but not really because, if you remember, they had the same depth as the volume we were convolving over and moved the same as the two-dimensional convolutions did—along the height and the width of the image.

Three-dimensional convolutions work a bit differently in that they convolve over the depth as well as the height and the width. This tells us that the depth of the kernel is smaller than the depth of the volume we want to convolve over, and at each step, it performs element-wise multiplication and addition, resulting in a single scalar value.

If we have volumetric data with a size of $21 \times 21 \times 15$ (as we did in the preceding section) and a three-dimensional kernel with a size of $5 \times 5 \times 5$ that takes a stride of 1, then the output will have a size of $16 \times 16 \times 11$.

Visually, this looks as follows:

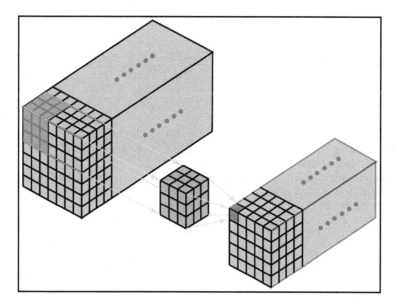

 We can calculate the output shape of the three-dimensional convolution in a similar way to as we did earlier in the two-dimensional case.

This type of convolution is used frequently in tasks that require us to find relationships in 3D. This is particularly used in the task of three-dimensional object segmentation and detecting actions/motion in videos.

Separable convolutions

Separable convolutions are a rather interesting type of convolution. They work on two-dimensional inputs and can be applied spatially or depthwise. The way this works is we decompose our k × k sized kernel into two smaller kernels with sizes of k × 1 and 1 × k. Instead of applying the k × k kernel, we would first apply the k × 1 kernel and then, to its output, the 1 × k kernel. The reason this is used is that it reduces the number of parameters in our network. With the original kernel, we would have had to carry out k^2 multiplications at each step, but with separable convolution, we only have to carry out 2,000 multiplications, which is a lot less.

Suppose we have a 3 × 3 kernel that we want to apply to a 6 × 6 input, as follows:

$$
\begin{bmatrix}
I_{1,1} & I_{1,2} & I_{1,3} & I_{1,4} & I_{1,5} & I_{1,6} \\
I_{2,1} & I_{2,2} & I_{2,3} & I_{2,4} & I_{2,5} & I_{2,6} \\
I_{3,1} & I_{3,2} & I_{3,3} & I_{3,4} & I_{3,5} & I_{3,6} \\
I_{4,1} & I_{4,2} & I_{4,3} & I_{4,4} & I_{4,5} & I_{4,6} \\
I_{5,1} & I_{5,2} & I_{5,3} & I_{5,4} & I_{5,5} & I_{5,6} \\
I_{6,1} & I_{6,2} & I_{6,3} & I_{6,4} & I_{6,5} & I_{6,6}
\end{bmatrix}
*
\begin{bmatrix}
K_{1,1} & K_{1,2} & K_{1,3} \\
K_{2,1} & K_{2,2} & K_{2,3} \\
K_{3,1} & K_{3,2} & K_{3,3}
\end{bmatrix}
=
\begin{bmatrix}
O_{1,1} & O_{1,2} & O_{1,3} & O_{1,4} \\
O_{2,1} & O_{2,2} & O_{2,3} & O_{2,4} \\
O_{3,1} & O_{3,2} & O_{3,3} & O_{3,4} \\
O_{4,1} & O_{4,2} & O_{4,3} & O_{4,4}
\end{bmatrix}
$$

In the preceding convolution, our kernel will have to perform nine multiplications at each of the 16 positions before it produces our output. This is a total of 144 multiplications.

Let's see how the separable convolution differs and compare its results. We will first decompose our kernel into k × 1 and 1 × k kernels:

$$
\begin{bmatrix}
K_{1,1} & K_{1,2} & K_{1,3} \\
K_{2,1} & K_{2,2} & K_{2,3} \\
K_{3,1} & K_{3,2} & K_{3,3}
\end{bmatrix}
=
\begin{bmatrix}
K_{1,1} \\
K_{2,1} \\
K_{3,1}
\end{bmatrix}
* [K_{1,1} \quad K_{1,2} \quad K_{1,3}]
$$

We will apply the kernels to our input in two steps. This looks as follows:

- Step 1:

$$
\begin{bmatrix}
I_{1,1} & I_{1,2} & I_{1,3} & I_{1,4} & I_{1,5} & I_{1,6} \\
I_{2,1} & I_{2,2} & I_{2,3} & I_{2,4} & I_{2,5} & I_{2,6} \\
I_{3,1} & I_{3,2} & I_{3,3} & I_{3,4} & I_{3,5} & I_{3,6} \\
I_{4,1} & I_{4,2} & I_{4,3} & I_{4,4} & I_{4,5} & I_{4,6} \\
I_{5,1} & I_{5,2} & I_{5,3} & I_{5,4} & I_{5,5} & I_{5,6} \\
I_{6,1} & I_{6,2} & I_{6,3} & I_{6,4} & I_{6,5} & I_{6,6}
\end{bmatrix}
*
\begin{bmatrix}
K_{1,1} \\
K_{2,1} \\
K_{3,1}
\end{bmatrix}
=
\begin{bmatrix}
O^1_{1,1} & O^1_{1,2} & O^1_{1,3} & O^1_{1,4} & O^1_{1,5} & O^1_{1,6} \\
O^1_{2,1} & O^1_{2,2} & O^1_{2,3} & O^1_{2,4} & O^1_{2,5} & O^1_{2,6} \\
O^1_{3,1} & O^1_{3,2} & O^1_{3,3} & O^1_{3,4} & O^1_{3,5} & O^1_{3,6} \\
O^1_{4,1} & O^1_{4,2} & O^1_{4,3} & O^1_{4,4} & O^1_{4,5} & O^1_{4,6}
\end{bmatrix}
$$

- Step 2:

$$
\begin{bmatrix}
O^1_{1,1} & O^1_{1,2} & O^1_{1,3} & O^1_{1,4} & O^1_{1,5} & O^1_{1,6} \\
O^1_{2,1} & O^1_{2,2} & O^1_{2,3} & O^1_{2,4} & O^1_{2,5} & O^1_{2,6} \\
O^1_{3,1} & O^1_{3,2} & O^1_{3,3} & O^1_{3,4} & O^1_{3,5} & O^1_{3,6} \\
O^1_{4,1} & O^1_{4,2} & O^1_{4,3} & O^1_{4,4} & O^1_{4,5} & O^1_{4,6}
\end{bmatrix}
* [K_{1,1} \quad K_{1,2} \quad K_{1,3}]
=
\begin{bmatrix}
O^2_{1,1} & O^2_{1,2} & O^2_{1,3} & O^2_{1,4} \\
O^2_{2,1} & O^2_{2,2} & O^2_{2,3} & O^2_{2,4} \\
O^2_{3,1} & O^2_{3,2} & O^2_{3,3} & O^2_{3,4} \\
O^2_{4,1} & O^2_{4,2} & O^2_{4,3} & O^2_{4,4}
\end{bmatrix}
$$

Here, $O^1_{i,j}$ is the output from the first convolution operation and $O^2_{i,j}$ is the output from the second. However, as you can see, we still get an output of the same size as before, but the number of multiplications that had to be carried out is fewer. The first convolution had to carry out three multiplications at each of the 24 positions for a total of 72 multiplications, and the second convolution also carried out three multiplications at each of the 16 positions for a total of 48 multiplications. By summing the total multiplications from both convolutions, we find that, together, they carried out 120 multiplications, which is fewer than the 144 that the k × k kernel had to do.

It is important to clarify that not every kernel is separable. As an example, let's take a look at the Sobel filter and its decomposition:

$$
\begin{bmatrix}
-1 & 0 & 1 \\
-2 & 0 & 2 \\
-1 & 0 & 1
\end{bmatrix}
=
\begin{bmatrix}
1 \\
2 \\
1
\end{bmatrix}
\times [-1 \quad 0 \quad 1]
$$

What we just learned was spatially separable convolution. Using what we have learned so far, how do you think depth-wise convolution would work?

You should recall that when we went through two-dimensional convolutions, we introduced a three-dimensional kernel for colored images, where the depth was the same as the image. So, if we had an input of $8 \times 8 \times 3$ and a kernel with a size of $3 \times 3 \times 3$, we would get an output of $6 \times 6 \times 1$. However, in depth-wise separable convolutions, we split the $3 \times 3 \times 3$ kernel into three kernels with a size of $3 \times 3 \times 1$ each, which convolves one of the channels. After applying our kernels to our input, we have an output with a size of $6 \times 6 \times 3$ and to this output, we will apply a kernel with a size of $1 \times 1 \times 3$, which produces an output of $6 \times 6 \times 1$.

If we want to increase the depth of the output to, say, 72, instead of applying 72 $3 \times 3 \times 3$ kernels, we would apply 72 $1 \times 1 \times 3$ convolutions.

Let's compare the two and see which is more computationally efficient. The number of multiplications that had to take place in order to compute our $6 \times 6 \times 72$ output using the $3 \times 3 \times 3$ kernel is $(3{\times}3{\times}3) \times (6{\times}6) \times 72 = 69{,}984$, which is a lot! To compute the same output using depth-wise separable convolution, the number of multiplications required is $(3{\times}3{\times}1) \times 3 \times (6{\times}6) + (1{\times}1{\times}3) \times (6{\times}6) \times 72 = 8{,}748$, which is a whole lot less and therefore a lot more efficient.

Transposed convolutions

We know that applying a convolution repeatedly to an image reduces its size, but what if we would like to go in the opposite direction; that is, go from the shape of the output to the shape of the input while still maintaining local connectivity. To do this, we use transposed convolution, which draws its name from matrix transposition (which you should remember from Chapter 1, *Vector Calculus*).

Let's suppose we have a 4×4 input and a 3×3 kernel. Then, we can rewrite the kernel as a 4×16 matrix, which we can use for matrix multiplications to carry out our convolutions. This looks as follows:

$$
\begin{bmatrix} K_{0,0} & K_{0,1} & K_{0,2} \\ K_{1,0} & K_{1,1} & K_{1,2} \\ K_{2,0} & K_{2,1} & K_{2,2} \end{bmatrix} \longrightarrow
\begin{bmatrix}
K_{0,0} & K_{0,1} & K_{0,2} & 0 & K_{1,0} & K_{1,1} & K_{1,2} & 0 & K_{2,0} & K_{2,1} & K_{2,2} & 0 & 0 & 0 & 0 & 0 \\
0 & K_{0,0} & K_{0,1} & K_{0,2} & 0 & K_{1,0} & K_{1,1} & K_{1,2} & 0 & K_{2,0} & K_{2,1} & K_{2,2} & 0 & 0 & 0 & 0 \\
0 & 0 & 0 & 0 & K_{0,0} & K_{0,1} & K_{0,2} & 0 & K_{1,0} & K_{1,1} & K_{1,2} & 0 & K_{2,0} & K_{2,1} & K_{2,2} & 0 \\
0 & 0 & 0 & 0 & 0 & K_{0,0} & K_{0,1} & K_{0,2} & 0 & K_{1,0} & K_{1,1} & K_{1,2} & 0 & K_{2,0} & K_{2,1} & K_{2,2}
\end{bmatrix}
$$

If you look closely, you will notice that each row represents one convolution operation.

To use this matrix, we rewrite our input as a 16×1 column vector, which looks as follows:

$$\begin{bmatrix} I_{0,0} \\ I_{0,1} \\ I_{0,2} \\ I_{0,3} \\ I_{1,0} \\ I_{1,1} \\ I_{1,2} \\ I_{1,3} \\ I_{2,0} \\ I_{2,1} \\ I_{2,2} \\ I_{2,3} \\ I_{3,0} \\ I_{3,1} \\ I_{3,2} \\ I_{3,3} \end{bmatrix}$$

$$\begin{bmatrix} I_{0,0} & I_{0,1} & I_{0,2} & I_{0,3} \\ I_{1,0} & I_{1,1} & I_{1,2} & I_{1,3} \\ I_{2,0} & I_{2,1} & I_{2,2} & I_{2,3} \\ I_{3,0} & I_{3,1} & I_{3,2} & I_{3,3} \end{bmatrix} \longrightarrow$$

Then, we can multiply our convolution matrix and column vector to get a 4×1 column vector, which looks as follows:

$$\begin{bmatrix} O_{0,0} \\ O_{0,1} \\ O_{1,0} \\ O_{1,1} \end{bmatrix}$$

We can rewrite this in the following form:

$$\begin{bmatrix} O_{0,0} & O_{0,1} \\ O_{1,0} & O_{1,1} \end{bmatrix}$$

This is the same as what we saw in the previous section.

You might now be wondering what this has to do with transposed convolution. It's simple—we use the same concept as before, but now we use the transpose of the convolution matrix to work our way backward from the output to the input.

Let's take the preceding convolution matrix and transpose it so that it becomes a matrix with a size of 16×4:

$$
\begin{bmatrix}
K_{0,0} & 0 & 0 & 0 \\
K_{0,1} & K_{0,0} & 0 & 0 \\
K_{0,2} & K_{0,1} & 0 & 0 \\
0 & K_{0,2} & 0 & 0 \\
K_{1,0} & 0 & K_{0,0} & 0 \\
K_{1,1} & K_{1,0} & K_{0,1} & K_{0,0} \\
K_{1,2} & K_{1,1} & K_{0,2} & K_{0,1} \\
0 & K_{1,2} & 0 & K_{0,2} \\
K_{2,0} & 0 & K_{1,0} & 0 \\
K_{2,1} & K_{2,0} & K_{1,1} & K_{1,0} \\
K_{2,2} & K_{2,1} & K_{1,2} & K_{1,1} \\
0 & K_{2,2} & 0 & K_{1,2} \\
0 & 0 & K_{2,0} & 0 \\
0 & 0 & K_{2,1} & K_{2,0} \\
0 & 0 & K_{2,2} & K_{2,1} \\
0 & 0 & 0 & K_{2,2}
\end{bmatrix}
$$

This time, the input vector we multiply with will be a 4×1 column vector:

$$
\begin{bmatrix}
I_{0,0} \\
I_{0,1} \\
I_{1,0} \\
I_{1,1}
\end{bmatrix}
$$

We can multiply them and get a 16×1 output vector, as follows:

$$
\begin{bmatrix}
K_{0,0} & 0 & 0 & 0 \\
K_{0,1} & K_{0,0} & 0 & 0 \\
K_{0,2} & K_{0,1} & 0 & 0 \\
0 & K_{0,2} & 0 & 0 \\
K_{1,0} & 0 & K_{0,0} & 0 \\
K_{1,1} & K_{1,0} & K_{0,1} & K_{0,0} \\
K_{1,2} & K_{1,1} & K_{0,2} & K_{0,1} \\
0 & K_{1,2} & 0 & K_{0,2} \\
K_{2,0} & 0 & K_{1,0} & 0 \\
K_{2,1} & K_{2,0} & K_{1,1} & K_{1,0} \\
K_{2,2} & K_{2,1} & K_{1,2} & K_{1,1} \\
0 & K_{2,2} & 0 & K_{1,2} \\
0 & 0 & K_{2,0} & 0 \\
0 & 0 & K_{2,1} & K_{2,0} \\
0 & 0 & K_{2,2} & K_{2,1} \\
0 & 0 & 0 & K_{2,2}
\end{bmatrix}
\begin{bmatrix}
I_{0,0} \\
I_{0,1} \\
I_{1,0} \\
I_{1,1}
\end{bmatrix}
\longrightarrow
\begin{bmatrix}
O_{0,0} \\
O_{0,1} \\
O_{0,2} \\
O_{0,3} \\
O_{1,0} \\
O_{1,1} \\
O_{1,2} \\
O_{1,3} \\
O_{2,0} \\
O_{2,1} \\
O_{2,2} \\
O_{2,3} \\
O_{3,0} \\
O_{3,1} \\
O_{3,2} \\
O_{3,3}
\end{bmatrix}
$$

We can rewrite our output vector into a 4 × 4 matrix, as follows:

$$
\begin{bmatrix} O_{0,0} \\ O_{0,1} \\ O_{0,2} \\ O_{0,3} \\ O_{1,0} \\ O_{1,1} \\ O_{1,2} \\ O_{1,3} \\ O_{2,0} \\ O_{2,1} \\ O_{2,2} \\ O_{2,3} \\ O_{3,0} \\ O_{3,1} \\ O_{3,2} \\ O_{3,3} \end{bmatrix} \longrightarrow \begin{bmatrix} O_{0,0} & O_{0,1} & O_{0,2} & O_{0,3} \\ O_{1,0} & O_{1,1} & O_{1,2} & O_{1,3} \\ O_{2,0} & O_{2,1} & O_{2,2} & O_{2,3} \\ O_{3,0} & O_{3,1} & O_{3,2} & O_{3,3} \end{bmatrix}
$$

Just like that, we can go from lower dimensional space to a higher dimensional space.

It is important to note that the padding and stride that were applied to the convolution operation can be used in transposed convolution as well.

We can then calculate the size of the output using the following formula:

$$
(s(n-1) + k - 2p) \times (s(n-1) + k - 2p)
$$

Here, the input is n × n, the kernel is k × k, p is the pooling, and s is the stride.

Pooling

Another often-used operation in CNNs is known as **pooling** (**subsampling** or **downsampling**). This works somewhat like the convolution operation, except it reduces the size of the feature map by sliding a window across the feature map and either averages all the values inside each window at each step or outputs the maximum value. The pooling operation differs from convolution in that it does not have any parameters and so cannot be learned or tuned. We can calculate the size of the feature map after pooling, as follows:

$$
(n \times n) * (r \times r) = \left(\left(\frac{n-r}{s} + 1 \right) \times \left(\frac{n-r}{s} + 1 \right) \right)
$$

Here, *I* is an n × n-shaped two-dimensional tensor, the pooling operation is an r × r-shaped two-dimensional tensor, and *s* is the stride.

Here is an example of maximum pooling with a stride of 1:

$$
\begin{bmatrix} 2 & 1 & 1 & 3 \\ 4 & 5 & 2 & 1 \\ 1 & 4 & 5 & 3 \\ 5 & 1 & 7 & 6 \end{bmatrix} \longrightarrow \begin{bmatrix} 5 & 5 & 3 \\ 5 & 5 & 5 \\ 5 & 7 & 7 \end{bmatrix}
$$

Here is an example of average pooling with a stride of 2:

$$
\begin{bmatrix} 2 & 1 & 1 & 3 \\ 4 & 5 & 2 & 1 \\ 1 & 4 & 5 & 3 \\ 5 & 1 & 7 & 6 \end{bmatrix} \longrightarrow \begin{bmatrix} 3 & 1.75 \\ 2.75 & 5.25 \end{bmatrix}
$$

As a rule of thumb, it has been found that the maximum pooling operation performs better.

 From this, you will probably notice that the output is quite different from the original and doesn't fully represent all the information. In fact, a lot of information has been lost. It is because of this that the pooling operation is used increasingly less in practice.

Global average pooling

Global average pooling is a variant of the pooling operation that we saw previously, where instead of sliding a subsampling kernel over the feature map, we just take the average of the entire feature map and output a single real value. Suppose we have a feature map with a size of 6 × 6 × 72. After applying this pooling operation, our output would have a size of 1 × 1 × 72.

This is generally used at the last layer, where, normally, we would apply the subsampling and feed the output into a fully connected layer; instead, this allows us to skip the fully connected layer and feed the output of the global average pool directly into our softmax for prediction.

The advantage of using this is that it significantly removes the number of parameters we have to train in our network. Had we flattened the preceding feature map and fed it into a layer of 500 nodes, it would have 1.296 million parameters. This also has the added benefit of reducing overfitting to the training data and improving our classification prediction because the output is closer to the classes.

Convolution and pooling size

Now that we know the various types of convolution and pooling, it is time to talk about a very important topic associated with them—their size. As you have seen, when we applied a convolution to an image, the output was of a smaller size than the input. The output size is determined by the size of the kernel, the stride, and whether or not we have padding. These are very important things to keep in mind when architecting CNNs.

There are several sizes of convolutions that are used in practice, the most commonly used ones being 7 × 7, 5 × 5, and 3 × 3. However, we can use other sizes as well, including—but not limited to—11 × 11, 13 × 13, 9 × 9, 17 × 17, and so on.

In practice, we generally use larger convolutions with a larger stride to generate a feature map of a smaller size to reduce the computational constraint and default to using 3 × 3 and 5 × 5 kernels the most. This is because they are computationally more feasible. Generally, having a larger kernel will allow us to look at a larger space in the image and capture more relationships, but having multiple 3 × 3 kernels has proven to have a similar performance while being less computationally intensive, which we prefer.

Working with the ConvNet architecture

Now that we know all the different components that make up a ConvNet, we can put it all together and see how to construct a deep CNN. In this section, we will build a full architecture and observe how forward propagation works and how we decide the depth of the network, the number of kernels to apply, when and why to use pooling, and so on. But before we dive in, let's explore some of the ways in which CNNs differ from FNNs. They are as follows:

- The neurons in CNNs have local connectivity, which means that each neuron in a successive layer receives input from a small local group of pixels from an image, instead of receiving the entire image, as a **feedforward neural network (FNN)** would.
- Each neuron in the layer of a CNN has the same weight parameters.
- The layers in CNNs can be normalized.
- CNNs are translation invariant, which allows us to detect the same object regardless of its position in the image.

- CNNs have fewer parameters because the convolution operation weighs the surrounding neurons and sums them into the neuron at the next layer, thereby smoothing the image.
- The activation functions typically used in CNNs are ReLU, PReLU, and ELU.

The CNN architecture isn't entirely dissimilar to the FNN architecture we saw earlier in this book, except instead of having fully connected layers, we have convolution layers that extract spatial relationships from the inputs and previous layers and learn features from the input at each layer.

In general, what the architecture learns can be demonstrated with the following flow:

input image → gradients + edges → textures → patterns → basic object features → object → output

As you can see from the preceding flow, the features grow in complexity in the latter layers. What this means is that the earliest layers (those closest to the input layer) learn very basic features, such as edges and lines, textures, or how certain colors differentiate. The latter layers take in the feature map from the previous layer as input and learn more complex patterns from it. For example, if we create a facial recognition model, the earliest layer would learn the simplest possible lines, curves, and gradients. The next layer would take in the feature maps from the previous layer and use it to learn more complex features, such as hair and eyebrows. The layer after that would learn even more complex features, such as eyes, noses, ears, and so on.

We can see what a neural network learns in the following diagram:

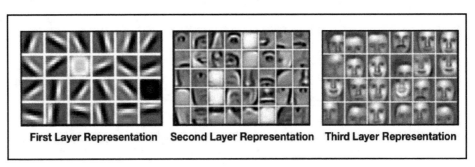

First Layer Representation   Second Layer Representation   Third Layer Representation

CNNs, like FNNs, have a structure that we can use as a guide when we build our own applications. It typically looks as follows:

input image → kernel(s) → nonlinearity → pooling → normalization → feature maps → ⋯ → flatten → fully connected → softmax

feature learning   classification

We are now going to break down one of the most popular CNN architectures, called AlexNet, which outperformed all other models in the ILSVRC in 2012 with 10% greater accuracy and kickstarted the deep learning revolution. It was created by Alex Krizhevsky, Ilya Sutskever, and Geoffrey Hinton. We can see its architecture in the following diagram:

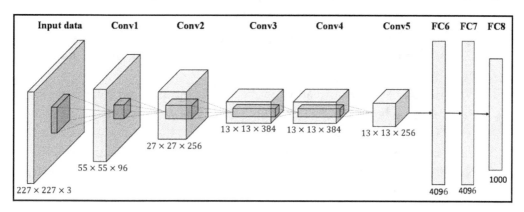

As you can see, the architecture contains eight trainable layers—five of which are convolutional layers and three of which are fully connected. The ImageNet dataset contains more than 15 million labeled images, but for ILSVRC, we have approximately 1.2 million images in the training set, 50,000 images in the validation set, 150,000 images in the testing set, and nearly 1,000 images for each of the 1,000 classes that the images belong to. Each of the images was rescaled to 256 × 256 × 3 because they all varied in size, and from these rescaled images, the authors generated random crops with a size of 256 × 256 × 3. Additionally, the creators of AlexNet used ReLU activations instead of **tanh** because they found that it sped up the training by as much as six times without sacrificing accuracy.

The operations applied to the image at each layer and their sizes are as follows:

- **Convolution layer 1**: 96 kernels of size 11 × 11 × 3 with a stride of 4. This results in a layer with a size of 55 × 55 × 96.
- **Nonlinearity 1**: ReLU activation applied to the output from convolution layer 1.
- **Subsampling layer 1**: Maximum pool with a size of 3 × 3 and a stride of 2. This results in a layer with a size of 27 × 27 × 96.
- **Convolution layer 2**: 256 kernels with a size of 5 × 5, a padding of 2, and a stride of 1. This results in a layer with a size of 27 × 27 × 256.
- **Nonlinearity 2**: ReLU activation applied to the output from convolution layer 2.
- **Subsampling layer 2**: Maximum pool with a size of 3 × 3 and a stride of 2. This results in a layer with a size of 13 × 13 × 256.

- **Convolution layer 3**: 384 kernels with a size of 3 × 3, a padding of 1, and a stride of 1. This results in a layer of size 13 × 13 × 384.
- **Nonlinearity 3**: ReLU activation applied to the output from convolution layer 3.
- **Convolution layer 4**: 384 kernels of size 3 × 3 with a padding of 1 and a stride of 1. This results in a layer with a size of 13 × 13 × 384.
- **Nonlinearity 4**: ReLU activation applied to the output from convolution layer 4.
- **Convolution layer 5**: 256 kernels with a size of 3 × 3, a padding of 1, and a stride of 1. This results in a layer with a size of 13 × 13 × 256.
- **Nonlinearity 5**: ReLU activation applied to the output from convolution layer 5.
- **Subsampling layer 3**: Maximum pool with a size of 3 × 3 and a stride of 2. This results in a layer with a size of 6 × 6 × 256.
- **Fully connected layer 1**: A fully connected layer with 4,096 neurons.
- **Nonlinearity 6**: ReLU activation applied to the output from fully connected layer 1.
- **Fully connected layer 2**: A fully connected layer with 4,096 neurons.
- **Nonlinearity 7**: ReLU activation applied to the output from fully connected layer 2.
- **Fully connected layer 3**: A fully connected layer with 1,000 neurons.
- **Nonlinearity 8**: ReLU activation applied to the output from fully connected layer 3.
- **Output layer**: Softmax applied to the 1,000 neurons to calculate the probability of it being one of the classes.

When building architectures, it is important to have an understanding of how many parameters are in the model. The formula we use to calculate the number of parameters at each layer is as follows:

$$(\text{kernel width} \times \text{kernel height}) \times (\text{input depth}) \times (\text{output depth})$$

Let's calculate the parameters of AlexNet. They are as follows:

- **Convolution layer 1**: 11 x 11 x 3 x 96 = 34,848
- **Convolution layer 2**: 5 x 5 x 96 x 256 = 614,400
- **Convolution layer 3**: 3 x 3 x 256 x 384 = 884,736
- **Convolution layer 4**: 3 x 3 x 384 x 384 = 1,327,104
- **Convolution layer 5**: 3 x 3 x 384 x 256 = 884,736

- **Fully connected layer 1**: 256 x 6 x 6 x 4096 = 37,748,736
- **Fully connected layer 2**: 4096 x 4096 = 16,777,216
- **Fully connected layer 3**: 4096 x 1000 = 4,096,000

Now, if we sum the parameters together, we find that AlexNet has a total of 62.3 million parameters. Roughly 6% of these parameters are from the convolution layers and the remaining 94% are from the fully connected layers. This should give you an idea of why CNNs are so effective and why we like them so much.

You may be wondering why we would use a CNN at all and why we wouldn't just use an FNN instead. Couldn't we just flatten the image into a fully connected layer and input every pixel into a single node? We could, but if we did, then our first layer would have 154,587 neurons and our overall network could have well over 1 million neurons and 500 million trainable parameters. This is massive and our network would likely underfit from not having enough training data. Additionally, FNNs do not have the translation-invariant property that CNNs have.

Using the preceding parameters, let's see whether we can generalize the architecture so that we have a framework to follow for future CNNs that we want to build or to understand how other architectures we come across work. The first thing you should have realized in the preceding architecture is that the size of each successive feature map reduces while its depth increases. Also, you may have noticed that the depth is always divisible by 2, many times over, and usually, we use 32, 64, 128, 256, 512, and so on in layers.

Just as we saw with FNNs previously, the deeper we go, the better our accuracy is, but this doesn't come without its own problems. Larger networks are much harder to train and can either overfit or underfit to the training data. This could be a result of a combination of being too small, being too large, having too much training data, or having too little training data. There is still no fixed recipe for exactly how many layers to use in our CNN; it is very much down to trial and error and building up some intuition after building and training several architectures for a variety of tasks.

Training and optimization

Now that we've got that sorted, it's time for us to dive into the really fun stuff. How do we train these fantastic architectures? Do we need a completely new algorithm to facilitate our training and optimization? No! We can still use backpropagation and gradient descent to calculate the error, differentiate it with respect to the previous layers, and update the weights to get us as close to the global optima as possible.

But before we go further, let's go through how backpropagation works in CNNs, particularly with kernels. Let's revisit the example we used earlier on in this chapter, where we convolved a 3 × 3 input with a 2 × 2 kernel, which looked as follows:

$$
\begin{bmatrix} I_{1,1} & I_{1,2} & I_{1,3} \\ I_{2,1} & I_{2,2} & I_{2,3} \\ I_{3,1} & I_{3,2} & I_{3,3} \end{bmatrix} * \begin{bmatrix} K_{1,1} & K_{1,2} \\ K_{2,1} & K_{2,2} \end{bmatrix} = \begin{bmatrix} O_{1,1} & O_{1,2} \\ O_{2,1} & O_{2,2} \end{bmatrix}
$$

We expressed each element in the output matrix as follows:

$$
O_{1,1} = I_{1,1}K_{1,1} + I_{1,2}K_{1,2} + I_{2,1}K_{2,1} + I_{2,2}K_{2,2}
$$
$$
O_{1,2} = I_{1,2}K_{1,1} + I_{1,3}K_{1,2} + I_{2,2}K_{2,1} + I_{2,3}K_{2,2}
$$
$$
O_{2,1} = I_{2,1}K_{1,1} + I_{2,2}K_{1,2} + I_{3,1}K_{2,1} + I_{3,2}K_{2,2}
$$
$$
O_{2,2} = I_{2,2}K_{1,1} + I_{2,3}K_{1,2} + I_{3,2}K_{2,1} + I_{3,3}K_{2,2}
$$

We should remember from `Chapter 7`, *Feedforward Networks*, where we introduced backpropagation, that we take derivatives of the loss (error) with respect to the weights and biases at the layers and then use this as a guide to update the parameters to reduce the error of prediction from our network. In CNNs, however, we find the gradient of the error with respect to the kernel. Since our kernel has four elements, the derivatives look as follows:

$$
\frac{\partial J}{\partial K_{1,1}} = \frac{\partial J}{\partial O_{1,1}} \frac{\partial O_{1,1}}{\partial K_{1,1}} + \frac{\partial J}{\partial O_{1,2}} \frac{\partial O_{1,2}}{\partial K_{1,1}} + \frac{\partial J}{\partial O_{2,1}} \frac{\partial O_{2,1}}{\partial K_{1,1}} + \frac{\partial J}{\partial O_{2,2}} \frac{\partial O_{2,2}}{\partial K_{1,1}}
$$

$$
\vdots
$$

$$
\frac{\partial J}{\partial K_{2,2}} = \frac{\partial J}{\partial O_{1,1}} \frac{\partial O_{1,1}}{\partial K_{2,2}} + \frac{\partial J}{\partial O_{1,2}} \frac{\partial O_{1,2}}{\partial K_{2,2}} + \frac{\partial J}{\partial O_{2,1}} \frac{\partial O_{2,1}}{\partial K_{2,2}} + \frac{\partial J}{\partial O_{2,2}} \frac{\partial O_{2,2}}{\partial K_{2,2}}
$$

If we observe these equations carefully, which represent the output from the feedforward computation, we can see that by taking the partial derivative with respect to each kernel element, we get the respective input element, $I_{i,j}$, that it depends on. If we substitute this value back into the derivatives, we can simplify them to get the following:

$$
\frac{\partial J}{\partial K_{1,1}} = \frac{\partial J}{\partial O_{1,1}} I_{1,1} + \frac{\partial J}{\partial O_{1,2}} I_{1,2} + \frac{\partial J}{\partial O_{2,1}} I_{2,1} + \frac{\partial J}{\partial O_{2,2}} I_{2,2}
$$

$$
\vdots
$$

$$
\frac{\partial J}{\partial K_{1,1}} = \frac{\partial J}{\partial O_{1,1}} I_{2,2} + \frac{\partial J}{\partial O_{1,2}} I_{2,3} + \frac{\partial J}{\partial O_{2,1}} I_{3,1} + \frac{\partial J}{\partial O_{2,2}} I_{3,3}
$$

We can simplify this further by rewriting it as a convolution operation. This looks as follows:

$$\begin{bmatrix} I_{1,1} & I_{1,2} & I_{1,3} \\ I_{2,1} & I_{2,2} & I_{2,3} \\ I_{3,1} & I_{3,2} & I_{3,3} \end{bmatrix} * \begin{bmatrix} \frac{\partial J}{\partial O_{1,1}} & \frac{\partial J}{\partial O_{1,2}} \\ \frac{\partial J}{\partial O_{2,1}} & \frac{\partial J}{\partial O_{2,2}} \end{bmatrix} = \begin{bmatrix} \frac{\partial J}{\partial K_{1,1}} & \frac{\partial J}{\partial K_{1,2}} \\ \frac{\partial J}{\partial K_{2,1}} & \frac{\partial J}{\partial K_{2,2}} \end{bmatrix}$$

But what if we wanted to find the derivative with respect to the input? Well, our Jacobian matrix would certainly look a bit different. We would have a 3 × 3 matrix since there are nine elements in the input matrix:

$$\begin{bmatrix} 0 & 0 & 0 & 0 \\ 0 & \frac{\partial J}{\partial O_{1,1}} & \frac{\partial J}{\partial O_{1,2}} & 0 \\ 0 & \frac{\partial J}{\partial O_{2,1}} & \frac{\partial J}{\partial O_{2,2}} & 0 \\ 0 & 0 & 0 & 0 \end{bmatrix} * \begin{bmatrix} K_{2,2} & K_{2,1} \\ K_{1,2} & K_{1,1} \end{bmatrix} = \begin{bmatrix} \frac{\partial J}{\partial I_{1,1}} & \frac{\partial J}{\partial I_{1,2}} & \frac{\partial J}{\partial I_{1,3}} \\ \frac{\partial J}{\partial I_{2,1}} & \frac{\partial J}{\partial I_{2,2}} & \frac{\partial J}{\partial I_{2,3}} \\ \frac{\partial J}{\partial I_{3,1}} & \frac{\partial J}{\partial I_{3,2}} & \frac{\partial J}{\partial I_{3,3}} \end{bmatrix}$$

We can verify this if we derive it ourselves by hand through the preceding equations, and I encourage you to try this out to get a good understanding of what's happening and why. However, let's now pay particular attention to the kernel we used. If we look carefully, it almost looks like the determinant, but that's not what it is. We just rotated (that is, transposed) the kernel by 180° so that we can compute the gradients.

This is a much-simplified view of how backpropagation works in CNNs; we have left it simple because the rest works exactly as it did in FNNs.

Exploring popular ConvNet architectures

Now that we know how CNNs are built and trained, it is time to explore some of the popular architectures that are used and understand what makes them so powerful.

VGG-16

The **VGG network** is a derivation of AlexNet that was created by Andrew Zisserman and Karen Simonyan at the **Visual Geometry Group** (VGG) at the University of Oxford in 2015. This architecture is simpler than the one we saw earlier, but it gives us a much better framework to work with. VGGNet was also trained on the ImageNet dataset, except it takes images with a size of 224 × 224 × 3 that are sampled from the rescaled images in the dataset as input. You may have noticed that we have headed this section *VGG-16*—this is because the VGG network has 16 layers. There are variants of this architecture that have 11, 13, and 19 layers.

We will first explore the basic building blocks of the network, known as VGG blocks. These blocks are made up of two to three convolutions, followed by a pooling layer. Each of the convolution layers throughout the network uses kernels with a size of 3×3 and a stride of 1; however, the number of kernels used in each block is the same but can vary from block to block. In the subsampling layer, we use a pooling with a size of 2×2, the same padding size, and a stride of 2.

The entire network can be broken down into the following operations:

- **Convolution layer 1**: 64 kernels with a size of 3×3, a stride of 1, and the same padding. This results in a layer with a size of $224 \times 224 \times 64$.
- **Nonlinearity 1**: ReLU activation applied to the output from convolution layer 1.
- **Convolution layer 2**: 64 kernels with a size of 3×3, a stride of 1, and the same padding. This results in a layer with a size of $224 \times 224 \times 64$.
- **Nonlinearity 2**: ReLU activation applied to the output from convolution layer 2.
- **Subsampling layer 1**: Maximum pool with a size of 2×2 and a stride of 2. This results in a layer with a size of $112 \times 112 \times 64$.
- **Convolution layer 3**: 128 kernels with a size of 3×3, a stride of 1, and the same padding. This results in a layer with a size of $112 \times 112 \times 128$.
- **Nonlinearity 3**: ReLU activation applied to the output from convolution layer 3.
- **Convolution layer 4**: 128 kernels with a size of 3×3, a stride of 1, and the same padding. This results in a layer with a size of $112 \times 112 \times 128$.
- **Nonlinearity 4**: ReLU activation applied to the output from convolution layer 4.
- **Subsampling layer 2**: Maximum pool with a size of 2×2 and a stride of 2. This results in a layer with a size of $56 \times 56 \times 128$.
- **Convolution layer 5**: 256 kernels with a size of 3×3, a stride of 1, and the same padding. This results in a layer with a size of $56 \times 56 \times 256$.
- **Nonlinearity 5**: ReLU activation applied to the output from convolution layer 5.
- **Convolution layer 6**: 256 kernels with a size of 3×3, a stride of 1, and the same padding. This results in a layer with a size of $56 \times 56 \times 256$.
- **Nonlinearity 6**: ReLU activation applied to the output from convolution layer 6.
- **Convolution layer 7**: 256 kernels with a size of 3×3, a stride of 1, and the same padding. This results in a layer with a size of $56 \times 56 \times 256$.
- **Nonlinearity 7**: ReLU activation applied to the output from convolution layer 7.
- **Subsampling layer 3**: Maximum pool with a size of 2×2 and a stride of 2. This results in a layer with a size of $28 \times 28 \times 256$.

- **Convolution layer 8**: 512 kernels with a size of 3 × 3, a stride of 1, and the same padding. This results in a layer with a size of 28 × 28 × 512.
- **Nonlinearity 8**: ReLU activation applied to the output from convolution layer 8.
- **Convolution layer 9**: 512 kernels with a size of 3 × 3, a stride of 1, and the same padding. This results in a layer with a size of 28 × 28 × 512.
- **Nonlinearity 9**: ReLU activation applied to the output from convolution layer 9.
- **Convolution layer 10**: 512 kernels with a size of 3 × 3, a stride of 1, and the same padding. This results in a layer with a size of 28 × 28 × 512.
- **Nonlinearity 10**: ReLU activation applied to the output from convolution layer 10.
- **Subsampling layer 4**: Maximum pool with a size of 2 × 2 and a stride of 2. This results in a layer with a size of 14 × 14 × 512.
- **Convolution layer 11**: 512 kernels with a size of 3×3, a stride of 1, and the same padding. This results in a layer with a size of 14 × 14 × 512.
- **Nonlinearity 11**: ReLU activation applied to the output from convolution layer 11.
- **Convolution layer 12**: 512 kernels with a size of 3 × 3, a stride of 1, and the same padding. This results in a layer with a size of 14 × 14 × 512.
- **Nonlinearity 12**: ReLU activation applied to the output from convolution layer 12.
- **Convolution layer 13**: 512 kernels with a size of 3 × 3, a stride of 1, and the same padding. This results in a layer with a size of 14 × 14 × 512.
- **Nonlinearity 13**: ReLU activation applied to the output from convolution layer 13.
- **Subsampling layer 5**: Maximum pool with a size of 2 × 2 and a stride of 2. This results in a layer with a size of 7 × 7 × 512.
- **Fully connected layer 1**: A fully connected layer with 4,096 neurons.
- **Nonlinearity 14**: ReLU activation applied to the output from fully connected layer 1.
- **Fully connected layer 2**: A fully connected layer with 4,096 neurons.
- **Nonlinearity 15**: ReLU activation applied to the output from fully connected layer 2.
- **Output layer**: Softmax applied to the 1,000 neurons to calculate the probability of it being one of the classes.

This network placed runner up in the 2014 ILSVRC and has approximately 138 million trainable parameters. So, it is very difficult to train.

Inception-v1

The InceptionNet architecture (often referred to as **GoogLeNet**) placed first in the 2014 ILSVRC and achieved near-human performance at 93.3% accuracy. The name **inception** is a reference to the movie *Inception*, particularly to the need to go deeper (in terms of layers). This architecture is a little different from the ones we saw earlier in that it makes use of Inception modules instead of layers. Each Inception block contains filters of three different sizes—1 × 1, 3 × 3, and 5 × 5. What this does is allow our network to capture sparse patterns through spatial information and variances at different scales, thereby allowing our network to learn even more complex information. However, previously, our networks consistently had a kernel of one size throughout the layer.

The Inception module looks as follows:

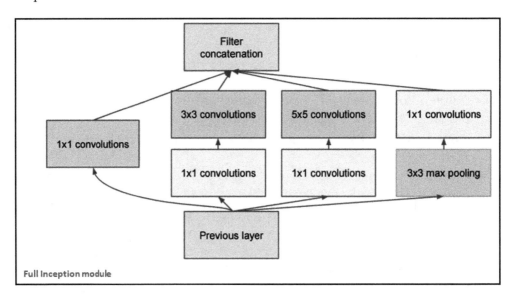

Full Inception module

As you can see, each block contains four parallel channels. The first channel contains a 1 × 1 kernel, the second channel contains a 1 × 1 kernel followed by a 3 × 3 kernel, the third channel contains a 1 × 1 kernel followed by a 5 × 5 kernel, and the fourth channel contains a 3 × 3 maximum pooling followed by a 1 × 1 kernel. The resulting feature maps are then concatenated and fed as input into the next block. The reason behind applying a 1 × 1 kernel before the larger kernels—such as the 3 × 3 and 5 × 5 kernels—is to reduce the dimensionality because larger kernels are more computationally expensive.

This network takes in images with a size of 224 × 224, mean subtraction, and 22 layers with trainable parameters (27 if you count the pooling layers).

The details of the architecture are displayed in the following table:

type	patch size/ stride	output size	depth	#1×1	#3×3 reduce	#3×3	#5×5 reduce	#5×5	pool proj	params	ops
convolution	7×7/2	112×112×64	1							2.7K	34M
max pool	3×3/2	56×56×64	0								
convolution	3×3/1	56×56×192	2		64	192				112K	360M
max pool	3×3/2	28×28×192	0								
inception (3a)		28×28×256	2	64	96	128	16	32	32	159K	128M
inception (3b)		28×28×480	2	128	128	192	32	96	64	380K	304M
max pool	3×3/2	14×14×480	0								
inception (4a)		14×14×512	2	192	96	208	16	48	64	364K	73M
inception (4b)		14×14×512	2	160	112	224	24	64	64	437K	88M
inception (4c)		14×14×512	2	128	128	256	24	64	64	463K	100M
inception (4d)		14×14×528	2	112	144	288	32	64	64	580K	119M
inception (4e)		14×14×832	2	256	160	320	32	128	128	840K	170M
max pool	3×3/2	7×7×832	0								
inception (5a)		7×7×832	2	256	160	320	32	128	128	1072K	54M
inception (5b)		7×7×1024	2	384	192	384	48	128	128	1388K	71M
avg pool	7×7/1	1×1×1024	0								
dropout (40%)		1×1×1024	0								
linear		1×1×1000	1							1000K	1M
softmax		1×1×1000	0								

The network looks as follows:

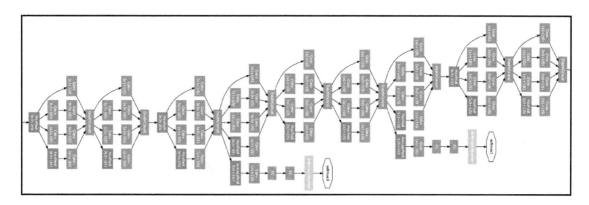

Interestingly, despite this being a much deeper network than AlexNet and VGG-16, there are a lot fewer parameters that we need to train because it uses kernels with smaller sizes, as well as depth reduction. Larger networks, as we know, do tend to perform better than shallower ones. The significance of this architecture is that despite being deep, it is relatively more simple to train that if it had many more parameters.

Summary

Congratulations! We have just finished learning about a powerful variant of neural networks known as CNNs, which are very effective in tasks relating to computer vision and time-series prediction. We will revisit CNNs later on in this book, but in the meantime, let's move on to the next chapter and learn about recurrent and recursive neural networks.

10
Recurrent Neural Networks

In this chapter, we will take an in-depth look at **Recurrent Neural Networks** (**RNNs**). In the previous chapter, we looked at **Convolutional Neural Networks** (**CNNs**), which are a powerful class of neural networks for computer vision tasks because of their ability to capture spatial relationships. The neural networks we will be studying in this chapter, however, are very effective for sequential data and are used in applications such as algorithmic trading, image captioning, sentiment classification, language translation, video classification, and so on.

In regular neural networks, all the inputs and outputs are assumed to be independent, but in RNNs, each output is dependent on the previous one, which allows them to capture dependencies in sequences, such as in language, where the next word depends on the previous word and the one before that.

We will start by taking a look at the vanilla RNN, then the bidirectional RNN, deep RNNs, **long short-term memory** (**LSTM**), and **gated recurrent units** (**GRUs**), as well as some of the state-of-the-art architectures used in industry today.

In this chapter, we will cover the following topics:

- The need for RNNs
- The types of data used in RNNs
- Understanding RNNs
- Long short-term memory
- Gated recurrent units
- Deep RNNs
- Training and optimization
- Popular architecture

The need for RNNs

In the previous chapter, we learned about CNNs and their effectiveness on image- and time series-related tasks that have data with a grid-like structure. We also saw how CNNs are inspired by how the human visual cortex processes visual input. Similarly, the RNNs that we will learn about in this chapter are also biologically inspired.

The need for this form of neural network arises from the fact that **fuzzy neural networks (FNNs)** are unable to capture time-based dependencies in data.

The first model of an RNN was created by John Hopfield in 1982 in an attempt to understand how associative memory in our brains works. This is known as a **Hopfield network**. It is a fully connected single-layer recurrent network and it stores and accesses information similarly to how we think our brains do.

The types of data used in RNNs

As mentioned in the introduction to this chapter, RNNs are used frequently for—and have brought about tremendous results in—tasks such as natural language processing, machine translation, and algorithmic trading. For these tasks, we need sequential or time-series data—that is, the data has a fixed order. For example, languages and music have a fixed order. When we speak or write sentences, they follow a framework, which is what enables us to understand them. If we break the rules and mix up words that do not correlate, then the sentence no longer makes sense.

Suppose we have the sentence `The greatest glory in living lies not in never falling, but in rising every time we fall` and we pass it through a sentence randomizer. The output that we get is `fall. falling, in every in not time but in greatest lies The we living glory rising never,` which clearly doesn't make sense. Another example is ordering stock prices by date and prices at opening and closing or daily prices at fixed time intervals (possibly every hour).

Other examples of sequential data are rainfall measurements over a number of successive days, nucleotide base pairs in a DNA strand, or the daily tick values for a stock.

We would structure this sort of data in a similar way to how we would for one-dimensional convolutions. However, instead of having a kernel that convolves over the data, the RNN (which we will become well acquainted with shortly) will take the same input, where the node corresponds to the time step of the data (this will become clearer momentarily).

Understanding RNNs

The word **recurrent** in the name of this neural network comes from the fact that it has cyclic connections and the same computation is performed on each element of the sequence. This allows it to learn (or memorize) parts of the data to make predictions about the future. An RNN's advantage is that it can scale to much longer sequences than non-sequence based models are able to.

Vanilla RNNs

Without further ado, let's take a look at the most basic version of an RNN, referred to as a vanilla RNN. It looks as follows:

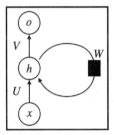

This looks somewhat familiar, doesn't it? It should. If we were to remove the loop, this would be the same as a traditional neural network, but with one hidden layer, which we've encountered already. Now, if we unroll the loop and view the full network, it looks as follows:

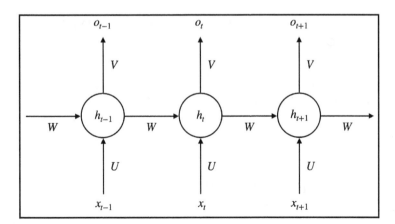

Here, we have the following parameters:

- x_t is the input at time step t
- h_t is the hidden state at time step t
- o_t is the output at time step t

From the preceding diagram, we can observe that the same calculation is performed on the input at each time step and this is what differentiates it from the FNNs we came across earlier. The parameters (weights and biases) at each layer of an FNN are different, but in this architecture, the parameters (U, V, and W) remain the same at each time step. Because of this, RNNs are more memory intensive and need to be trained for longer in comparison to CNNs. It is also important that you note that in RNNs, the time step doesn't necessarily correspond to the time in the real world; it merely means the input sequence is of length t.

But why do these weights remain the same across all the time steps? Why can't we have separate parameters that need to be learned at different time steps? The reason for this is that separate parameters are unable to generalize to sequence lengths that aren't encountered during the training process. Having the same three weights shared across the sequence and at different time steps enables the network to deal with information that can occur at multiple positions, as it tends to in language. For example, the can appear at a number of positions in a given sentence and the RNN should be able to recognize and extract it regardless of the position(s) it is in. This shared statistical strength property is advantageous in comparison to an FNN because an FNN would need to learn the language's rules at every position, which—as you can imagine—can be very challenging to train.

Intuitively, we can think of this as having a sequence $(x_1, x_2, \cdots, x_t)$ where we are trying to find $P(x_{t+1} \mid x_t, x_{t-1}, \cdots, x_1)$, which we are already familiar with from Chapter 3, *Probability and Statistics*. This is not exactly what is happening; we have simplified it to help you understand what the RNN is trying to learn to do.

Using the knowledge we have now gained, we can create some very complex RNNs for a variety of tasks, such as language translation or converting audio into text. Depending on the type of task we want to build our model for, we can choose from one of the following types of RNNs:

- One-to-one (one input and one output)
- One-to-many (one input and many outputs)
- Many-to-one (many inputs and one output)

- Many-to-many (multiple inputs and outputs, where the number of inputs and outputs are equal)
- Many-to-many (multiple inputs and outputs, where the number of inputs and outputs are not equal)

Let's take a deeper dive into RNNs and see what is happening at each time step from the input to the output through all the hidden layers.

Mathematically, we can calculate the hidden state at each time step using the following equation:

$$h_t = f_1(Wh_{t-1} + Ux_t + a)$$

Here, f_1 is a non-linearity, such as ReLU, tanh, or sigmoid. The output is calculated as follows:

$$o_t = Vh_t + b.$$

We can calculate the probability vector of the output using a nonlinear function, f_2, (such as softmax), as follows:

$$\hat{y}_t = f_2(o_t)$$

By using these equations and applying them repeatedly, we can calculate the hidden states and outputs at each time step.

So, the RNN then looks as follows:

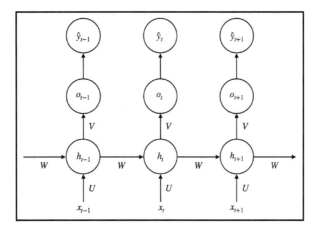

By looking at the preceding diagram and the equations, you should be able to venture a guess as to the shape of our weight matrices and our bias vectors—$U \in \mathbb{R}^{h_t \times x_t}$ (connects the input to the hidden layer), $W \in \mathbb{R}^{h_t \times h_{t-1}}$ (connects the previously hidden layer to the current hidden layer), $V \in \mathbb{R}^{o_t \times h_t}$ (connects the hidden layer and the output), $a \in \mathbb{R}^{h_t}$ (the bias vector for the hidden layer), and $b \in \mathbb{R}^{o_t}$ (the bias vector for the output layer).

From the preceding equations, we can clearly tell that the hidden state at time step t depends on the current input and the previous hidden state. However, the initial hidden state, h_0, must be initialized in a similar way to how we initialized the weights and kernels in FNNs and CNNs. The output at each time step, on the other hand, is dependent on the current hidden state. Additionally, a and b are biases and so they are trainable parameters.

In RNNs, h_t contains information about everything that has occurred at the previous time steps (but in practice, we limit this to a few time steps, instead of all previous ones, because of the vanishing/exploding gradient problem) and o_t is calculated based on the most recent information. This allows the RNN to exploit relationships between the sequence and use it to predict the most likely output, which is not entirely dissimilar to how CNNs capture spatial relationships in sequential data using one-dimensional convolutions.

However, this isn't the only way to construct RNNs. Instead of passing outputs from hidden layer to hidden layer ($h_{t-1} \rightarrow h_t$) as in the preceding diagram, we could pass the output from the previous output into the next hidden state ($o_{t-1} \rightarrow h_t$), changing how we calculate the hidden state. It now becomes the following:

$$h_t = f_1(Wo_{t-1} + Ux_t + a)$$

In the following diagram, we can see the various operations taking place in a hidden state cell at time step t:

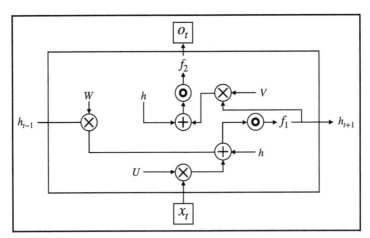

When working with FNNs, we calculate the loss at the end of each forward pass through the network and then backpropagate the errors to update the weights. However, in RNNs, we calculate the loss at each time step, as follows:

$$L(\hat{y}, y) = \sum_{t=1}^{\tau} L(\hat{y}_t, y_t) = \sum_{t=1}^{\tau} -y_t \log \hat{y}_t - (1 - y_t) \log(1 - \hat{y}_t)$$

Here, L is the cross-entropy loss function (which we are already familiar with), y_t is the target, $\hat{y}_t$ is a probability vector, and n is the number of outputs/targets.

While effective, these vanilla RNNs aren't perfect. They do have a few problems that we usually encounter during training, particularly the vanishing gradient problem. This occurs when the weights become very small, preventing the neuron from firing, which prevents hidden neurons at later time steps from firing because each one depends on the last, and the one before that, and so on.

To get a better understanding of this, let's consider the following example. Suppose we have a very simple vanilla RNN without any nonlinear activations and or inputs. We can express this network as $h_t = (W)^t h_0$. As you can see, we are applying the same weight over and over again at each unit from time step to time step. However, let's focus our attention on the weights.

To understand the vanishing and exploding gradient problem, let's suppose that our weight matrix has a shape of 2 × 2 and is diagonalizable. You should remember from Chapter 2, *Linear Algebra*, that if our matrix is diagonalizable, then it can be decomposed into the form $W = Q^{-1} \Lambda Q$, where Q is a matrix containing the eigenvectors and Λ is a square matrix that contains eigenvalues along the diagonal. As previously, if we have eight hidden layers, then our weight would be $W^8 = Q^{-1} \Lambda^8 Q$. We can see this as follows:

$$\Lambda = \begin{bmatrix} -0.3 & 0 \\ 0 & 1.8 \end{bmatrix} \longrightarrow \Lambda^8 = \begin{bmatrix} 0.000066 & 0 \\ 0 & 110.199 \end{bmatrix}$$

In the preceding equation, we get a good glimpse of both the vanishing and the exploding gradient problems. We assumed we have eight hidden units and by multiplying them over and over, we can see that the values become either very small or very large, which makes training RNNs rather challenging because of their instability. The small weights make it difficult for our RNN to learn long-term dependencies and is why innovations in the cells, such as **Long short-term models (LSTMs)** and **gated recurrent units (GRUs)** were created (we'll learn about these two RNN cell variants shortly).

Now, if we have an RNN with 20 time steps or more and we want our network to remember the first, second, or third input, it is more than likely it won't be able to remember them, but it will remember the most recent inputs. For example, we could have the sentence `I remember when I visited Naples a few years ago...I had the best pizza of my life`. In this case, we need to understand the context of Naples from further back to understand where this magnificent pizza is from, but looking this far back is challenging for RNNs.

Similarly, if our weight is greater than 1, it can get much larger, which results in exploding gradients. We can, however, deal with this by using gradient clipping, where we rescale the weights so that the norm is at most η. We use the following formula to do so:

$$g \leftarrow \frac{\eta g}{\|g\|}$$

Bidirectional RNNs

Now that we know how RNNs work at their most basic level, let's take a look at a variant of them—the bidirectional RNN. The preceding RNN is feedforward; that is, the data passes through the network from left ($t = 0$) to right ($t = \tau$), which creates a dependency on the past. However, for some of the problems that we may want to work with, it could help to look into the future, as well.

This allows us to feed the network training data both forward and backward into two separate recurrent layers, respectively. It is important to note that both of these layers share the same output layer. This approach allows us to contextualize the input data with respect to the past and the future, which produces much better results than the previous, unidirectional RNN for tasks relating to speech and translation. Naturally, however, bidirectional RNNs are not the answer to every time-series task, such as predicting stock prices, because we don't know what will happen in the future.

In the following diagram, we can see what a bidirectional RNN looks like:

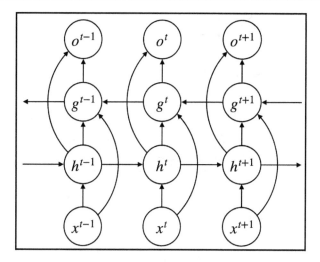

As you can see, the network now contains two parallel layers running in opposite directions and there are now six different sets of weights applied at every time step; namely, input-to-hidden (*U* and *C*), hidden-to-hidden (*A* and *W*), and hidden-to-output (*V* and *B*). It is important that we note that there is no information shared between the forward layer and the backward layer.

Now, the operations taking place at each of the hidden states at time t are as follows:

- $h_t = f_1(Wh_{t-1} + Ux_t + a)$
- $g_t = f_1(Ag_{t+1} + Cx_t + b)$

Here, f_1 is a non-linearity and a and b are biases. The output unit can be calculated as follows:

$$o_t = Vh_t + Bg_t + d$$

Here, d is a bias. Then, we can find the probability vector using the following equation:

$$\hat{y}_t = f_2(o_t)$$

The preceding equations show us that the hidden states in the forward layer receive information from the previous hidden states and the hidden states in the backward layer receive information from the future states.

Long short-term memory

As we saw earlier, the standard RNN does have some limitations; in particular, they suffer from the vanishing gradient problem. The LSTM architecture was proposed by Jürgen Schmidhuber (ftp://ftp.idsia.ch/pub/juergen/lstm.pdf) as a solution to the long-term dependency problem that RNNs face.

LSTM cells differ from vanilla RNN cells in a few ways. Firstly, they contain what we call a memory block, which is basically a set of recurrently connected subnets. Secondly, each of the memory blocks contains not only self-connected memory cells but also three multiplicative units that represent the input, output, and forget gates.

Let's take a look at what a single LSTM cell looks like, then we will dive into the nitty-gritty of it to gain a better understanding. In the following diagram, you can see what an LSTM block looks like and the operations that take place inside it:

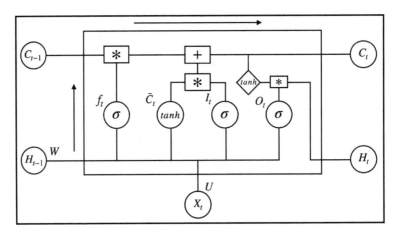

As you can see in the preceding LSTM cell, a bunch of operations take place at each time step and it has the following components:

- f: The forget gate (an NN with sigmoid)
- $\bar{c}$: The candidate layer (an NN with tanh)
- I: The input gate (an NN with sigmoid)
- O: The output gate (an NN with sigmoid)
- H: The hidden state (a vector)
- C: The memory state (a vector)
- W and U: The weights for the forget gate, candidate, input gate, and output gate

At each time step, the memory cell takes the current input (X_t), the previous hidden state (H_{t-1}), and the previous memory state (C_{t-1}) as input and it outputs the current hidden state (H_t) and the current memory state (C_t).

As you can see in the preceding diagram, there are a lot more operations happening here than were taking place in the hidden cell of the vanilla RNN. The significance of this is that it preserves the gradients throughout the network and allows longer-term dependencies, as well as providing a solution to the vanishing gradient problem.

But how exactly do LSTMs do this? Let's find out. The memory state stores information and continues to do so until the old information is overridden by the new information. Each cell can make a decision as to whether or not it wants to output this information or store it. Before we go deeper into the explanations, let's first take a look at the mathematical operations that take place in each LSTM cell. They are as follows:

- $f_t = \sigma(X_t U_f + H_{t-1} W_f + b_f)$
- $\bar{C} = \tanh(X_t U_c + H_{t-1} W_c + b_c)$
- $I_t = \sigma(X_t U_i + H_{t-1} W_i + b_i)$
- $O_t = \sigma(X_t U_o + H_{t-1} W_o + b_o)$
- $C_t = f_t C_{t-1} + I_t \bar{C}_t$
- $H_t = O_t \tanh(C_t)$

Now that we know the different operations that take place in each cell, let's really understand what each of the preceding equations represents. They are as follows:

- The candidate layer ($\tilde{C}$) takes as input a word (X_t) and the output from the previous hidden state H_{t-1} and creates a new memory, which includes the new word.
- The input gate (I) performs a very important function. It determines whether or not the new input word is worth preserving based on the output of the previous hidden state.
- The forget gate (f), even though it looks very similar to the input gate, performs a different function. It determines the relevance (or usefulness) of the previous memory cell when computing the current one.

- The memory state (sometimes referred to as the final memory) is produced after taking in the forget gate and the input gate as input and then gates the new memory and sums the output to product C_t.
- The output gate differentiates the memory from the hidden state and determines how much of the information present in the memory should be present in the hidden state. This produces O_t, which we then use to gate tanh (C_t).

Gated recurrent units

Similar to the LSTM, GRUs are also an improvement on the hidden cells in vanilla RNNs. GRUs were also created to address the vanishing gradient problem by storing memory from the past to help make better future decisions. The motivation for the GRU stemmed from questioning whether all the components that are present in the LSTM are necessary for controlling the forgetfulness and time scale of units.

The main difference here is that this architecture uses one gating unit to decide what to forget and when to update the state, which gives it a more persistent memory.

In the following diagram, you can see what the GRU architecture looks like:

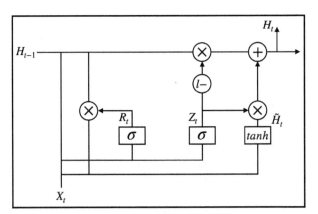

As you can see in the preceding diagram, it takes in the current input (X_t) and the previous hidden state (H_{t-1}), and there are a lot fewer operations that take place here in comparison to the preceding LSTM. It has the following components:

- Z_t: The update gate
- R_t: The reset gate

- $\tilde{H}_t$: The new memory
- H_t: The hidden state

To produce the current hidden state, the GRU uses the following operations:

- $Z_t = \sigma(W_z X_t + U_z h_{t-1})$
- $R_t = \sigma(W_r X_t + U_r H_{t-1})$
- $\tilde{H}_t = \tanh(R_t * U H_{t-1} + W X_t)$
- $H_t = (1 - Z_t) * \tilde{H}_t + Z_t * H_{t-1}$

Now, let's break down the preceding equations to get a better idea of what the GRU is doing to its two inputs. They are as follows:

- The GRU takes in the current input (X_t) and the previous hidden state (H_{t-1}) and contextualizes the word based on the information it has about the previous words to produce $\tilde{H}_t$—the new memory.
- The reset gate (R_t) decides the importance of the previous hidden state in computing the current hidden state; that is, whether or not it is relevant to obtaining the new memory, which helps capture short-term dependencies.
- The update gate (Z_t) determines how much of the previous hidden state should be passed on to the next state to capture long-term dependencies. In a nutshell, if $Z_t \approx 1$, then most of the previous hidden state is incorporated into the current hidden state; but if $Z_t \approx 0$, then most of the new memory is passed forward.
- Finally, the present hidden state (H_t) is computed using the new memory and the previous hidden state, contingent on the results of the update gate.

Deep RNNs

In the previous chapters, we saw how adding depth to our neural networks helps achieve much greater results; the same is true with RNNs, where adding more layers allows us to learn even more complex information.

Now that we have seen what RNNs are and have an understanding of how they work, let's go deeper and see what deep RNNs look like and what kind of benefits we gain from adding additional layers. Going deeper into RNNs is not as straightforward as it was when we were dealing with FNNs and CNNs; we have to make a few different kinds of considerations here, particularly about how and where we should add the nonlinearity between layers.

If we want to go deeper, we can stack more hidden recurrent layers on top of each other, which allows our architecture to capture and learn complex information at multiple timescales, and before the information is passed from layer to layer, we can add either non-linearity or gates.

Let's start with a two-hidden-layer bidirectional RNN, which is shown in the following diagram:

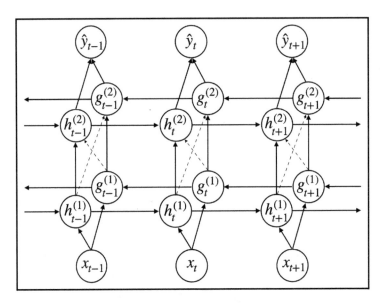

As you can see, it looks like three **multilayer perceptrons** (**MLPs**) stacked together side by side, and the hidden layers are connected, as before, forming a lattice. There are also no connections between the forward and backward hidden units in the same layer. Each hidden node feeds into the node directly above it at the same time step and each hidden node takes two parameters from the correlated hidden node in the previous layer as input—one from the forward layer and the other from the backward layer.

We can generalize and write the equations for the deep bidirectional RNN as follows:

- In the forward layer, we have the following:

$$h_t^{(i)} = f_1(W^{(i)} h_{t-1}^{(i)} + U^{(i)} h_t^{(i-1)} + M^{(i)} g_t^{(i-1)} + a^{(i)})$$

- In the backward layer, we have the following:

$$g_t^{(i)} = f_1(A^{(i)} g_{t+1}^{(i)} + C^{(i)} g_t^{(i-1)} + N^{(i)} h_t^{(i-1)} + b^{(i)})$$

- In the output layer, we have the following:

$$\hat{y}_t = f_2(Vh_t^{(L+1)} + Bg_t^{(L+1)} + d)$$

Using this as a guideline, we can do the same for LSTMs or GRUs and add them in.

Training and optimization

As in the neural networks we have already encountered, RNNs also update their parameters using backpropagation by finding the gradient of the error (loss) with respect to the weights. Here, however, it is referred to as **Backpropagation Through Time (BPTT)** because each node in the RNN has a time step. I know the name sounds cool, but it has nothing to do with time travel—it's still just good old backpropagation with gradient descent for the parameter updates.

Here, using BPTT, we want to find out how much the hidden units and output affect the total error, as well as how much changing the weights (U, V, W) affects the output. W, as we know, is constant throughout the network, so we need to traverse all the way back to the initial time step to make an update to it.

When backpropagating in RNNs, we again apply the chain rule. What makes training RNNs tricky is that the loss function is dependent not only on the activation of the output layer but also on the activation of the current hidden layer and its effect on the hidden layer at the next time step. In the following equation, we can see how backpropagation works in RNNs.

As you can see, we first find the cross-entropy loss (defined in the *Vanilla RNNs* section); our total error is as follows:

$$\frac{\partial E}{\partial W} = \sum_{i=1}^{\tau} \frac{\partial E_t}{\partial W}$$

We can expand the preceding equation using the chain rule with respect to the losses and hidden layers, as follows:

$$\frac{\partial E_t}{\partial W} = \sum_{k=1}^{t} \frac{\partial E_t}{\partial y_t} \frac{\partial y_t}{\partial h_t} \frac{\partial h_t}{\partial h_k} \frac{\partial h_k}{\partial W}$$

Let's focus in on the third term on the right-hand side and expand on it:

$$\frac{\partial h_t}{\partial h_j} = \prod_{j=k+1}^{t} \frac{\partial h_j}{\partial h_{j-1}}$$

You should note that each partial here is a Jacobian matrix.

We can now combine the preceding equations together to get a holistic view of how to calculate the error, which looks as follows:

$$\frac{\partial E}{\partial W} = \sum_{i=1}^{\tau} \sum_{k=1}^{t} \frac{\partial E_t}{\partial y_t} \frac{\partial y_t}{\partial h_t} \left(\prod_{j=k+1}^{t} \frac{\partial h_j}{\partial h_{j-1}} \right) \frac{\partial h_k}{\partial W}$$

We know from earlier on in this chapter that h_t is calculated using the following equation:

$$h_t = f_1(Wh_{t-1} + Ux_t + a)$$

So, we can calculate the gradient of h_t, as shown:

$$\frac{\partial h_t}{\partial h_{t-1}} = W^{\mathrm{T}} \mathrm{diag}(f_1'(Wh_{t-1} + Ux_t + a))$$

Since the hidden neurons also take x_t as input, we need to take the derivative with respect to U as well. We can do this as follows:

$$\frac{\partial E_t}{\partial U} = \frac{\partial E_t}{\partial y_t} \frac{\partial y_t}{\partial h_t} \frac{\partial h_t}{\partial U}$$

But wait—the hidden units, as we have seen, take in two inputs. So, let's backpropagate one time step using what we have just seen and see how it works:

$$\frac{\partial E_t}{\partial U} = \frac{\partial E_t}{\partial y_t} \frac{\partial y_t}{\partial h_t} \frac{\partial h_t}{\partial U} + \frac{\partial E_t}{\partial y_t} \frac{\partial y_t}{\partial h_t} \frac{\partial h_t}{\partial h_{t-1}} \frac{\partial h_{t-1}}{\partial U}$$

Using this, we can now sum over all the previous gradients up to the present one, as follows:

$$\frac{E_t}{\partial U} = \sum_{t=1}^{\tau} \frac{\partial E_t}{\partial y_t} \frac{\partial y_t}{\partial h_t} \frac{\partial h_t}{\partial h_{t-1}} \frac{\partial h_{t-1}}{\partial U}$$

The backward pass in LSTM or GRU is much like what we did with regular RNNs, but there are some additional complexities here because of the gates (we will not go through the differences between the backward passes in LSTMs or GRUs here).

Popular architecture

Now that we have learned about all the components that are used to contrast RNNs, let's explore a popular architecture that has been developed by researchers in the field—the **clockwork RNN (CW-RNN)**.

Clockwork RNNs

As we have learned, it is very challenging to discover long-term dependencies in RNNs, and LSTMs and GRUs were designed to overcome this limitation. CW-RNN, created by a group at IDSIA led by Jürgen Schmidhuber, modifies the vanilla RNN module such that the hidden layer is partitioned into separate modules, each of which processes its inputs at different temporal granularities. What this means is that the hidden layers perform computations at their preset clock rate (which is where the name comes from). The effect of this is a reduced number of trainable parameters and greater accuracy when compared to regular RNNs and LSTMs.

Just as our earlier RNNs had input-to-hidden and hidden-to-output connections, a CW-RNN also has the same, except the neurons in the hidden layer are partitioned into g modules of size k, each of which has an assigned clock period, $T_n = \{T_1, \cdots, T_g\}$.

These modules are fully connected together, but the recurrent connections from modules j to i are not if period $T_i < T_j$. These modules are sorted by increasing period and, therefore, the connections move from slower to faster (right to left).

In the following diagram, we can see the architecture of the CW-RNN:

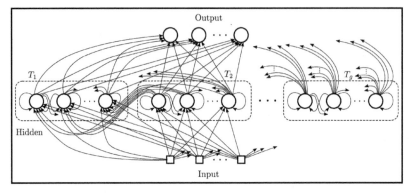

The clock period of module i can be calculated as follows:

$$T_i = 2^{i-1}$$

The input and hidden weight matrices are partitioned into g block rows, as follows:

$$W = \begin{pmatrix} W_1 \\ \vdots \\ W_g \end{pmatrix} \text{ and } U = \begin{pmatrix} U_1 \\ \vdots \\ U_g \end{pmatrix}$$

In the preceding equation, W is an upper-triangular matrix and each W_i value is partitioned into block columns:

$$\{0_1, \cdots, 0_{i-1}, W_{i,i}, \cdots, W_{i,g}\}$$

During the forward pass, only the block rows of the hidden weight matrix and the input weight matrix correspond to the executed modules, where the following is true:

$$W_i = \begin{cases} W_i & \text{for } (t \mod T_i) = 0 \\ 0 & \text{otherwise} \end{cases}$$

The modules with lower clock rates learn and maintain long-term information from the input and the modules with the higher clock rates learn local information.

We mentioned in the preceding equation that each hidden layer is partitioned into g modules of size k, which means there are a total of $n = kg$ neurons. Since neurons are only connected to those that have a similar or larger period, the number of parameters within the hidden-to-hidden matrix is as follows:

$$N_H = \sum_{i=1}^{g} \sum_{g=1}^{k} = k(g - i + 1) = \frac{n^2}{2} + \frac{nk}{2}$$

Let's compare this with our vanilla RNNs, which have n^2 parameters. Let's see how this is the case:

$$\frac{N_H}{n^2} = \frac{\frac{n^2}{2} + \frac{nk}{2}}{n^2} = \frac{n + k}{2n} = \frac{g + 1}{2g} \approx \frac{1}{2}$$

The CW-RNN has approximately half as many parameters.

Summary

In this chapter, we covered a very powerful type of neural network—RNNs. We also learned about several variations of the RNN cell, such as LSTM cells and GRUs. Like the neural networks in prior chapters, these too can be extended to deep neural networks, which have several advantages. In particular, they can learn a lot more complex information about sequential data, for example, in language.

In the next chapter, we will learn about attention mechanisms and their increasing popularity in language- and vision-related tasks.

3
Section 3: Advanced Deep Learning Concepts Simplified

Having built a sound understanding of the fundamental ideas behind deep learning in the previous section, in this section, you will learn about a variety of deep learning networks; namely, networks that are used to process images, text, and sequences, as well as to generate items.

This section is comprised of the following chapters:

- Chapter 11, *Attention Mechanisms*
- Chapter 12, *Generative Models*
- Chapter 13, *Transfer and Meta Learning*
- Chapter 14, *Geometric Deep Learning*

11
Attention Mechanisms

In the preceding two chapters, we learned about convolutional neural networks and recurrent neural networks, both of which have been very effective for sequential tasks such as machine translation, image captioning, object recognition, and so on. But we have also seen that they have limitations. RNNs have problems with long-term dependencies. In this chapter, we will cover attention mechanisms, which have been increasing in popularity and have shown incredible results in language- and vision-related tasks.

The following topics will be covered in this chapter:

- Overview of attention
- Understanding neural Turing machines
- Exploring the types of attention
- Transformers

Let's get started!

Overview of attention

When we go about our lives (in the real world), our brains don't observe every detail in our environment at all times; instead, we focus on (or pay greater attention to) information that is relevant to the task at hand. For example, when we are driving, we are able to adjust our focal length to focus on different details, some of which are closer and others are further away, and then act on what we observe. Similarly, when we are conversing with others, we usually don't listen carefully to each and every word; we listen to only part of what is spoken and use it to infer the relationships with some of the words to figure out what the other person is saying. Often, when we are reading/listening to someone, we can use some words to infer what the person is going to say next based on what we have already read/heard.

But why do we need these attention mechanisms in deep learning? Let's take a stroll down memory lane to `Chapter 10`, *Recurrent Neural Networks*, where we learned about sequence-to-sequence models (RNNs), which, as we saw, can be used for tasks such as language-to-language translation. We should recall that these types of models have an encoder-decoder architecture where the encoder takes in the input and compresses the information into an embedding space (or context vector), while the decoder takes in the context vector and transforms it back into the desired output. Both the encoder and decoder are RNNs (possibly with LSTMs or GRUs for long-term memory).

In the previous chapter, we also came across a few limitations that RNNs have – in particular, the problem of vanishing or exploding gradients, which hinders long-term dependencies. And thus, the attention mechanism was created. It was created for the sole purpose of solving this very problem of memorizing long sentences that RNNs face.

In RNNs, the hidden state at each time step takes the previous hidden state as input (which contains the context of the sequence it has seen so far) and the input for that time step, and then the final hidden state is passed to the decoder sequence. Attention mechanisms differ by creating connections between the context vector and the whole sequence of inputs. This way, we no longer have to worry about how much will end up being forgotten. And similar to all the other connections in ANNs, these attention connections are weighted, which means they can be adjusted for each output. Essentially, the context vector controls the alignment between the input and target (output).

Let's suppose we have an input, $\mathbf{x} = [x_1, x_2, \cdots, x_n]$, and a target, $\mathbf{y} = [y_1, y_2, \cdots, y_m]$, where the hidden states produced by the encoder (a vanilla RNN for simplicity, though this could be any RNN architecture) will be $\mathbf{h} = [h_1, h_2, \cdots, h_n]$. The hidden states for the decoder here are slightly different from what we have previously seen:

$$s_t = f(s_{t-1}, y_{t-1}, c_t)$$

For all $t = 1, 2, \cdots, m$. Here, c_t (the context vector) is a sum of all hidden states from the input. This is weighted by the alignment scores so that $c_t = \sum_{i=1}^{n} \alpha_{t,i} h_i$ and

$\alpha_{t,i} = \dfrac{e^{\text{score}(s_{t-1}, h_i)}}{\sum_{i'=1}^{n} e^{\text{score}(s_{t-1}, h_{i'})}}$, which determine the alignment of y_t and x_i by assigning a score based on how well the two match. Each $\alpha_{t,i}$ here is a weight that decides the extent to which each source's hidden state should have an impact on each output.

The preceding score function is parameterized by an MLP with a single hidden layer and is calculated using the following equation:

$$\text{score}(s_t, h_i) = \mathbf{V}_a^T \tanh(\mathbf{W}_a[s_t; h_i])$$

Here, $\mathbf{V}_a$ and $\mathbf{W}_a$ are weight matrices to be learned.

Before we dive deep into the inner workings of various attention mechanisms, let's take a look at neural Turing machines.

Understanding neural Turing machines

The **Turing machine (TM)** was proposed by Alan Turing in 1936, and it is a mathematical model of computation made up of an infinitely long tape and a head that interacts with the tape by reading, editing, and moving symbols on it. It works by manipulating symbols on the strip according to a predefined set of rules. The tape is made up of an endless number of cells, each of which can contain one of three symbols – 0, 1, or blank (" "). Therefore, this is referred to as a **three-symbol Turing machine**. Regardless of how simple it seems, it is capable of simulating any computer algorithm, regardless of complexity. The tape that these computations are done on can be considered to be the machine's memory, akin to how our modern-day computers have memory. However, the Turing machine differs from modern-day computers as it has limited memory and computational limitations.

In `Chapter 10`, *Recurrent Neural Networks*, we learned that this type of ANN is Turing complete, which means that when they are properly trained, they can simulate any arbitrary procedure. But this is only in theory. In practice, we have seen that this is not the case because they do have their limitations. To overcome these limitations, in 2014, Alex Graves et al. proposed augmenting an RNN with a large, addressable memory (similar to the tape in a TM), thereby giving it the name **neural Turing machine (NTM)**. This model, as the authors stated, *is a differentiable computer that can be trained by gradient descent, yielding a practical mechanism for learning programs.*

The NTM borrows the idea of working memory (a process in human cognition), which is the same as short-term memory, and applies it to RNNs, thereby giving it the ability to selectively read from and write to memory using an attentional controller. We can see what the NTM looks like in the following diagram:

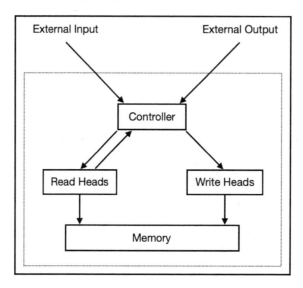

In the preceding diagram, we can see that there are two main components to the NTM – the controller, which is a neural network, and the memory, which contains processed information. The controller interacts with the external world by receiving an input vector and outputting an output vector, but it differs from the ANNs from previous chapters in that it also interacts with the memory matrix using the selective read and write operations.

Reading

Let's suppose our memory is an NxM matrix and that it is denoted by $\mathbf{M}_t \in \mathbb{R}^{N \times M}$, where t is the time step, N is the number of rows (memory locations), and M is the size of the vector at each location. Then, we have another vector of weights, $\mathbf{w}_t$, which determines how much attention to designate to various locations in the memory (that is, the rows of the matrix). Each of the N weightings in the weight vector is normalized, which tells us that $\sum_i w_t(i) = 1$ and that for all i, we have $0 \le w_t(i) \le 1$, where $w_t(i)$ is the ith element of $\mathbf{w}_t$.

The read vector, $\mathbf{r}_t$, which is returned by the head, can be calculated as follows:

$$\mathbf{r}_t = \sum_i w_t(i) \mathbf{M}_t(i)$$

Here, $\mathbf{M}_t(i)$ is the ith memory vector. From the preceding equation, we can also see that $\mathbf{r}_t$ can be differentiated with respect to both the weight and the memory.

Writing

The writing operation takes inspiration from the input and forget gates of LSTMs, where some information is erased and then replaced (or added).

The memory is then updated using two formulas, the first of which erases the memory and the second of which adds memory:

- $\tilde{\mathbf{M}}_t(i) = \mathbf{M}_{t-1}(i)[\mathbf{1} - w_t(i)\mathbf{e}_t]$
- $\mathbf{M}_t(i) = \tilde{\mathbf{M}}_t(i) + w_t(i)\mathbf{a}_t$

Here, $\mathbf{e}_t \in (0, 1)$ is the erase vector, $\mathbf{a}_t$ is the add vector, and $\mathbf{1}$ is a vector containing only ones. From these equations, we can see that the memory at a specific location is only erased when both the weight and erase vector are equal to one, and it is left unchanged otherwise. Since both the erase and add operations are differentiable, so is the entire write operation.

Addressing mechanisms

Now that we know how the reading and writing operations work, let's dive into how the weights are produced. The weights are outputs that are a combination of two mechanisms—a content-based addressing mechanism and a location-based addressing mechanism.

Content-based addressing mechanism

This addressing mechanism focuses on the similarity between the key values, $\mathbf{k}_t$, which are output by the controller based on the input it receives, and the memory rows. Based on this similarity, it creates an attention vector. It is calculated using the following equation:

$$w_i^c(i) = \text{softmax}(\beta_t \cdot \text{cosine}[\mathbf{k}_t, \mathbf{M}_t(i)]) = \frac{e^{\beta_t \frac{\mathbf{k}_t \cdot \mathbf{M}_t(i)}{\|\mathbf{k}_t\| \cdot \|\mathbf{M}_t(i)\|}}}{\sum_{j=1}^{N} e^{\beta_t \frac{\mathbf{k}_t \cdot \mathbf{M}_t(j)}{\|\mathbf{k}_t\| \cdot \|\mathbf{M}_t(j)\|}}}$$

Here, w_t^c is a normalized weight and β_t is a strength multiplier.

Location-based address mechanism

Before we learn how location-based addressing works, we need to define our interpolation gate, which blends together the content-based attention at the current time step with the weights in the attention vector from the previous time step. This can be done using the following formula:

$$\mathbf{w}_t^g = g_t \mathbf{w}_t^c + (1 - g_t)\mathbf{w}_{t-1}$$

Here, $g_t \in (0, 1)$ is the scalar interpolation gate.

Location-based addressing works by summing the values in the attention vector, each of which are weighted by a shifting weight, $\mathbf{s}_t$, which is a distribution of the allowable integer shifts. For example, if it can shift between -1 and +1, then the allowable shifts that can be performed are -1, 0, and +1. Now, we can formulate this rotation so that the shifting weight applies to $\mathbf{w}_t^g$ as a circular convolution. We can observe this in the following equation:

$$\tilde{w}_t(i) = \sum_{j=0}^{N-1} w_t^g(j) s_t(i - j)$$

To prevent any leakage or blurriness being caused by the shifting weight, we sharpen the attention vector, $\mathbf{w}_t$, using the following equation:

$$w_t(i) = \frac{\tilde{w}_t(i)^{\gamma_t}}{\sum_j \tilde{w}_t(j)^{\gamma_t}}$$

Here, $\gamma_t \geq 1$ is a positive scalar value.

And lastly, the values that are output by the controller are unique for each read and write head.

Exploring the types of attention

Attention has proven to be so effective in machine translation that it has been expanded into natural language processing, statistical learning, speech understanding, object detection and recognition, image captioning, and visual question answering.

The purpose of attention is to estimate how correlated (connected) two or more elements are to one another.

However, there isn't just one kind of attention. There are many types, such as the following:

- **Self-attention**: Captures the relationship between different positions of a sequence of inputs
- **Global or soft attention**: Focuses on the entire sequence of inputs
- **Local or hard attention**: Focuses on only part of the sequence of inputs

Let's take a look at these in more detail.

Self-attention

Self-attention finds relationships between different positions of the input sequence and then computes a representation of the same sequence of inputs. You can think of this as summarizing the input. This is somewhat similar to how the LSTM we saw in the previous chapter works, where it tries to learn a correlation between the previous inputs and the current one and decide what is relevant and what isn't.

Comparing hard and soft attention

These types of attention were created for generating captions for images. A CNN is first used to extract features and then compress them into an encoding. To decode it, an LSTM is used to produce words that describe the image. But that isn't important right now—distinguishing between soft and hard attention is.

In soft attention, the alignment weights that are learned during training are softly placed over patches in an image so that it focuses on part(s) of an image more than others.

On the other hand, in hard attention, we focus only on part of the image at a time. This only makes a binary decision about where to focus on, and it is much harder to train in comparison to soft attention. This is because it is non-differentiable and needs to be trained using reinforcement learning. Since reinforcement learning is beyond the scope of this book, we won't be covering hard attention.

Comparing global and local attention

Global attention shares some similarities with how soft attention works in that it takes all of the input into consideration.

Local attention differs from global attention as it can be seen as a mix of hard and soft attention and considers only a subset of the input. It starts by predicting a single aligned position for the current output. Then, a window centered around the current input is used to create a context vector.

Transformers

For those of you who got excited at the title (transformers), this section sadly has nothing to do with Optimus Prime or Bumblebee. In all seriousness now, we have seen that attention mechanisms work well with architectures such as RNNs and CNNs, but they are also powerful enough to be used on their own, as evidenced by Vaswani in 2017, in his paper *Attention Is All you Need*.

The transformer model is made entirely out of self-attention mechanisms to perform sequence-to-sequence tasks without the need for any form of recurrent unit. Wait, but how? Let's break down the architecture and find out how this is possible.

RNNs take in the encoded input and then decode it in order to map it to a target output. However, the transformer differs here by instead treating the encoding as a set of key-value pairs ($\mathbf{K}$, $\mathbf{V}$) which has dimensions ($=n$) equal to the length of (the sequence of) the inputs. The decoder is treated as a query, Q, that has dimensions ($=m$) equal to the length of (the sequence of) the outputs. Each output is created by mapping the key-value pair to a query.

The attention here is calculated using a scaled dot product that calculates the weighted sum of the values using the formula:

$$\text{attention}(\mathbf{Q}, \mathbf{K}, \mathbf{V}) = \text{softmax}\left(\frac{\mathbf{Q}\mathbf{K}^{\mathrm{T}}}{\sqrt{n}}\right)\mathbf{V}$$

Now, instead of calculating the attention just once, we do it multiple times in parallel. This is referred to as multi-head attention. In the following diagram, we can see a visualization of the scaled-dot product attention and multi-head attention calculations:

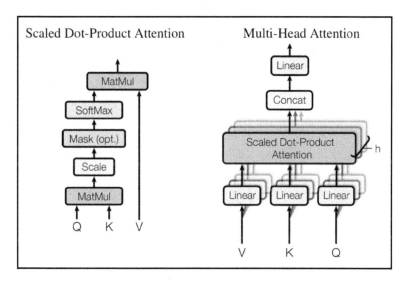

The output from each of these attention calculations is then concatenated and we apply a linear transformation to them to ensure their dimensions match what is expected. The reason for this is that multi-head attention enables the model to focus on information from different subspaces at different positions at the same time, which single attention is unable to do. This works as follows:

$$\text{multihead}(\mathbf{Q}, \mathbf{K}, \mathbf{V}) = [\text{head}_1, \text{head}_2, \cdots, \text{head}_h]\mathbf{W}^o$$

Here, each head is calculated as follows:

$$\text{head}_i = \text{attention}(\mathbf{Q}\mathbf{W}_i^Q, \mathbf{K}\mathbf{W}_i^K, \mathbf{V}\mathbf{W}_i^V)$$

Here, $\mathbf{W}_i^Q \in \mathbb{R}^{d_{\text{model}} \times d_k}$, $\mathbf{W}_i^K \in \mathbb{R}^{d_{\text{model}} \times d_k}$, $\mathbf{W}_i^V \in \mathbb{R}^{d_{\text{model}} \times d_v}$, and $\mathbf{W}^o \in \mathbb{R}^{h d_v \times d_{\text{model}}}$ are trainable parameters.

Let's now turn our attention to the encoder and decoder.

The encoder is composed of a stack of six identical layers, each of which is made up of two sub-layers. The first of these sub-layers is a multi-head self-attention layer, while the second is an FNN that applies identical weights individually to each element in the entire sequence. This is similar to a convolution, which would apply the same kernel at each position. The FNN can be represented as follows:

$$\text{FNN}(\mathbf{x}) = \max(0, \mathbf{x}\mathbf{W}_1 + \mathbf{b}_1)\mathbf{W}_2 + \mathbf{b}_2$$

Each has a residual connection to a layer normalization. What this does is identify particular pieces of information in the text/image from the whole, that is, the most important parts that we need to pay greater attention to. The computation for this encoder is as follows:

$$\text{layer norm}(\mathbf{x} + \text{sub layer}(\mathbf{x}))$$

The encoder architecture looks as follows:

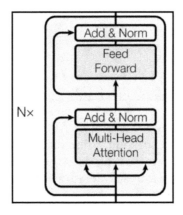

The preceding layer normalization transforms the input so that it has zero mean and a variance of one. It does this using the following formulas:

- $$\mu^l = \frac{1}{H}\sum_{i=1}^{H} a_i^l$$

- $$\sigma^l = \sqrt{\frac{1}{H}\sum_{i=1}^{H}(a_i^l - \mu^l)^2}$$

$$h_i = f\left(\frac{g_i}{\sigma_i}(a_i - \mu_i) + b_i\right)$$

Here,

The decoder (whose architecture is shown in the following diagram) is also composed of a stack of six identical layers; however, each of these layers is made up of three sub-layers. The first two of these sub-layers is a multi-head attention layer, and each is followed by a layer normalization, which is where the residual connection is. The first of the sub-layers is modified with a mask so that the positions don't go to the subsequent positions and try to use future predictions to predict the current one:

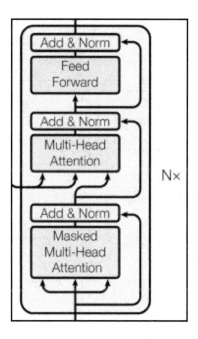

The output of the decoder is then passed to a linear layer, which is what we apply a softmax to.

In the architecture, we can quite easily notice that there are no convolutions or recurrent connections for the model to make use of in the sequence, which is where it sees this information. To deal with this, the authors of this method used positional encodings to inject information about the absolute and relative positions of the elements in the sequence into the input embeddings of the input embeddings, which are at the bottom of the encoder and decoder.

This gives us the full transformer architecture, which can be seen in the following diagram:

The position encodings are calculated using the following two equations:

- $$PE(pos, 2i) = \sin\left(\frac{pos}{10000^{\frac{2i}{d_{model}}}}\right)$$

- $$PE(pos, 2i + 1) = \cos\left(\frac{pos}{10000^{\frac{2i}{d_{model}}}}\right)$$

Here, *pos* is the position and *i* is the dimension.

Now, let's conclude this chapter.

Summary

In this chapter, we learned about a hot new area in deep learning known as attention mechanisms. These are used to allow networks to focus on specific parts of input. This helps the network overcome the problem of long-term dependencies. We also learned about how these attention mechanisms can be used instead of sequential models such as RNNs to produce state-of-the-art results on tasks such as machine translation and sentence generation. However, they can also be used to focus on relevant parts of images. This can be used for tasks such as visual question answering, where we may want our network to tell us what is happening in a given scene.

In the next chapter, we will learn about generative models.

12
Generative Models

So far in this book, we have covered the three main types of neural networks—**feedforward neural networks (FNNs)**, **convolutional neural networks (CNNs)**, and **recurrent neural networks (RNNs)**. Each of them are discriminative models; that is, they learned to discriminate (differentiate) between the classes we wanted them to be able to predict, such as *is this language French or English?*, *is this song classic rock or 90s pop?*, and *what are the objects present in this scene?*. However, deep neural networks don't just stop there. They can also be used to improve image or video resolution or generate entirely new images and data. These types of models are known as **generative models**.

In this chapter, we will cover the following topics related to generative models:

- Why we need generative models
- Autoencoders
- Generative adversarial networks
- Flow-based networks

Why we need generative models

All the various neural network architectures we have learned about in this book have served a specific purpose—to make a prediction about some given data. Each of these neural networks has its own respective strengths for various tasks. A CNN is very effective for object recognition tasks or music genre classification, an RNN is very effective for language translation or time series prediction, and FNNs are great for regression or classification. Generative models, on the other hand, are those that model the data, $p(x)$, that we can sample data from, which is different from discriminative models, which learn to estimate conditional distributions, such as $p(\bullet|x)$.

But how does this benefit us? What can we use generative models for? Well, there are a couple of reasons why it is important for us to understand how generative models work. To start, in image recognition, we have to learn to estimate a high-dimensional space of the $p(y_i \mid x)$ form, which we can use to predict which class our data belongs to. You should remember that these models require a lot of training data. Now, what we could do instead is make it so that our data is generated from a low-dimensional latent variable, z, which makes our probability function come to $p(x) \int p(x \mid z)p(z)\mathrm{d}z$. What we need to do now is change our prediction problem top, $(y_i \mid z)$. Another way that we can make use of generative models is to understand what our neural networks have learned. As we know, deep neural networks are quite complex and knowing what exactly they have or haven't learned is quite challenging to figure out. So, what we can do is sample from them and compare these drawn samples to the real data. Lastly, we can use generative models to create synthetic data to train our models on if we have a shortage of data.

Now that we know what generative models can be used for, let's explore some of the more popular ones and learn how they work.

Autoencoders

An **autoencoder** is an unsupervised type of FNN that learns to reconstruct high-dimensional data using latent-encoded data. You can think of it as trying to learn an identity function (that is, take x as input and then predict x).

Let's start by taking a look at the following diagram, which shows you what an autoencoder looks like:

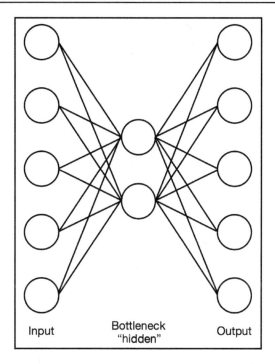

As you can see, the network is split into two components—an encoder and a decoder—which are mirror images of each other. The two components are connected to each other through a bottleneck layer (sometimes referred to as either a latent-space representation or compression) that has dimensions that are a lot smaller than the input. You should note that the network architecture is symmetric, but that doesn't necessarily mean its weights need be. But why? What does this network learn and how does it do it? Let's take a look at both networks and explore what they're doing.

The encoder network takes in high-dimensional input and reduces it to lower-dimensional latent code (that is, it learns the patterns in the input data). This works similarly to principal component analysis and matrix factorization. It works as follows:

$$\mathbf{z} = f_\theta(\mathbf{x})$$

The decoder network takes as input the lower-dimensional latent code (the patterns), which contains all the main information about the input, and reconstructs the original input (or as close to the original input as possible) from it. It works as follows:

$$\mathbf{x}' = g_\phi(\mathbf{z})$$

We can combine the preceding two equations and express the autoencoder as follows:

$$\mathbf{x}' = g_\phi(f_\theta(\mathbf{x}))$$

Our goal is for the original input to be as close (ideally, identical) to the reconstructed output—that is, $\mathbf{x} \approx \mathbf{x}'$.

Both the encoder and decoder have separate weights, but we learn the parameters together to output the reconstructed data, which is nearly identical to the original input. During training, we can use the **MSE** loss:

$$L_{AE}(\theta, \phi) = \frac{1}{n}\sum_{i=1}^{n}(x_i - g_\phi(f_\theta(x_i)))$$

This type of autoencoder is commonly referred to as an **undercomplete autoencoder** because the bottleneck layer is much smaller than the dimensions of the input and the output layer.

But what goes on in this bottleneck layer that allows the decoder to reconstruct the input from it? This latent coding, which is a high-dimensional space being mapped to a lower-dimensional one, learns a manifold, which is a topological space that resembles Euclidean space at each point (we will shine more light on topological spaces and manifolds in `Chapter 12`, *Geometric Deep Learning*). We can represent this manifold as a vector field and visualize the data clusters. It is this vector field that the autoencoder is learning to reconstruct inputs from. Each data point can be found on this manifold and we can project this back into higher-dimensional space to reconstruct it.

Let's suppose we have the MNIST dataset, which contains images of handwritten digits from 0-9. In the following screenshot, we can see some of the images from the dataset:

The encoder network takes this data as input and encodes it into a lower-dimensional latent bottleneck layer, which contains a compressed representation of this higher-dimensional input and shows it to us in two dimensions. This embedding space looks as follows, where each of the colors represents a specific digit:

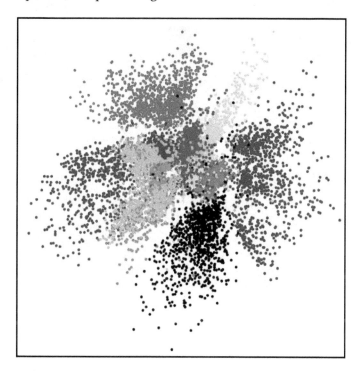

About now, you are probably wondering what purpose an architecture such as this serves. What could we gain from training a model to recreate and output its own input? A number of things, as it turns out—we could use it to compress data and store it to save space and reconstruct it when we need to access it, we could remove noise from images or audio files, or we could use it for dimensionality reduction for data visualization.

However, just because this architecture can be used to compress images, doesn't mean this is similar to a data compression algorithm such as MP3 or JPEG. An autoencoder is only able to compress data that it has seen during training, so if it was trained on images of cars, it would be quite ineffective in compressing images of horses since the features it has learned are specific to cars, which don't generalize well to horses. Compression algorithms such as MP3 and JPEG, on the other hand, don't learn the features of the inputs they receive; they make general assumptions about their inputs.

In the following diagram, you can see an autoencoder compressing an image into latent space and reconstructing it in the output:

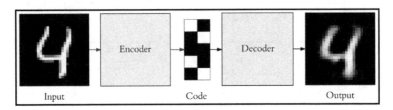

You can see, in the diagram, that the autoencoder has managed to reconstruct the input image and it still looks like the number four, but it isn't an exact replica; some of the information has been lost. This isn't an error in training; this is by design. Autoencoders are designed to be *lossy* and only approximately copy the input data so that it can extract only what is necessary by prioritizing what it deems more useful.

As we have seen so far in this book, adding layers and going deeper into autoencoders does have its advantages; it allows our neural network to capture greater complexities and reduces the required computational cost (in comparison to going wider and shallower). Similarly, we can add additional layers to our encoder and decoder. This is particularly true in the case of dealing with images because we know that convolutional layers bring better results than flattening the image and using it as input.

Let's now explore some of the variations of autoencoders that allow us to achieve the aforementioned tasks.

The denoising autoencoder

The **denoising autoencoder** (**DAE**) is a variation of the preceding autoencoder as it learns to reconstruct corrupted or noisy inputs with near certainty. Suppose we have an image and, for some reason, it is blurry or some of the pixels have been corrupted and we'd like to improve the resolution of the image (kind of how they do in the movies when they can find clues in images with relatively low resolution). We can pass it through our DAE and get back a fully reconstructed image.

We start by corrupting the initial input using a conditional distribution, $C(\tilde{\mathbf{x}} \mid \mathbf{x})$—which is basically a stochastic mapping—and it returns back to us the corrupted samples. Now that we have our new input, our autoencoder will learn how to reconstruct the uncorrupted data—that is, $p(\mathbf{x} \mid \tilde{\mathbf{x}})$—and to train this, our data will be the $(x_i, \tilde{x}_i)$ pairs. What we want the decoder to learn is $p(\mathbf{x} \mid \tilde{\mathbf{x}}) = p(\mathbf{x} \mid \mathbf{z})$, where as before, z was the output of the encoder.

The preceding corruption works as follows:

$$C(\tilde{\mathbf{x}} = \tilde{x} \mid x) = \mathcal{N}(\tilde{x}; \mu = x, \Sigma = \sigma^2 I)$$

Here, σ^2 is the variance of the noise.

We can train our DAE just as any other FNN and perform gradient descent on the following:

$$-\mathbb{E}_{\mathbf{x} \sim \hat{p}(\mathbf{x})} \, \mathbb{E}_{\tilde{\mathbf{x}} \sim C(\tilde{\mathbf{x}}|\mathbf{x})} \log p(\mathbf{x} \mid \mathbf{z} = f(\tilde{\mathbf{x}}))$$

Here, $\hat{p}(\mathbf{x})$ is the distribution of the training data.

As mentioned, the encoder projects high-dimensional data into a lower-dimensional space, called **latent space**, and learns the shape of the manifold. It then tries to map the corrupted data onto or near to this manifold to figure out what it could be and then pieces it together in the reconstruction process to obtain x by estimating $\mathbb{E}_{\mathbf{x},\tilde{\mathbf{x}} \sim p(\mathbf{x})C(\tilde{\mathbf{x}}|\mathbf{x})} [\mathbf{x} \mid \tilde{x}]$ and minimizing the square error, $\|g(f(\tilde{x})) - x\|^2$.

We can view this process in the following diagram:

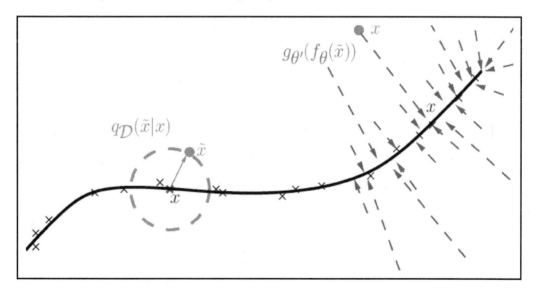

Here, the black curve is the learned manifold in the latent space and you can see the noisy points, $\tilde{x}$, are projected onto the closest point on the manifold to estimate what it could be.

The variational autoencoder

The **variational autoencoder** (**VAE**) is another type of autoencoder, but with some particular differences. In fact, instead of learning functions, $f()$ and $g()$, it learns the probability density function of the input data.

Let's suppose we have a distribution, p_θ, and it is parameterized by θ. Here, we can express the relationship between x and z as follows:

- $p_\theta(z)$: The prior
- $p_\theta(x \mid z)$: The likelihood (the distribution of the input given the latent space)
- $p_\theta(z \mid x)$: The posterior (the distribution of the latent space given the input)

The aforementioned distributions are parameterized by neural networks, which enables them to capture complex nonlinearities and, as we know, we train them using gradient descent.

But why did the authors of this method decide to deviate from the previous approach to learning a distribution? There are a few reasons why this is more effective. To start, the data we would often be dealing with is noisy and so instead, modelling the distribution is better for us. The goal here, as you may have guessed, is to generate data that has a statistic that is similar to that of the input.

Before we move further, let's take a look at what a VAE looks like:

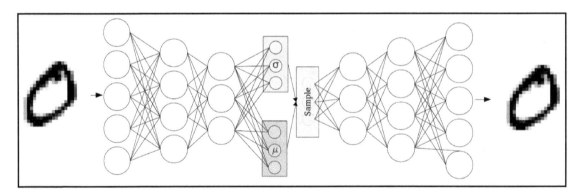

As you can see, it shares some similarities with the autoencoder but, as we mentioned, instead of $z = f(x)$ and $x' = g(z)$, we learn $p = (z \mid x)$ and $p = (x \mid z)$, respectively. However, because there is now a random variable in between the input and the output, this architecture cannot be trained through regular backpropagation; we instead do backpropagation through the latent distribution's parameters.

Once we know the prior and likelihood distributions and the real parameters, θ^*, we can generate samples by repeatedly doing the following:

- Randomly generate samples from $z_i \sim p_{\theta^*}(\mathbf{z})$.
- Generate a $x_i \sim p(\mathbf{x} \mid \mathbf{z} = \mathbf{z}_i)$ sample.

Using our knowledge of probability from Chapter 3, *Probability and Statistics*, we know that θ^* should maximize the probability of a real data sample being generated; that is,

$$\theta^* = \arg\max_{\theta} \prod_{i=1}^{n} p_\theta(\mathbf{x}_i)$$

.

The equation used to generate the data now is as follows:

$$p_\theta(\mathbf{x}_i) = \int p_\theta(\mathbf{x}_i \mid \mathbf{z}) p_\theta(\mathbf{z}) \mathrm{d}\mathbf{z}$$

Now, suppose we can approximate the distribution of x by repeatedly sampling z_i, as follows:

$$p(\mathbf{x}) \approx \frac{1}{n} \sum_{i=1}^{n} p(\mathbf{x} \mid \mathbf{z}_i)$$

But, in order to do this, we would need a lot of samples, the majority of which would likely be zero or close to zero. This is intractable (that is, not computationally practical). So, what we do instead is learn another distribution (that is tractable)—$q_\phi(\mathbf{z} \mid \mathbf{x})$—to approximate the posterior, $p_\theta(\mathbf{z} \mid \mathbf{x})$. Naturally, we want these two distributions to be close to each other so that they are able to better approximate the posterior distribution; so, we use **Kullback-Leibler (KL) divergence** to measure the distance between them and try to minimize it with respect to φ. We can see how we do this in the following equations:

$$D_{KL}\left(q_\phi(\mathbf{z} \mid \mathbf{x}) \| p_\theta(\mathbf{z} \mid \mathbf{x})\right) = \mathbb{E}_{\mathbf{z} \sim q_\phi(\mathbf{z} \mid \mathbf{x})}\left[\log q_\phi(\mathbf{z} \mid \mathbf{x}) - \log p_\theta(\mathbf{z} \mid \mathbf{x})\right]$$

From Bayes' rule, we know the following:

$$p(\mathbf{z} \mid \mathbf{x}) = \frac{p(\mathbf{x} \mid \mathbf{z})p(\mathbf{z})}{p(\mathbf{x})}$$

If we take its logarithm, we get the following:

$$\log[p(\mathbf{z} \mid \mathbf{x})] = \log[p(\mathbf{x} \mid \mathbf{z})] + \log[p(\mathbf{z})] - \log[p(\mathbf{x})]$$

We can plug this back into the equation for KL divergence and get the following:

$$D_{KL}(q_\phi(\mathbf{z} \mid \mathbf{x}) \| p_\theta(\mathbf{z} \mid \mathbf{x})) = \mathbb{E}_{\mathbf{z} \sim q_\phi(\mathbf{z}|\mathbf{x})}[\log q_\phi(\mathbf{z} \mid \mathbf{x}) - \log p_\theta(\mathbf{x} \mid \mathbf{z}) - \log p(\mathbf{z})] + \log[p(\mathbf{x})]$$

 Since $p(x)$ doesn't depend on z, we can keep it on the outside.

We can now rearrange the equation into the following form:

$$\log p_\theta(\mathbf{x}) - D_{KL}(q_\phi(\mathbf{z} \mid \mathbf{x}) \| p_\theta(\mathbf{z} \mid \mathbf{x})) = \mathbb{E}_{\mathbf{z} \sim q_\phi(\mathbf{z}|\mathbf{x})} \log p_\theta(\mathbf{x} \mid \mathbf{z}) - D_{KL}(q_\phi(\mathbf{z} \mid \mathbf{x}) \| p_\theta(\mathbf{z}))$$

Since $\mathbb{E}_{\mathbf{z} \sim q_\phi(\mathbf{z}|\mathbf{x})}[\log q(\mathbf{z} \mid \mathbf{x}) - \log p_\theta(\mathbf{z})] = D_{KL}(q_\phi(\mathbf{z} \mid \mathbf{x}) \| p_\theta(\mathbf{z}))$, the goal here is to maximize the lower bound of $\log p_\theta(\mathbf{x})$ because $\log p_\theta(\mathbf{x}) > \log p_\theta(\mathbf{x}) - D_{KL}(q_\phi(\mathbf{z} \mid \mathbf{x}) \| p_\theta(\mathbf{z} \mid \mathbf{x}))$, and we do so because the output of KL divergence is non-zero and non-negative.

But wait—what is the encoder and what is the decoder? This is an autoencoder, after all. Interestingly, it has been right in front of us all along. The encoder in a VAE is $q_\phi(\mathbf{z} \mid \mathbf{x})$ and is usually assumed to be Gaussian:

$$q_\phi(\mathbf{z} \mid \mathbf{x}) = \mathcal{N}(\mathbf{z}; \mu, \Sigma^2 I)$$

The decoder is $p_\theta(\mathbf{x} \mid \mathbf{z})$. Both of these are modeled using neural networks.

Generative adversarial networks

The **generative adversarial network** (**GAN**) is a game theory-inspired neural network architecture that was created by Ian Goodfellow in 2014. It comprises two networks—a generator network and a critic network—both of which compete against each other in a minimax game, which allows both of them to improve simultaneously by trying to better the other.

In the last couple of years, GANs have produced some phenomenal results in tasks such as creating images that are indistinguishable from real images, generating music when given some recordings, and even generating text. But these models are known for being notoriously difficult to train. Let's now find out what exactly GANs are, how they bring about such tremendous results, and what makes them so challenging to train.

As we know, discriminative models learn a conditional distribution and try to predict a label given input data—that is, $P(Y \mid X)$. Generative models, on the other hand, model a joint distribution—that is, $P(X, Y)$—and, using Bayes' rule, they can, when given the label, generate the data. So, like VAEs, they learn the distribution, $P(X)$.

The critic network is a discriminator (D) with parameters, $\theta^{(D)}$, and its job is to determine whether the data being fed into it is real or fake. The generator network is a generator (G) with parameters, $\theta^{(G)}$, whose job is to learn to create synthetic data samples from noise that can fool the discriminator into thinking the synthetic data is real with a high probability.

As we have seen in this book, discriminator models are brilliant at learning to map input data to a desired label (output) and can determine whether an object is present in an image, as well as tracking an object in a video and translating languages. However, they are unable to use what they have learned to generate entirely new data the way we are able to use our imagination.

Before we proceed, let's take a look at what this architecture looks like. In the following diagram, you can see how GANs are structured:

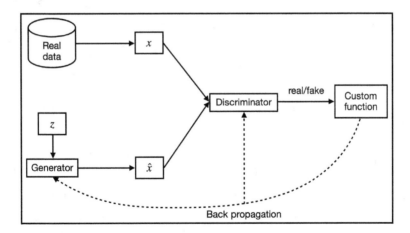

Now that we know what GANs look like, let's see how they work. We can summarize a GAN with the following equation:

$$\min_G \max_D L(G, D) = \mathbb{E}_{x \sim p(x)} [\log D(x)] + \mathbb{E}_{z \sim q(z)} [\log(1 - D(G(z)))]$$

The discriminator's goal is for $D(x) = 1$ and $D(G(z)) = 0$, while the generator's goal is for $D(G(z)) = 1$.

Since the generator and discriminator have different goals, naturally, they would have different cost functions. The respective losses for the discriminator and the generator are as follows:

- $L^{(D)}(\theta^{(D)}, \theta^{(G)})$
- $L^{(G)}(\theta^{(D)}, \theta^{(G)})$

Naturally, neither of the two networks has a direct effect on the parameters of the other. As mentioned, since this is a game-theoretic-inspired architecture, we treat this as a two-player game and our objective is to find the Nash equilibria for cases where x is as follows:

$$p_{\text{data}}(x) = p_{\text{gen}}(x)$$

This is a saddle point. When we achieve this, the discriminator is unable to differentiate between the real data and the generated data.

How do we now find the optimal value for the discriminator? Well, to start, we know the loss function and from it, we can find the optimal $D(x)$ value:

$$L = \mathbb{E}_{x \sim p(x)} [\log D(x)] + \mathbb{E}_{z \sim q(z)} [\log(1 - D(G(z)))]$$

However, when trained, the generator ideally outputs x, so we can rewrite the loss function as follows:

$$L = \mathbb{E}_{x \sim p_r(x)} [\log D(x)] + \mathbb{E}_{x \sim p_g(x)} [\log(1 - D(x))]$$

Here, p_r is the real data distribution and p_g is the generated data distribution. Now, we have the following:

$$L = \int_x (p_r(x) \log(D(x)) + p_g(x) \log(1 - D(x))) \, dx$$

To make life a bit easier, let's substitute parts of our equation with the following variables:

- $x' = D(x)$
- $A = p_r(x)$
- $B = p_g(x)$

Since we are sampling over all the possible values of x, we can write the preceding three variables as follows:

$$f(x') = A\log x' + B\log(1 - x')$$

$$\frac{\mathrm{d}f(x')}{\mathrm{d}x'} = A\frac{1}{\log 10}\frac{1}{x'} - B\frac{1}{\log 10}\frac{1}{1 - x'}$$

$$\frac{\mathrm{d}f(x')}{\mathrm{d}x'} = \frac{1}{\log 10}\left(\frac{A}{x'} - \frac{B}{1 - x'}\right)$$

$$\frac{\mathrm{d}f(x')}{\mathrm{d}x'} = \frac{1}{\log 10}\left(\frac{A - (A + B)x'}{x'(1 - x')}\right)$$

Now, to find the optimal value of the discriminator, we equate the preceding derivative to 0 and get the following:

$$D^*(x) = x'^* = \frac{A}{A + B} = \frac{p_r(x)}{p_r(x) + p_g(x)}$$

So, when $p_r(x) = p_g(x)$, $D^*(x) = \frac{1}{2}$, which satisfies our condition. The loss function now becomes the following:

$$L = \int_x \left(p_r(x)\log(D^*(x)) + p_g(x)\log(1 - D^*(x))\right)\mathrm{d}x$$

$$L = \log\frac{1}{2}\int_x p_r(x)\mathrm{d}x + \log\frac{1}{2}\int_x p_g(x)\mathrm{d}x = -\log 4$$

Now that we know how to find the optimal discriminator, naturally, you may be wondering how we can find the optimal generator. Our goal here is to minimize the **Jensen–Shannon (JS)** divergence between the true and generated distributions, which is as follows:

$$D_{JS}(p_r\|p_g) = \frac{1}{2}D_{KL}\left(p_r\|\frac{p_r + p_g}{2}\right) + \frac{1}{2}D_{KL}\left(p_g\|\frac{p_r + p_g}{2}\right)$$

$$D_{JS}(p_r\|p_g) = \frac{1}{2}\left(\log 2 + \int_x p_r(x)\log\frac{p_r(x)}{p_r(x) + p_g(x)}\mathrm{d}x\right) + \frac{1}{2}\left(\log 2 + \int_x p_g(x)\log\frac{p_g(x)}{p_r(x) + p_g(x)}\mathrm{d}x\right)$$

$$D_{JS}(p_r\|p_g) = \frac{1}{2}(\log 4 + L(G, D^*))$$

So, $L(G, D^*) = 2D_{JS}(p_r \| p_g) - \log 4$, which tells us that if our generator is in fact optimal, then $L(G^*, D^*) = -\log 4$.

There you have it—that's how GANs work. However, there are certain problems associated with GANs. In particular, the convergence of the two networks is not guaranteed since the gradient descent of either model does not directly impact the other, and model parameters tend to oscillate and destabilize. Another problem is mode collapse, which is a result of improper convergence, which means the generator only outputs a select few generated samples, which it knows will trick the discriminator into thinking are real. Since the generator starts to output the same few samples over and over again, the discriminator learns to classify them as fake. Mode collapse is a rather challenging problem to solve. Lastly, our discriminator could become so good that the gradient of the generator vanishes and it ends up not learning anything at all.

If we were to compare VAEs and GANs, both of which are generative models, we would see that with GANs, our goal is to minimize the divergence between the two distributions, while with VAEs, our objective is to minimize a bound on the divergence of the two distributions. This is a much easier task, but it doesn't produce results in quite the same way as the GAN.

Wasserstein GANs

In the preceding section, we learned about GANs, how they work, and how they face some problems during training. Now, we will learn about the **Wasserstein GAN (WGAN)**, which makes use of the Wasserstein distance. It is a function that measures the distance between two probability distributions on a given metric space. Imagine we're on a beach and we decide to model a three-dimensional probability distribution in the sand. The Wasserstein distance measures the least amount of energy that would be required to move and reshape the distribution into another one. So, we can say that the cost is the product of the total mass of sand we moved and the distance it was moved.

What this does for GANs is it smoothens the gradient and prevents the discriminator from being overtrained. The losses of our discriminator and generator are now, respectively, as follows:

- $L_D = \mathbb{E}_{x \sim p(x)} D(x) - \mathbb{E}_{z \sim p(z)} D(G(z))$
- $L_G = \mathbb{E}_{z \sim p(z)} D(G(z))$

Why does this perform better than JS and KL divergence? Let's find out using the following example.

We have two distributions, P and Q, with the following parameters:

$$\text{for all } (x, y) \in P, x = 0, \text{and } y \sim U(0, 1)$$
$$\text{for all } (x, y) \in Q, x = \theta, 0 \leq \theta \leq 1 \text{ and } y \sim U(0, 1)$$

Now, let's compare KL divergence with JS divergence with the Wasserstein distance. If $\theta \neq 0$, then we can observe the following:

$$D_{KL}(P\|Q) = \sum_{x=0, y\sim U(0,1)} 1 \cdot \log \frac{1}{0} = \infty$$

$$D_{KL}(Q\|P) = \sum_{x=\theta, y\sim U(0,1)} 1 \cdot \log \frac{1}{0} = \infty$$

$$D_{JS}(P, Q) = \frac{1}{2} \left(\sum_{x=0, y\sim U(0,1)} 1 \cdot \log \frac{1}{1/2} + \sum_{x=0, y\sim U(0,1)} 1 \cdot \log \frac{1}{1/2} \right) = \log 2$$

$$W(P, Q) = |\theta|$$

When $\theta = 0$, we can observe the following:

$$D_{KL}(P\|Q) = D_{KL}(Q\|P) = D_{JS}(P, Q) = 0$$
$$W(P, Q) = 0$$

As you can see, the Wasserstein distance has some clear advantages over KL and JS divergence in that it is differentiable with respect to θ, which improves the stability of the learning. So, the loss function now becomes the following:

$$W(p_r, p_g) = \frac{1}{K} \sup_{\|f\|_L \leq K} \mathbb{E}_{x\sim p_r}[f(x)] - \mathbb{E}_{x\sim p_g}[f(x)]$$

This is K-Lipschitz continuous—that is, $|f(x_1) - f(x_2)| \leq K|x_1 - x_2|$ for $K \geq 0$ and $x_1, x_2 \in \mathbb{R}$.

Sadly, despite the benefits of WGAN over GAN, it is still difficult to train. There are a number of variants of GAN that attempt to address this problem.

Flow-based networks

So far in this chapter, we have studied two kinds of generative models—GANs and VAEs—but there is also another kind, known as **flow-based generative models**, which directly learn the probability density function of the data distribution, which is something that the previous models do not do. Flow-based models make use of normalizing flows, which overcomes the difficulty that GANs and VAEs face in trying to learn the distribution. This approach can transform a simple distribution into a more complex one through a series of invertible mappings. We repeatedly apply the change of variables rule, which allows the initial probability density to flow through the series of invertible mappings, and at the end, we get the target probability distribution.

Normalizing flows

Before we can proceed with understanding how flow-based models work, let's recap some concepts such as the Jacobian matrix, calculating the determinant of a matrix and the change of the variable theorem in probability, and then go on to understand what a normalizing flow is.

As a refresher, the Jacobian matrix is an *m×n*-dimensional matrix that contains the first derivatives of a function, which maps an *n*-dimensional vector to an *m*-dimensional vector. Each element of this matrix is represented by $J_{i,j} = \frac{\partial f_i}{\partial x_j}$.

The determinant can only be found for a square matrix. So, let's suppose we have an *n×n* matrix, *M*. Its determinant can be found using the following:

$$|M| = \sum_j (-1)^{\sigma(j)} a_{1j_1} a_{2j_2} \cdots a_{nj_n}$$

Here, the sum is calculated over all *n*! permutations, $j = (j_1, j_2, \cdots, j_n)$ of $(1, 2, \cdots, n)$, and σ(•) tells us the signature of the permutation. However, if $|M| = 0$, then *M* is not invertible.

Now, let's say we have a random variable, z, whose probability density function is $z \sim \pi(z)$. Using this, we can make a new random variable as the result of a one-to-one mapping, $x = f(z)$. Since this function is invertible, we know that $z = f^1(x)$. But what, then, is the probability density function of our new random variable? From our knowledge of probability distributions, we know that the following is true:

$$\int p(x)\mathrm{d}x = \int \pi(x)\mathrm{d}z = 1$$

From Chapter 1, *Vector Calculus*, we should remember that an integral is the area under a curve and in probability, this is always equal to 1. This area under the curve can be sliced into infinitesimal rectangles of $\triangle z$ width and the height of this rectangle at z is $\pi(z)$.

Knowing $z=f'(x)$ tells us that the ratio of a small change in z with respect to a small change in x gives us the following:

$$\frac{\triangle z}{\triangle x} = (f^{-1}(x))'$$

We can rewrite this as follows:

$$\triangle z = (f^{-1}(x))'\triangle x$$

Now, we can rewrite our preceding distribution as follows:

$$p(x) = \pi(x)\left|\frac{\mathrm{d}z}{\mathrm{d}x}\right| = \pi(f^{-1}(x))\left|\frac{\mathrm{d}f^{-1}}{\mathrm{d}x}\right|$$

Since we'll we working with vectors, we can express the preceding equation in terms of multiple variables, as follows:

$$p(\mathbf{x}) = \pi(\mathbf{z})\left|\det\frac{\mathrm{d}\mathbf{z}}{\mathrm{d}\mathbf{x}}\right| = \pi(f^{-1}(\mathbf{x}))\left|\det\frac{\mathrm{d}f^{-1}}{\mathrm{d}\mathbf{x}}\right|$$

Great! Now that we have those concepts fresh in our memory, let's move on to understanding what exactly a normalizing flow is.

Getting a good probability density estimation is quite important in deep learning, but it is often very challenging to do. So instead, we use a normalizing flow to approximate the distribution more efficiently by transforming a simple distribution into a more complex one by applying a series of invertible functions on it. The name comes from the fact that the change of variable normalizes the probability density after applying a mapping and the flow means that these simpler transformations can be applied continuously to create a much more complex transformation. It is also required for these transformation functions to be easily invertible and the determinant needs to be simple to compute.

Let's take an initial distribution, apply K transformations (or mappings) to it, and see how we obtain x from it. It works as follows:

$$\mathbf{z}_0 \xrightarrow{f_1()} \mathbf{z}_1 \xrightarrow{f_2()} \cdots \xrightarrow{f_i()} \mathbf{z}_i \xrightarrow{f_{i+1}()} \cdots \xrightarrow{f_K()} \mathbf{z}_K = \mathbf{x}$$

We can also use the following:

$$\mathbf{x} = \mathbf{z}_K = f_K \circ f_{K-1} \circ \cdots f_3 \circ f_2 \circ f_1(\mathbf{z}_0)$$

Here, we have the following parameters:

- $\mathbf{z}_{i-1} \sim p_{i-1}(\mathbf{z}_{i-1})$
- $\mathbf{z}_i = f_i(\mathbf{z}_{i-1})$
- $\mathbf{z}_{i-1} = f_i^{-1}(\mathbf{z}_i)$
- $p_i(\mathbf{z}_i) = p_{i-1}(f_i^{-1}(\mathbf{z}_i)) \left| \det \dfrac{\partial f_i^{-1}}{\partial \mathbf{z}_i} \right|$ (from the change of variables theorem)

 The determinant is a Jacobian matrix.

Let's expand on the fourth equation that we used to find $p_i(z_i)$ to get a clearer picture of it:

$$p_i(\mathbf{z}_i) = p_{i-1}(f_i^{-1}(\mathbf{z}_i)) \left| \det \frac{\partial f_i^{-1}}{\partial \mathbf{z}_i} \right|$$

$$p_i(\mathbf{z}_i) = p_{i-1}(\mathbf{z}_{i-1}) \left| \det \left(\frac{\partial f_i}{\partial \mathbf{z}_{i-1}} \right)^{-1} \right|$$

$$p_i(\mathbf{z}_i) = p_{i-1}(\mathbf{z}_{i-1}) \left| \det \frac{\partial f_i}{\partial \mathbf{z}_{i-1}} \right|^{-1}$$

If we take the logarithm of both sides, we get the following:

$$\log p_i(\mathbf{z}_i) = \log p_{i-1}(\mathbf{z}_{i-1}) - \log \left| \det \frac{\partial f_i}{\partial \mathbf{z}_{i-1}} \right|$$

This tells us the relationship that exists between the sequence of variables and from this, we can obtain the relationship between x and the initial distribution, z_0, through expansion, which looks as follows:

$$\log p(\mathbf{x}) = \log p_K(\mathbf{z}_K) = \log p_0(\mathbf{z}_0) - \sum_{i=1}^{K} \log \left| \det \frac{\partial f_i}{\partial \mathbf{z}_{i-1}} \right|$$

It is this process that is referred to as **normalizing the flow**.

Real-valued non-volume preserving

So far in this chapter, we have covered two very popular generative neural network architectures—VAEs and GANs—both of which are quite powerful and have brought about tremendous results in generating new data. However, both of these architectures also have their challenges. Flow-based generative models, on the other hand, while not as popular, do have their merits.

Some of the advantages of flow-based generative models are as follows:

- They have exact latent-variable inference and log-likelihood evaluation, whereas in VAEs, we can only approximately infer from latent variables, and GANs cannot infer the latent as they do not have an encoder.
- They are efficient to parallelize for both synthesis and inference.
- They have a useful latent space for downstream tasks and so are able to interpolate between data points and modify existing data points.
- They are much more memory-efficient in comparison to GANs and VAEs.

In this section, we will take an in-depth look at a generative probabilistic model known as **real-valued non-volume preserving** (**real NVP**) transformations, which can tractably model high-dimensional data. This model works by stacking together a sequence of invertible bijective transformations.

Let's suppose we have a D-dimensional input, x, it is split into two parts by $d < D$, and the output, y, is computed using the following two equations:

- $y_{1:d} = x_{1:d}$
- $y_{d+1:D} = x_{d+1:D} \odot e^{s(x_{1:d})} + t(x_{1:d})$

Here, $\odot$ is an element-wise product; $s(\bullet)$ and $t(\bullet)$ are scale and translation functions that map $\mathbb{R}^d \to \mathbb{R}^{D-d}$.

Using our knowledge of normalizing flows, we know that this method must satisfy two properties—it must be easily invertible and its Jacobian matrix must be simple to compute. Let's now check whether this method fits both of these criteria.

In the following equation, we can see that it is, in fact, quite simple to find the inverse:

$$\begin{cases} y_{1:d} = x_{1:d} \\ y_{d+1:D} = x_{d+1:D} \odot e^{s(x_{1:d})} + t(x_{1:d}) \end{cases} \Leftrightarrow \begin{cases} x_{1:d} = y_{1:d} \\ x_{d+1:D} = (y_{d+1:D} - t(y_{1:d})) \odot e^{-s(y_{1:d})} \end{cases}$$

Computing the inverse of the coupling layer doesn't require us to compute the inverse of $s(\bullet)$ and $t(\bullet)$, which is great because in this case, both of those functions are CNNs and would be very difficult to invert.

Now, we can determine how easy the Jacobian matrix is to compute:

$$J = \begin{bmatrix} I_d & 0_{d \times (D-d)} \\ \frac{\partial y_{d+1:D}}{\partial x_{1:d}} & \text{diag}(e^{s(x_{1:d})}) \end{bmatrix}$$

This is a lower-triangular matrix. Should we want to find the determinant of the Jacobian matrix, we can do so using the following formula:

$$\det(J) = e^{\sum_{j=1}^{D-d} s(x_{1:d})_j}$$

These two equations for the mapping tell us that when we combine the coupling layers during a forward compute, some of the parts remain unaffected. To overcome this, the authors of this method coupled the layers using an alternating pattern so that all of the parts are updated eventually.

Summary

In this section, we covered a variety of generative models that learn the distribution of true data and try to generate data that is indistinguishable from it. We started with a simple autoencoder and built on it to understand a variant of it that uses variational inference to generate data similar to the input. We then went on to learn about GANs, which pit two models—a discriminator and a generator—against each other in a game so that the generator tries to learn to create data that looks real enough to fool the discriminator into thinking it is real.

Finally, we learned about flow-based networks, which approximate a complex probability density using a simpler one by applying several invertible transformations on it. These models are used in a variety of tasks, including—but not limited to—synthetic data generation to overcome data limitations and extracting insights from data.

In the next chapter, we will learn about transfer and meta-learning, which cover various methods involving transferring the knowledge a network has already learned for one task to bootstrap learning for another task. We will make a distinction between these two methods.

13
Transfer and Meta Learning

So far in this book, we have studied a variety of neural networks and, as we have seen, each of them has its own strengths and weaknesses with regard to a variety of tasks. We have also learned that deep learning architectures require a large amount of training data because of their size and their large number of trainable parameters. As you can imagine, for a lot of the problems that we want to build models for, it may not be possible to collect enough data, and even if we are able to do so, this would be very difficult and time-consuming—perhaps even costly—to carry out. One way to combat this is to use generative models to create synthetic data (something we encountered in Chapter 8, *Regularization*) that is generated from a small dataset that we collect for our task.

In this chapter, we will cover two topics that have recently grown in popularity and are likely to continue to be more widely used in the field (and rightfully so). They are known as **transfer learning** and **meta learning**. The difference between them is that transfer learning is where we try to use what one model has learned to try and solve another different—but similar—problem, whereas meta learning is where we try to create models that can learn to learn new concepts. The literature on transfer learning is very sparse and it is a more hacky practice; we have mostly introduced it because it is important to understand the differences between transfer and meta learning since they are similar but quite different and are often confused. However, the focus of this chapter is meta learning. We will dive deeper into their distinctions as we progress through the chapter.

We will cover the following topics in this chapter:

- Transfer learning
- Meta learning

Transfer learning

We humans have an amazing ability to learn, and then we take what we have learned and apply the knowledge to different types of tasks. The more closely related the new task is to tasks we already know, the easier it is for us to solve the new task. Basically, we never really have to start from scratch when learning something new.

However, neural networks aren't afforded this same luxury; they need to be trained from scratch for each individual task we want to apply them to. As we have seen in previous chapters, neural networks are very good at learning how to do one thing very well, and because they only learn what lies within an interpolation of the distribution they have been trained to recognize, they are unable to generalize their knowledge to deal with tasks beyond what they have encountered in the training dataset.

In addition, deep neural networks can require tens of millions of data samples in order to learn the latent patterns in the data before they are able to perform well. For this reason, researchers in the field created transfer learning—a way to transfer what one neural network has learned to another neural network, essentially bootstrapping the learning process. This is very handy when we have a project that we want to build or a hypothesis that we would like to test but we don't have the resources (such as GPUs, enough data, and so on) to build and train a network from scratch. Instead, we can use an existing model that works on a similar task and leverage it for our own task.

Let's think back to Chapter 9, *Convolutional Neural Networks*, for a moment. The architectures we saw all had an input layer that took in images of a certain size ($h \times w \times c$), and then we had multiple convolutional layers followed by an optional pooling (or subsampling) layer. Toward the end of the network, we unrolled the feature map into a fully connected layer, and then the output layer had as many nodes as classes we wanted to detect. We also learned that **Convolutional Neural Networks** (**CNNs**) can extract their own features and each layer learns different kinds or levels of features. The layers closer to the input learn very granular features, such as edges, curves, color blobs, and so on, while the layers closer to the output learn larger features, such as eyes, ears, tails, mouths, and so on.

What we can do is take an existing trained CNN and remove the last few layers (that is, the fully connected layers and the output layer) and treat this CNN as a feature extractor for the new dataset we are building a model for. Alternatively, what we could also do is use an existing trained CNN for a new problem by fine-tuning it on the new dataset we want to create a CNN for. We can do this by freezing the earlier layers (since they learn very granular or generic features) and fine-tuning the latter layers using backpropagation so that the CNN learns more complex features that are specific to the new dataset.

Before we get into the details of transfer learning, it is important that we have a clear understanding of it. We will use the definition given by Zhuang et al; but before that, let's revisit the definitions of a domain and a task.

A **domain**, $\mathcal{D}$, is composed of two parts; that is, a feature space, $\mathcal{X}$, and a marginal distribution, $P(X)$. In other words, $\mathcal{D} = \{\mathcal{X}, P(X)\}$, where X denotes a data sample, which is defined as $X = \{\mathbf{x} \mid \mathbf{x}_i \in \mathcal{X}, i = 1, \cdots, n\}$.

A **task**, $\mathcal{T}$, consists of a label space, $\mathcal{Y}$, and a mapping function, f; that is, $\mathcal{T} = \{\mathcal{Y}, f\}$. The mapping function (our model) is an implicit one that is expected to be learned from the sample data.

In the case of transfer learning, we have two distinct domains and tasks—each corresponding to a source and a target—where our goal is to transfer what a model has learned in the source domain to a model in the target domain in order to improve its overall performance.

Before we go further into the details of this, there are four concepts that are important for us to understand. They are as follows:

- The feature space of the target domain, $\mathcal{X}_t$, and the source domain, $\mathcal{X}_s$, are not the same.
- The label space of the target domain, $\mathcal{Y}_t$, and source domain, $\mathcal{Y}_s$, are not the same.
- Domain adaptation—this is where the marginal probabilities of the target domain, $P(X_t)$, and the source domain, $P(X_s)$, are not equal.
- The conditional probabilities of the target domain, $P(Y_t | X_t)$, and the source domain, $P(Y_s | X_s)$, are not equal.

As you can imagine, there are some limitations here as to what can be done. You cannot use just any pre-trained model of arbitrary size on another task. Consideration of the type of pre-trained network to use largely depends on whether the dataset we have for our task is similar to the one that the pre-trained model was trained on, and on the size of the dataset available to us for the current task at hand. For example, if we have an object detection task, we cannot use a pre-trained GAN or RNN for it since they are meant for different tasks. Additionally, if the model has been trained on images to recognize various farm animals, it will not perform well on a new task that wants our network to recognize the make and model of aircraft and cars.

Meta learning

Meta learning—also known as **learning to learn**—is another fascinating topic within deep learning and is considered by many to be a promising path toward **Artificial General Intelligence (AGI)**. For those of you who do not know what AGI is, it is when artificial intelligence reaches the capacity to understand and learn to do any type of intelligent task that a human is capable of doing, which is the goal of artificial intelligence.

Deep neural networks, as we know, are very data-hungry and require a lot of training time (depending on the size of the model), which can sometimes be several weeks, whereas humans are able to learn new concepts and skills a lot faster and more efficiently. For example, as kids, we can quickly learn to tell the difference between a donkey, a horse, and a zebra with absolute certainty after only seeing them once or a handful of times; however, a neural network would likely need a few hundred thousand to 1 million data samples to be able to learn to differentiate between the three classes to expert-level accuracy.

Approaches to meta learning

The question we are trying to answer with meta learning is whether we can create a model that can learn as we do—that is, learn new concepts and skills to deal with new tasks with only a handful of training samples. So, in a nutshell, we want to find similarities between what we have learned and use this to learn to do new tasks faster. A good meta learning model is one that is trained on a number of tasks and has been optimized to perform well on them, as well as on tasks that it has not been trained on.

The deep neural networks that we have seen throughout this book so far all required millions of data samples, sometimes even several hundreds of millions. However, in meta learning, we want our model to learn using only a few samples; we refer to this as few-shot learning.

The problem of learning using only a few data samples is known as **few-shot learning** or **k-shot learning** (where k is the number of data samples for each class of the dataset). Suppose we have an image recognition problem with three classes—a donkey, a horse, and a zebra. If each class has 10 samples, then this is referred to as 10-shot learning. However, if each class has only 1 sample, then this is 1-shot learning. There could also be another interesting case where we have no data samples, which is known as **zero-shot learning**. (That's right, we can train a neural network without any data... just kidding! We use metadata instead; we'll learn about this soon.)

If we have multiple classes in our dataset and we want to carry out few-shot learning, this is known as **n-way k-shot learning**, where n is the number of classes. In our case, we have 3 classes and 10 samples for each, so we are carrying out 3-way 10-shot learning.

Each of the preceding tasks will have an associated dataset, $\mathcal{D} = (x_i, y_i)$ (consisting of the data samples and the respective labels). As we know, our model, f, has trainable parameters, θ, so we can represent the model as learning the following:

$$P_\theta(y \mid x)$$

Here, $\theta^* = \arg\max_\theta \mathbb{E}_{(x,y)\in\mathcal{D}} [P_\theta(y \mid x)]$.

For meta learning, we split our dataset into two portions—a support set, S, and a query set, B—such that $\mathcal{D} = (S, B)$. Then, we take a subset of the $Y \in \mathcal{Y}$ labels, such that $S^Y, B^Y \in \mathcal{D}$. We then train our model on the support set while testing on the query set, which we do in an episodic fashion. The support set is built through sampling from each of the classes of $\mathcal{D}$ and the prediction set is built similarly using other samples from the same dataset. By using this method, our model gradually learns to learn from smaller datasets. We then calculate the loss of the model and optimize it using backpropagation using the training set, exactly as we did before.

The objective now looks as follows:

$$\theta = \arg\max_\theta \mathbb{E}_{Y \in \mathcal{Y}} \left[\mathbb{E}_{S^Y \subset \mathcal{D}, B^Y \subset \mathcal{D}} \left[\sum_{(x,y)\in B^Y} P_\theta(x, y, S^Y) \right] \right]$$

As you can see, this is somewhat similar to transfer learning, except it goes a step further by optimizing to perform well over several tasks instead of just one.

There are three types of meta learning approaches used in practice, as follows:

- Model-based
- Metric-based
- Optimization-based

Model-based meta learning

In model-based meta learning, we want to create a model that is able to learn and update its parameters quickly using only a handful of training steps. We can do this internally (within the model) or externally (using another model). Let's now explore some of the methods.

Memory-augmented neural networks

As the name suggests, **Memory-Augmented Neural Networks (MANNs)** are augmented using external memory (a storage buffer), which makes it easier for the model to learn and retain new information so as to not forget it later on. One of the approaches that is used is training a **Neural Turing Machine (NTM)** to learn a learning algorithm by altering the training setup and memory retrieval.

To adapt an NTM for meta learning, we need it to be able to encode information related to new tasks quickly, while also ensuring that the stored information can be accessed quickly. The way this works is we pass the information at the present time step and the corresponding label at the next time step, which forces the network to retain information for longer. So, at each time step, the network receives the following:

$$(x_{t+1}, y_t)$$

In the following diagram, we can observe what the network looks like:

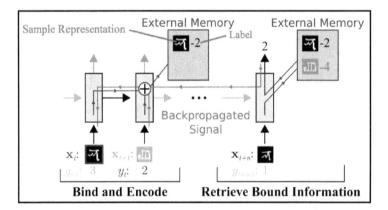

By providing the label later, the network is forced to memorize information so that when it is given the label, it can look back and recall the data to make a prediction. To ensure the model is best suited for meta learning, the reading and writing mechanisms have also been altered.

Reading works using content similarity, as follows:

$$r_i = \sum_{i=1}^{N} w_t^r(i) M_t(i)$$

Here, $w_t^r(i) = \text{softmax}\left(\dfrac{k_t \cdot M_t(i)}{\|k_t\| \cdot \|M_t(i)\|} \right)$, k_t is a key feature vector output by the controller at the tth time step, w_t^r is a read weight over N elements calculated through the cosine similarity between each of the rows in memory, k_t and r_t are the sum of the weighted memory records, and M_t is the memory matrix (while $M_t(i)$ is its ith row).

Now, to write to memory, we use **Least Recently Used Access (LRUA)**, which writes new information to the location where either the **Least Recently Used (LRU)** memory or **Most Frequently Used (MRU)** memory is stored. The reasoning for this is that by replacing the LRU memory, we will be able to maintain information that is used more frequently, and once the MRU memory is retrieved, it likely won't be needed for a while, so we can write over it.

We compute LRUA using the following equations:

- $w_t^u = \gamma w_{t-1}^u + w_t^r + w_t^w$
- $w_t^r = \text{softmax}(\text{cosine}(k_t, M_t(i)))$
- $w_t^w = \sigma(\alpha)w_{t-1}^r + (1 - \sigma(\alpha))w_{t-1}^{lu}$
- $w_t^{lu} = 1_{w_t^u(i) \le m(w_t^u, n)}$, where $m(w_t^u, n)$ is the nth smallest element in w_t^u

In the last update equations, when the LRU memory is set to 0, each of the rows in memory is updated using the following equation:

$$M_t(i) = M_{t-1}(i) + w_t^2(i)k_t$$

Now that we have seen how meta learning can work using external memory to learn new information by overriding the information it hasn't used in a while, we will move on to another model-based meta learning approach, which uses its internal architecture to rapidly learn new information.

Meta Networks

Meta Networks (**MetaNet**) is an architecture created to generalize across tasks quickly; it uses fast weights to do so. The reason they are called fast weights is that instead of using gradient descent to update weights as we normally do, we use a neural network to predict the weights for another neural network. The weights the other neural network generates are referred to as fast weights, while the weights that rely on gradient descent are referred to as slow weights. The effect of this is that it supports meta-level continual learning.

In the following figure, you can see the overall architecture of MetaNet:

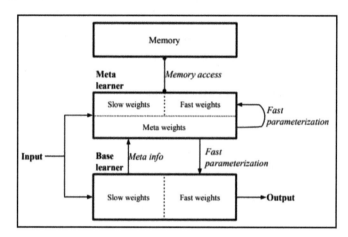

MetaNet is comprised of two components—a meta learner, which learns an embedding function, f_θ, to help determine the similarity between two data inputs and verify whether both inputs belong to the same class, and a base learner, g_φ, which carries out the actual learning. As you can see in the preceding diagram, both the fast weights and the slow weights are summed together and input back into the model. Both the meta learner and the base learner have their own respective fast weights.

This requires two neural networks—F_w (an LSTM whose inputs are the embedding loss of f) and G_v (an ANN)—each of which outputs the fast weights for f_θ and g_φ. The fast weights corresponding to f_θ and g_θ are θ^* and φ^*, respectively. The difference between the two is that the input to F_w is the gradient of the embedding loss of f, while G_v learns using the gradients of the loss of g.

As you can see, this means we have to learn four different sets of parameters (θ, ϕ, w, v). To train our networks, we make use of two datasets—a training set, $\{x_i, y_i\}_{i=1}^L$, and a support set, $\{x_i', y_i'\}_{i=1}^N$.

The overall training of this network can be broken down into three distinct parts:

- Acquiring the meta information
- Generating the fast weights
- Optimizing the slow weights

We start by creating a sequence of tasks, each of which has a training set and a support set, and randomly sample T input pairs, $(\mathbf{x}_i', y_i)$ and $(\mathbf{x}_j', y_j)$, from the support—where $T < N$—and then calculate the cross-entropy loss for the embeddings for the verification task.

We then compute the fast weights for the task level, $\theta^+ = F_w(\nabla_\theta L_{embed,1}, \nabla_\theta L_{embed,T})$. Once this is complete, we compute the fast weights at the example level, $\phi^+ = G_v(\nabla_\phi L_{task,1}, \cdots, \nabla_\phi L_{task,T})$, from the support set and update the ith location of the value memory, M, (for the meta learned) with ϕ_i^+. Then, we encode the sampled point from the support set into the task space with fast and slow weights using $r_i' = f_{\theta,\theta'}(\mathbf{x}_i')$, which is updated at the ith location of the key memory, R (for the base learner).

Once this is done, we sample from the test set and encode them into the task space using $r_j = f_{\theta,\theta'}(\mathbf{x}_j)$, then we calculate the cosine similarity to find out how similar the memory index and the input embedding are.

Metric-based meta learning

Metric-based meta learning uses a concept similar to what is used in clustering, where we try to learn the distance between objects. This is similar to kernel density estimation, where we use a kernel function, k_θ, to calculate weight or how similar two samples are, then find the predicted probability over the labels:

$$P_\theta(y \mid x, S) = \sum_{(x_i, y_i) \in S} k_\theta(x, x_i) y_i$$

This class of meta learning algorithms explicitly learns the embedding of the data to create optimal kernels.

Prototypical networks

Prototypical networks are a type of meta learning algorithm used for few-shot learning. The way this works is we use an encoding function, f_θ, to encode each of the D-dimensional inputs into an M-dimensional vector. This prototype vector is defined as follows:

$$v_c = \frac{1}{|S_c|} \sum_{(x_i, y_i) \in S_c} f_\theta(x_i)$$

This is the case for each class of $c \in C$. We then calculate the distance, $d : \mathbb{R}^M \times \mathbb{R}^M \to [0, +\infty)$, between the embedding of the test data and the prototype vector, then use it to calculate the probability distribution over the classes, as follows:

$$P(y = c \mid x) = \mathrm{softmax}(-d_\phi(f_\theta(x)), v_c) = \frac{e^{(-d_\phi(f_\theta(x)), v_c)}}{\sum_{c' \in C} e^{(-d_\phi(f_\theta(x)), v_{c'})}}$$

Here, d_φ is the distance function, but φ must be differentiable.

In the following diagram, we can see the prototypical network compute the few-shot prototypes and the zero-shot prototypes:

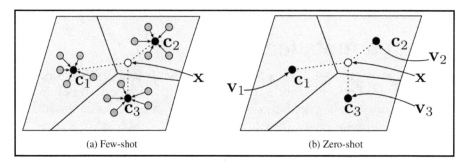

(a) Few-shot   (b) Zero-shot

Siamese neural networks

The Siamese neural network is an architecture that is comprised of two identical neural networks with shared weights, and their parameters are trained to determine the similarity between two data samples using a distance metric on the embeddings. This architecture has proven to be effective for one-shot image classification where the network learns to tell whether or not two images belong to the same class.

In the following diagram, we can see that the network takes in two images and each passes through an identical CNN (f_θ) to generate feature vectors (the embeddings):

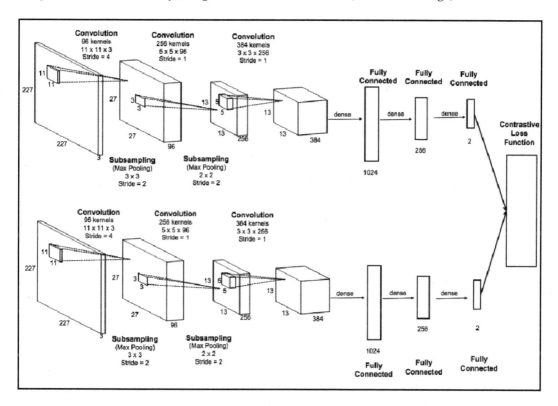

Once the embeddings are calculated, we can then calculate the distance between the two embeddings, as follows:

$$\| f_\theta(x_i) - f_\theta(x_j) \|_2^2$$

The output from the distance is passed through a **multilayer perceptron (MLP)** with a sigmoid function to compute the probability of whether the two inputs belong to the same class.

Since the labels for the image are binary (*1* for yes and *0* for no), we calculate the loss using cross-entropy:

$$L(x_i, x_j) = \sum_{x_i, y_i, x_j, y_j} \mathbf{1}_{y_i = y_j} \log p(x_i, x_j) + (1 - \mathbf{1}_{y_i = y_j} \log(1 - p(x_i, x_j)))$$

We calculate the probability of which class it belongs to using the following:

$$\hat{c}_S(x) = c(\arg\max_{x_i \in S} P(x, x_i))$$

Here, S is a support set, x is a test image, $c(x)$ is the label corresponding to the image, and $\hat{c}(\cdot)$ is the class prediction.

Optimization-based meta learning

In Chapter 7, *Feedforward Neural Networks*, we covered backpropagation and gradient descent as a way to optimize the parameters of our model to reduce the loss; but we also saw that it is quite slow and requires a lot of training samples and so a lot of compute power. To overcome this, we use optimization-based meta learning, where we learn the optimization process. But how do we do that?

Long Short-Term Memory meta learners

Let's think back to when we learned about gradient-based optimization for a moment. What happened there? We started at an initial point in the parameter space and then calculated the gradient and took a step toward the local/global minima, then repeated these steps. In gradient descent, with momentum, we used the history of previous updates to guide the next one. If you think about it carefully, this is slightly similar to RNNs and **Long Short-Term Memory** (**LSTM**), so we can just replace the entire process of gradient descent with an RNN. This approach is known as **learning to learn by gradient descent**. The reasoning behind this name is that we train RNNs using gradient descent and then we use the RNN to perform the gradient descent. In this scenario, we call the RNN the optimizer and the base model the optimizee.

As we know, vanilla RNNs have their problems (vanishing gradient), so here, we are going to cover optimizing the model using LSTM cells. But first, let's revisit how parameter optimization works. It looks as follows:

$$\theta_t = \theta_{t-1} - \alpha_t \nabla_{\theta_{t-1}} L_t$$

Let's compare this with the updates in an LSTM cell:

$$C_t = f_t C_{t-1} + I_t \tilde{C}_t$$

Here, $C_t = \theta_t$, $f_t = 1$, $I_t = \alpha_t$ and $\tilde{C}_t = -\nabla_{\theta_{t-1}} L_t$. However, the forget gate and input gate do not have to be fixed; they can be learned so that we can adapt them for other tasks. The calculations for the forget gate, input gate, candidate layer, and memory state now become the following, respectively:

- $f_t = \sigma(W_f \cdot [\nabla_{\theta_{t-1}} L_t, L_t, \theta_{t-1}, f_{t-1}] + b_f)$
- $I_t = \sigma(W_I \cdot [\nabla_{\theta_{t-1}} L_t, L_t, \theta_{t-1}, I_{t-1}] + b_I)$
- $\tilde{\theta}_t = -\nabla_{\theta_{t-1}} L_t$
- $\theta_t = f_t \theta_{t-1} + I_t \tilde{\theta}_t$

In the following diagram, we can see how the LSTM meta learner is structured:

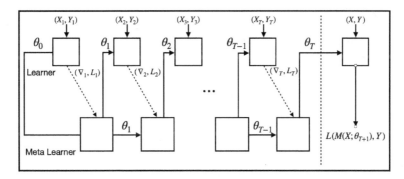

During the training process, we want to try and mimic what will happen during the testing process, and during training, we sample a dataset as follows:

$$\mathcal{D} = (\mathcal{D}_{\text{train}}, \mathcal{D}_{\text{test}}) \in \hat{\mathcal{D}}_{\text{meta-train}}$$

Following this, we sample from $\mathcal{D}_{\text{train}}$ to update the parameters of the model by a total number of T iterations and calculate the loss with respect to the weights of the base model (θ), as well as feeding the loss, gradients, and meta learner parameter (φ) to the optimizer (meta learner). The meta learner will then output the new cell state, which we use to update the parameters of the base model.

Once we have completed T iterations, we can expect to have found an optimal parameter for the base model. To test the goodness of θ_T and update the parameters of the meta learner, we find the loss on the test data with respect to θ_T, then find the gradients of the test loss with respect to φ, to perform updates to φ for N iterations.

Model-agnostic meta learning

Model-Agnostic Meta Learning (MAML) is an optimization algorithm that can work on any type of neural network that is trained using gradient descent. Suppose we have a model, f, with parameters, θ, and a task, τ_i, that has a corresponding dataset $(\mathcal{D}^{(i)}_{\text{train}}, \mathcal{D}^{(i)}_{\text{test}})$. Then, we can make updates to the model using a single or several gradient descent steps. A single step in this algorithm works as follows:

$$\theta'_i = \theta - \nabla_\theta L^{(0)}_{\tau_i}(f_\theta)$$

The preceding step learns to optimize a single task, but we would like to optimize multiple tasks. So, we can change the task to find the optimal parameters over multiple tasks as follows:

$$\theta^* = \arg\min_\theta \sum_{\tau_i \sim p(\tau)} L^{(1)}_{\tau_i}(f_{\theta'_i}) = \arg\min_\theta \sum_{\tau_i \sim p(\tau)} L^{(1)}_{\tau_i}\left(f_{\theta - \alpha\nabla_\theta L^{(0)}_{\tau_i}(f_\theta)}\right)$$

$$\theta \leftarrow \theta - \beta\nabla_\theta \sum_{\tau_i \sim p(\tau)} L^{(1)}_{\tau_i}\left(f_{\theta - \alpha\nabla_\theta L^{(0)}_{\tau_i}(f_\theta)}\right)$$

Here, $L^{(0)}$ is the loss corresponding to the initial training batch and $L^{(1)}$ is the loss for the next training batch.

This looks pretty similar to the gradient descent we know, so what's special about it? What this is doing is learning the parameters associated with other tasks and attempting to learn the best initial parameters to use for the next task to reduce the training time. However, this uses second-order optimization, which is a bit more computationally intensive, so instead, we can use a first-order method, which is more feasible. This method is known as **First-Order Model-Agnostic Meta Learning (FOMAML)**. Let's see the difference between the two in the following calculations.

Let's consider a case where we perform n gradient descent steps, where $n \geq 1$. Our starting point is θ_{meta} and the steps are as follows:

$$\theta_0 = \theta_{\text{meta}}$$
$$\theta_1 = \theta_0 - \alpha\nabla_\theta L^{(0)}(\theta_0)$$
$$\vdots$$
$$\theta_n = \theta_{n-1} - \alpha\nabla_\theta L^{(0)}(\theta_{n-1})$$

Once n steps are computed, we sample the next batch and perform updates over it. This then becomes the following:

$$\theta_{\text{meta}} \leftarrow \theta_{\text{meta}} - \beta g_{\text{MAML}}$$

Here,
$$g_{\text{MAML}} = \nabla_{\theta_k} L^{(1)}(\theta_k) \prod_{i=1}^{k} (I - \alpha \nabla_{\theta_{i-1}}(\nabla_\theta L^{(0)}(\theta_{i-1}))) \quad .$$

However, the gradient in FOMAML is as follows:

$$g_{\text{FOMAML}} = \nabla_{\theta_k} L^{(1)}(\theta_k)$$

Congratulations—you have now completed this chapter on transfer learning and meta learning!

Summary

In this chapter, we covered two very fascinating areas within the field of deep learning—transfer learning and meta learning—both of which hold the promise of furthering the field of not only deep learning but also artificial intelligence by enabling neural networks to learn additional tasks and generalize over unseen distributions. We explored several meta learning approaches, including model-based, metric-based, and optimization-based, and explored how they differ.

In the next chapter, we will learn about geometric deep learning.

14
Geometric Deep Learning

Throughout this book, we have learned about various types of neural networks that are used in deep learning, such as convolutional neural networks and recurrent neural networks, and they have achieved some tremendous results in a variety of tasks, such as computer vision, image reconstruction, synthetic data generation, speech recognition, language translation, and so on. All of the models we have looked at so far have been trained on Euclidean data, that is, data that can be represented in grid (matrix) format—images, text, audio, and so on.

However, many of the tasks that we would like to apply deep learning to use non-Euclidean data (more on this shortly) – the kind that the neural networks we have come across so far are unable to process and deal with. This includes dealing with sensor networks, mesh surfaces, point clouds, objects (the kind used in computer graphics), social networks, and so on. In general, geometric deep learning is designed to help deep neural networks generalize to graphs and manifolds (we learned about graphs in `Chapter 5`, *Graph Theory*, and we will learn about manifolds shortly in this chapter).

We will cover the following topics in this chapter:

- Comparing Euclidean and non-Euclidean data
- Graph neural networks
- Spectral graph CNNs
- Mixture model networks
- Facial recognition in 3D

Let's get started!

Comparing Euclidean and non-Euclidean data

Before we learn about geometric deep learning techniques, it is important for us to understand the differences between Euclidean and non-Euclidean data, and why we need a separate approach to deal with it.

Deep learning architectures such as FNNs, CNNs, and RNNs have proven successful for a variety of tasks, such as speech recognition, machine translation, image reconstruction, object recognition and segmentation, and motion tracking, in the last 8 years. This is because of their ability to exploit and use the local statistical properties that exist within data. These properties include stationarity, locality, and compositionality. In the case of CNNs, the data they take as input can be represented in a grid form (such as images, which can be represented by matrices and tensors).

The stationarity, in this case (images), comes from the fact that CNNs have the following:

- Shift invariance, owing to the use of convolutions.
- The locality can be attributed to local connectivity since the kernels are observing not just singular pixels but neighboring pixels as well.
- The compositionality comes from it being made up of multiple scales (or hierarchies) where simpler structures are combined to represent more abstract structures.

However, not all data can be expressed in the format required for deep neural networks, and if it can be contorted into grid form, this means that we have had to sacrifice a lot of the relationships that existed in the complex data in favor of a much more simple representation that our neural networks can take as input.

These three properties limit what neural networks can learn and the kinds of problems we can use them for.

A lot of the data that exists in the real world, as you may have guessed, cannot be properly captured in a grid. This kind of data can, however, be represented using graphs or manifolds. Examples of data that can be represented by graphs include social networks, academic paper citation networks, communication networks, knowledge graphs, molecules, and road maps. On the other hand, we can make use of Riemannian manifolds (more on this in the next section) to represent three-dimensional objects (which are volumetric) such as animals, human bodies, faces, airplanes, chairs, and so on. In a nutshell, both are methods of capturing the relationships that may exist between nodes.

This type of data is difficult for neural networks to deal with because it lacks the structure they are used to being fed during training. For example, we may want to use the weight (or strength) between two nodes to represent the closeness of two people in a social network. In this scenario, we would do this to make a suggestion regarding a new friend for a user to add to their existing network. However, there is no straightforward method we can use to represent this information in a feature vector.

Before we learn about the methods used in geometric deep learning, let's learn what exactly a manifold is.

Manifolds

A **manifold** is any topological space where, in the neighborhood of any point, (p), it is topologically equivalent (or homeomorphic) to a k-dimensional Euclidean space. We encountered the term manifold earlier in this book, but we didn't define it properly, so we will do that now. The preceding definition probably sounds a bit daunting, but it will make a lot more sense in a moment.

Suppose we have a one-dimensional manifold. For simplicity, we will work with a circle, or a disk, (which we denote as S^1) that exists in $\mathbb{R}^2$ (there are other one-dimensional manifolds, as well, such as parabolas, hyperbolas, and cubic curves, but that doesn't concern us right now).

Let's suppose we have the following manifold:

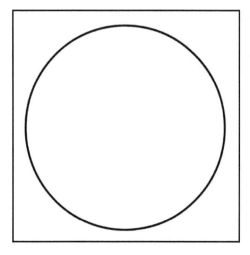

Now, if we were to zoom into the curve of the circle on the top-left quadrant a bunch of times, eventually, we would arrive at a magnification where the curve appears to look like a straight line (sort of like a tangent at that point):

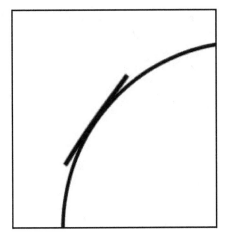

As shown in the preceding image, we have zoomed into the top left and have drawn a tangent at a point, and at that point, the curve is almost parallel to the tangent line. The more we zoom in, the more the line appears to be straight.

Similarly, if we have a two-dimensional manifold such as a sphere (which we denote as S^2) that exists in $\mathbb{R}^3$ and we zoom into it, then at any point on the surface, it will appear to look like a flat disk. A manifold does not necessarily have to be a sphere; it can be any topological space that has the characteristics of a manifold. To visualize this, consider the Earth to be a manifold. From anywhere you stand and look, the Earth appears to look flat (or planar), even though it is curved.

We can write the unit circle and unit sphere, respectively, as follows:

- $S^1 = \{(x, y) \in \mathbb{R}^2 \mid x^2 + y^2 = 1\}$
- $S^2 = \{(x, y, z) \in \mathbb{R}^3 \mid x^2 + y^2 + z^2 = 1\}$

Similarly, we can also write higher-dimensional manifolds as follows:

$$S^n = \{x \in \mathbb{R}^{n+1} \mid \|x\| = 1\}$$

Formally, a (differentiable) k-dimensional manifold M in $\mathbb{R}^n$ is a set of points in $\mathbb{R}^n$ where for every point, $p \in M$, there is a small open neighborhood, U, of p, a vector-valued differentiable function, $F : \mathbb{R}^k \rightarrow \mathbb{R}^n$, and an open set, $V \in \mathbb{R}^k$, with the following:

- $F(V) = U \cap M$
- The Jacobian of F has rank, k, at each of the points in V, where the Jacobian of F is an $n \times k$ matrix that looks as follows:

$$
J = \begin{bmatrix}
\frac{\partial f_1}{\partial x_1} & \frac{\partial f_1}{\partial x_2} & \cdots & \frac{\partial f_1}{\partial x_k} \\
\frac{\partial f_2}{\partial x_1} & \frac{\partial f_2}{\partial x_2} & \cdots & \frac{\partial f_2}{\partial x_k} \\
\vdots & \vdots & \ddots & \vdots \\
\frac{\partial f_n}{\partial x_1} & \frac{\partial f_n}{\partial x_2} & \cdots & \frac{\partial f_n}{\partial x_k}
\end{bmatrix}
$$

Here, F is the local parameterization of the manifold.

We can also use existing topological spaces to create new ones using Cartesian products. Suppose we have two topological spaces, X and Y, and that their Cartesian product is $X \times Y$, where each $x \in X$ and $y \in Y$ generates a point, $(x, y) \in X \times Y$. A familiar Cartesian product is a three-dimensional Euclidean space, where $\mathbb{R} \times \mathbb{R} \times \mathbb{R} = \mathbb{R}^3$. However, it is important to note that $S^1 \times S^1 \neq S^2$ (it is actually equal to T^2, which is a ring torus, but we will avoid going into why since that goes beyond the scope of this book).

In computer graphics, we use two-dimensional manifolds embedded in $\mathbb{R}^3$ to represent boundary surfaces of three-dimensional objects.

Since these parametric manifolds are objects, they will have an orientation, and to define this, we will need what is known as the tangent space to the manifold. However, before we're able to define the tangent space, we need to clarify some concepts. Suppose again that we have a k-dimensional manifold, M, defined in $\mathbb{R}^n$ (where $k < n$). Here, for each $p \in M$, there is an open set, U, containing p and $(n-k)$ real-valued $\rho_1, \cdots, \rho_{n-k}$ functions, defined on U such that $(\rho_1 = 0) \cap \cdots \cap (\rho_{n-k} = 0) = M \cap U$ and at each point, $q \in M \cap U$, we have the following linearly independent vectors:

$$
\nabla \rho_1(q), \cdots, \nabla \rho_{n-k}(q)
$$

Now, the normal space to M at p is written as $N_p(M)$ and is spanned by the following vectors:

$$\nabla \rho_1(p), \cdots, \nabla \rho_{n-k}(p)$$

As we already know, tangents are perpendicular to normal vectors, and so the tangent space, $T_p(M)$, to the manifold at p consists of all the vectors, $\mathbf{v} \in \mathbb{R}^n$, that are perpendicular to each of the normal vectors, $N_p(M)$. However, $\mathbf{v} = (v_1, \cdots, v_n)$ is only in $T_p(M)$ if—and only if—for all of $i = 1, \cdots, n - k$, we have the following:

$$\mathbf{v} \cdot \nabla \rho_i(p) = \sum_{j=1}^{n} \frac{\partial \rho_i(p)}{\partial x_j} v_j = 0$$

Once we have our tangent space, we can use it to define a Riemannian metric, which is as follows:

$$\langle \cdot, \cdot \rangle_{T_p(M)} : T_p(M) \times T_p(M) \to \mathbb{R}$$

This metric allows us to perform local measurements of angles, distances, and volumes, as well as any manifold that this metric is defined on. This is known as a **Riemannian manifold**.

Before we move on, there are two terms that are important for us to become familiar with:

- **Isometry**: Metric preserving shape deformation
- **Geodesic**: Shortest path on M between p and p'

Interestingly, we can define manifolds using scalar fields and vector fields, which means we can extend calculus to manifolds. In this case, we need to introduce three new concepts, as follows:

- **Scalar field**: $f : M \to \mathbb{R}$

- **Vector field**: $F : M \to TM$

- **Hilbert space with inner products**:

$$\langle f, g \rangle_{L^2(M)} = \int_M f(p)g(p)\mathrm{d}p$$
$$\langle F, G \rangle_{L^2(TM)} = \int_M \langle F(p), G(p) \rangle_{T_pM} \mathrm{d}p$$

A Hilbert space is an abstract vector space that merely generalizes the concept of Euclidean space. So, the methods we learned about regarding vector algebra and calculus can be extended from two-dimensional and three-dimensional Euclidean space to an arbitrary or infinite number of dimensions.

Naturally, if we are going to define calculus on manifolds, we want to be able to take derivatives, but this isn't as clear as it is for curves. For manifolds, we make use of the tangent space, such that $df(p) = \langle \nabla f(p), \cdot \rangle_{T_p M}$ and the directional derivative is $df(p)F(p) = \langle \nabla f(p), F(p) \rangle_{T_p M}$, which tells us how much f changes at point p in the direction $F(p)$. And the intrinsic gradient operator, which tells us the direction that the change of f is most steep in, is calculated from the following equation:

$$\nabla f : L^2(M) \to L^2(TM)$$

The intrinsic divergence operator calculates the net flow of the field, F, at point p through the following equation:

$$\text{div} : L^2(TM) \to L^2(M)$$

Using this, we can find the formal adjoint of the gradient, as follows:

$$\langle F, \nabla f \rangle_{L^2(TM)} = \langle \nabla^* F, f \rangle_{L^2(M)} = \langle -\text{div}F, f \rangle_{L^2(M)}$$

Now, we can find the Laplacian, $\triangle : L^2(M) \to L^2(M)$, which calculates the difference between $f(x)$ and the average value of f in the vicinity of point p using $\triangle f = -\text{div}(\nabla f)$, which tells us that the Laplacian is isometry-invariant (an isometry is a distance preserving transformation between metric spaces. However, in geometry, we sometimes want the shape of an object to be defined in a way that is invariant to isometries. This means the object can be deformed so that it gets bent but not stretched, thus not affecting the intrinsic distances), positive-definite, and symmetric, as follows:

$$\langle \triangle f, g \rangle_{L^2(M)} = \langle f, \triangle g \rangle_{L^2(M)}$$

Discrete manifolds

For a moment, let's think back to `Chapter 5`, *Graph Theory*, where we learned about graph theory. As a quick refresher, a graph, G, is made up of vertices, $V = \{1, 2, \cdots, n\}$, and edges, $E \subseteq V \times V$, and the undirected edge, $(i, j) \in E$ iff $(j, i) \in E$. The edges of weighted graphs have weights, $w_{i,j} \geq 0$ for all $(i, j) \in E$, and vertexes can have weights as well for all $i \in V$, the vertex weight, $a_i > 0$.

The reason we care about graphs here is because we can also do calculus on graphs. To do this, we will need to define a vertex field, $f : V \to \mathbb{R}$, and an edge field, $f : E \to \mathbb{R}$ (we also assume that $F_{i,j} = -F_{j,i}$). The Hilbert spaces with inner products are $\langle f, g \rangle_{L^2(V)} = \sum_{i \in V} a_i f_i g_i$ and $\langle F, G \rangle_{L^2(E)} = \sum_{i \in E} w_{i,j} F_{i,j} G_{i,j}$.

As we no doubt know by now, in calculus, we are very fond of gradients, and naturally, we can define a gradient operator for graphs, $\nabla : L^2(V) \to L^2(E)$, giving us $(\nabla f)_{i,j} = f_i - f_j$ and a divergence operator, $\mathrm{div} : L^2(E) \to L^2(V)$, that produces $(\mathrm{div} F)_i = \frac{1}{a_i} \sum_{j:(i,j) \in E} w_{i,j} F_{i,j}$ and is adjoint to the gradient operator, $\langle F, \nabla f \rangle_{L^2(E)} = \langle \nabla^* F, f \rangle_{L^2(V)} = \langle -\mathrm{div} F, f \rangle_{L^2(V)}$.

The graph Laplacian operator, $\triangle : L^2(V) \to L^2(V)$, is defined as $\triangle = -\mathrm{div} \nabla$. By combining the preceding two equations, we can obtain the following:

$$(\triangle f)_i = \frac{1}{a_i} \sum_{j:(i,j) \in E} w_{i,j}(f_i - f_j)$$

As in the case of manifolds, this calculates the difference between f and its local average (that is, of the neighboring nodes). We can rewrite this as a positive semi-definite square matrix:

$$\triangle = A^{-1}(D - W)$$

We can also write this as an unnormalized Laplacian, where $A = I$:

$$\triangle = D - W$$

Finally, we can write it for the random walk Laplacian, where $A = D$:

$$\triangle = D^{-1}(D - W)$$

Here, $W = (w_{i,j})$, $A = \text{diag}(a_1, a_2, \cdots, a_n)$, and $D = \text{diag}\left(\sum_{j \neq i} w_{i,j}\right)$.

Using graphs, we can formulate discrete manifolds, that is, describe three-dimensional objects using vertices, $V = \{1, \cdots, n\}$, edges, $E \subseteq V \times V$, and faces, $F = \{(i, j, k) \in V \times V \times V : (i, j), (j, k), (k, i) \in E\}$. This is generally referred to as a triangular mesh. In a manifold mesh, each edge is shared by two faces and each vertex has one loop.

Before we move on, let's redefine the Laplacian on triangular meshes using the cotangent formula, which can be defined for an embedded mesh that has the coordinates $\{x_1, \cdots, x_n\}$ and in terms of the lengths of the edges.

The cotangent Laplacian for the embedded mesh is as follows:

$$(\triangle f)_i = \frac{1}{a_i} \sum_{(i,j) \in E} \frac{\cot \alpha_{i,j} + \cot \beta_{i,j}}{2} (f_i - f_j)$$

Here, $a_i = \frac{1}{3}$ (since we're dealing with triangles) and the cotangent Laplacian, in terms of edge length, is as follows:

$$(\triangle f)_i = \frac{1}{a_i} \sum_{(i,j) \in E} \left(\frac{-l_{i,j}^2 + l_{j,k}^2 + l_{i,k}^2}{8a_{i,j,k}} + \frac{-l_{i,j}^2 + l_{j,h}^2 + l_{i,h}^2}{8a_{i,j,h}}\right) (f_i - f_j)$$

Here, $a_{i,j,k} = \sqrt{s(s - l_{i,j})(s - l_{j,k})(s - l_{i,k})}$, s is a semi-perimeter, and $l_{i,j} = \|x_i - x_j\|_2$.

Spectral decomposition

To understand spectral analysis, we must first define the Laplacian on a compact manifold, M, which has countably many eigenfunctions:

$$\triangle \phi_k(x) = \lambda_k \phi_k(x)$$

This is for $k = 1, 2, \cdots$.

Due to the symmetry property, the eigenfunctions will be both real and orthonormal, which gives us the following:

$$\langle \phi_k, \phi_{k'} \rangle_{L^2(M)} = \delta_{k,k'}$$

Here, the eigenvalues are non-negative, that is, $0 = \lambda_1 \leq \lambda_2 \leq \cdots$.

For two-dimensional manifolds, we often use Weyl's law to describe the asymptotic behavior of eigenvalues, which looks as follows:

$$\lim_{k \to \infty} \frac{k}{\lambda_k} = \frac{1}{3\pi} \text{area}(M)$$

Using the eigenfunctions and eigenvalues, we can eigendecompose the graph Laplacian into the following:

$$\triangle \Phi = \Phi \Lambda$$

Here, $\Phi = (\phi_1, \cdots, \phi_n)$ and $\Lambda = \text{diag}(\lambda_1, \cdots, \lambda_n)$.

Now, if we were to pose this as a generalized eigenproblem, we would obtain the following from the preceding equation with A-orthogonal eigenvectors, $\Phi^T A \Phi = I$:

$$(D - W)\Phi = A\Phi\Lambda$$

If we were to change the variables through substituting, $\Psi = A^{-\frac{1}{2}}\Phi$, we would find ourselves with the standard eigenproblem:

$$A^{-\frac{1}{2}}(D - W)A^{-\frac{1}{2}}\Psi = \Psi\Lambda$$

Here, the eigenvectors are orthogonal, that is, $\Psi^T \Psi = I$.

Graph neural networks

Graph neural networks are the quintessential neural network for geometric deep learning, and, as the name suggests, they work particularly well on graph-based data such as meshes.

Now, let's assume we have a graph, G, that has a binary adjacency matrix, A. Then, we have another matrix, X, that contains all the node features. These features could be text, images, or categorical, node degrees, clustering coefficients, indicator vectors, and so on. The goal here is to generate node embeddings using local neighborhoods.

As we know, nodes on graphs have neighboring nodes, and, in this case, each node tries to aggregate the information from its neighbors using a neural network. We can think of the network neighborhood as a computation graph. Since each node has edges with different nodes, each node has a unique computation graph.

If we think back to convolutional neural networks, we learned that convolutions are a window of sorts and that we can slide across the input and summarize the data into a reduced form. The aggregator operation works similarly to how the convolution operation works.

Let's dive right in and see how they work mathematically.

At each layer, nodes have embeddings, and initial embeddings are equivalent to the node features:

$$h_v^0 = x_v$$

The embedding of the kth layer embedding of v is as follows:

$$h_v^k = \sigma \left(W_k \sum_{u \in N(v)} \frac{h_u^{k-1}}{|N(v)|} + B_k h_v^{k-1} \right)$$

This is done for all $k > 0$, where h_v^{k-1} is the previous layer embedding of v and $\sum \frac{h_u^{k-1}}{|N(v)|}$ is the average of the neighbor's previous layer embeddings. During training, the model learns W_k and B_k, and the output embeddings for each node after K layers of neighborhood aggregation is as follows:

$$z_v = h_v^K$$

To generate embeddings that are of a high quality, we define a loss function on z_v and feed the embeddings into it, after which we perform gradient descent to train the aggregation parameters.

In the case of a supervised task, we can define the loss as follows:

$$L = \sum_{v \in V} y_v \log(\sigma(z_v \theta)) + (1 - y_v) \log(1 - \sigma(z_v \theta))$$

Let's suppose we have the following undirected graph:

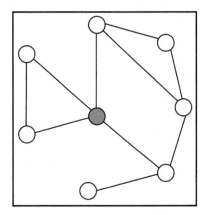

With this, we want to calculate the update for the solid node, as follows:

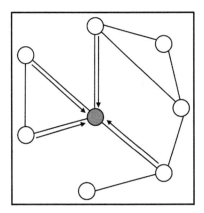

To calculate the update, we can use the following equation:

$$h_i^{(l+1)} = \sigma \left(h_i^{(l)} W_0^{(l)} + \sum_{j \in N(i)} \frac{1}{c_{i,j}} h_j^{(l)} W_1^{(l)} \right)$$

Here, $N^{(i)}$ is the neighbor of node i and $c_{i,j}$ is the normalized constant.

Spectral graph CNNs

Spectral graph CNNs, as the name suggests, use a spectral convolution, which we defined as follows:

$$f * g = \sum_{k \geq 1} \underbrace{\langle f, \phi_k \rangle_{L^2(M)} \langle g, \phi_k \rangle_{L^2(M)}}_{\text{product in the Fourier domain}} \phi_k$$

$$\underbrace{\phantom{\sum_{k \geq 1} \langle f, \phi_k \rangle_{L^2(M)} \langle g, \phi_k \rangle_{L^2(M)} \phi_k}}_{\text{inverse Fourier transform}}$$

Here, $f, g \in L^2(M)$. We can rewrite this in matrix form as follows:

$$f * g = \Phi(\Phi^T g) \circ (\Phi^T f) = \underbrace{\Phi \text{diag}(\hat{g}_1, \cdots, \hat{g}_n) \Phi^T}_{G} f$$

This is not shift-invariant since G does not have a circulant structure.

Now, in the spectral domain, we define a convolutional layer as follows:

$$g_l = \xi \left(\sum_{l'=1}^{p} \Phi W_{l,l'} \Phi^T f_{l'} \right)$$

Here, $l = 1, \cdots, q$, $l' = 1, \cdots, p$, and $W_{l,l'}$ is an n×n diagonal matrix of spectral filter coefficients (which are basis-dependent, meaning that they don't generalize over different graphs and are limited to a single domain), and ξ is the nonlinearity that's applied to the vertex-wise function values.

What this means is that if we learn a convolutional filter with the basis Φ on one domain, it will not be transferable or applicable to another task that has the basis Ψ. This isn't to say we can't create bases that can be used for different domains—we can—however, this requires using a joint diagonalizable procedure. But doing this would require having prior knowledge of both domains and how they relate to one another.

We can also define the pooling function in non-Euclidean domains. We refer to this as graph coarsening, and in it, only a fraction, $\alpha < 1$, of the vertices of the graph are left. If we were to have the eigenvectors of graph Laplacians at different resolutions, then they would be related through the following equation:

$$\tilde{\Phi} \approx P\Phi \begin{pmatrix} I_{\alpha n} \\ 0 \end{pmatrix}$$

Here, Φ is an $n \times n$ matrix, $\tilde{\Phi}$ is an $\alpha n \times \alpha n$ matrix, and P is an $\alpha n \times n$ binary matrix representing the position of the ith vertex of the coarsened graph on the original graph.

Graph neural networks, like the neural networks we learned about in previous chapters, can also overfit, and in an effort to avoid this from happening, we adapt the learning complexity to try and reduce the total number of free parameters in the model. For this, we use spatial localization of the filters in the frequency domain. In the Euclidean domain, we can write this as follows:

$$\int_{-\infty}^{+\infty} |x|^{2k} |f(x)|^2 \, dx = \int_{-\infty}^{+\infty} \left| \frac{\partial^k \hat{f}(\omega)}{\partial \omega^k} \right|^2 d\omega$$

What this tells us is that in order to learn a layer in which the features aren't just well localized in the original domain but also shared across other locations, we must learn smooth spectral multipliers. Spectral multipliers are parameterized as follows:

$$\text{diag}(\Gamma_{l,l'}) = B\alpha_{l,l'}$$

Here, $B = (b_{i,j}) = (\beta_j(\lambda_i))$, which is a fixed interpolation matrix of size $k \times q$, and α is a vector of interpolation coefficients of size q.

Mixture model networks

Now that we've seen a few examples of how GNNs work, let's go a step further and see how we can apply neural networks to meshes.

First, we use a patch that is defined at each point in a local system of d-dimensional pseudo-coordinates, $u(x, x')$, around x. This is referred to as a geodesic polar. On each of these coordinates, we apply a set of parametric kernels, $v_1(u), \cdots, v_J(u)$, that produces local weights.

The kernels here differ in that they are Gaussian and not fixed, and are produced using the following equation:

$$v_j(u) = e^{-\frac{1}{2}(u-\mu_j)^{\mathsf{T}} \Sigma_j^{-1}(u-\mu_j)}$$

These parameters (Σ_j and μ_j) are trainable and learned.

A spatial convolution with a filter, g, can be defined as follows:

$$(f * g)(x) \propto \sum_{j=1}^{J} g_j \underbrace{\int_M v_j(u(x, x')) f(x') dx'}_{\text{patch operator}}$$

Here, $x_i \in \mathbb{R}^d$ is a feature at vertex i.

Previously, we mentioned geodesic polar coordinates, but what are they? Let's define them and find out. We can write them as follows:

$$u_{i,j} = (\rho_{i,j}, \theta_{i,j})$$

Here, $\rho_{i,j}$ is the geodesic distance between i and j and $\theta_{i,j}$ is the direction of the geodesic from i to j. However, here, the orientation is somewhat ambiguous.

Now, we can define angular max-pooling (which is a rotating filter), as follows:

$$(f * g)(x) \propto \max_{\triangle\theta \in [0, 2\pi)} \sum_{j=1}^{J} g_j \int_M v_j(\rho(x, x'), \theta(x, x') + \triangle\theta) f(x') dx'$$

Facial recognition in 3D

Let's go ahead and see how this translates to a real-world problem such as 3D facial recognition, which is used in phones, security, and so on. In 2D images, this would be largely dependent on the pose and illumination, and we don't have access to depth information. Because of this limitation, we use 3D faces instead so that we don't have to worry about lighting conditions, head orientation, and various facial expressions. For this task, the data we will be using is meshes.

In this case, our meshes make up an undirected, connected graph, $G = (V, E, A)$, where $|V|$ = n is the vertices, E is a set of edges, and $A \in \mathbb{R}^{N \times N \times d}$ contains the d-dimensional pseudo-coordinates, $u(i, j) \in \mathbb{R}^d$, where $j \in N(i)$. The node feature matrix is denoted $F \in \mathbb{R}^{N \times d}$ as , where each of the nodes contains d-dimensional features. We then define the lth channel of the feature map as f_l, of which the ith node is denoted as $f_l(i)$.

The pseudo-coordinates, $u(i, j)$, determine how the features in the mesh are aggregated, and since, as we know, meshes are constructed from smaller triangles, we can compute the pseudo-coordinates from all the nodes, i to node j. Here, we will use the globally normalized Cartesian coordinates:

$$u(i, j) = 0.5 + \frac{\text{pos}_j - \text{pos}_i}{2 \max_{(v,w) \in E} |\text{pos}_w - \text{pos}_v|}$$

This gives us the ability to map spatial relations to fixed regions.

We initialize the weights using $\mathcal{N}\left(0, \sqrt{\frac{2}{l_{in}}}\right)$, where l_{in} is the dimensions of the input feature for the kth layer.

Now, we can compute the feature aggregation into node i from the neighboring nodes, $j \in N(i)$, as follows:

$$g_{l'}(i) = \frac{1}{|N(i)|} \sum_{l=1}^{C^{k_1}} \left(\sum_{j \in N(i)} f_l(i) \sum_{p \in P(u(i,j))} W_{p,l,l'} \prod_{k=1}^{d} N_{k,p_i}^{m}(u_k) + b_{l,l'} \right)$$

Here, $l' = 1, \cdots, C^{k_2}$. N_{k,p_i}^{m} is the basis of the B-spline over degree m, and $W_{p,l,l'}$ are parameters that can be learned.

This being a classification task, we will use cross-entropy as our loss function. We do this as follows:

$$L(X, Y) = \frac{1}{N} \sum_{i=1}^{N} l_i(x, y)$$

Here, $l_i(x, y) = -\log\left(\frac{e^{x[y]}}{\sum_j e^{x[j]}}\right)$ and Y is the label matrix.

And with that, we can conclude this chapter on geometric deep learning.

Summary

In this chapter, we learned about some important mathematical topics, such as the difference between Euclidean and non-Euclidean data and manifolds. We then went on to learn about a few fascinating and emerging topics in the field of deep learning that have widespread applications in a plethora of domains in which traditional deep learning algorithms have proved to be ineffective. This new class of neural networks, known as graph neural networks, greatly expand on the usefulness of deep learning by extending it to work on non-Euclidean data. Toward the end of this chapter, we saw an example use case for graph neural networks—facial recognition in 3D.

This brings us to the end of this book. Congratulations on successfully completing the lessons that were provided!

Other Books You May Enjoy

If you enjoyed this book, you may be interested in these other books by Packt:

Advanced Deep Learning with Python
Ivan Vasilev

ISBN: 978-1-78995-617-7

- Cover advanced and state-of-the-art neural network architectures
- Understand the theory and math behind neural networks
- Train DNNs and apply them to modern deep learning problems
- Use CNNs for object detection and image segmentation
- Implement generative adversarial networks (GANs) and variational autoencoders to generate new images
- Solve natural language processing (NLP) tasks, such as machine translation, using sequence-to-sequence models
- Understand DL techniques, such as meta-learning and graph neural networks

Advanced Deep Learning with TensorFlow 2 and Keras

Rowel Atienza

ISBN: 978-1-83882-165-4

- Use mutual information maximization techniques to perform unsupervised learning
- Use segmentation to identify the pixel-wise class of each object in an image
- Identify both the bounding box and class of objects in an image using object detection
- Learn the building blocks for advanced techniques—MLPss, CNN, and RNNs
- Understand deep neural networks—including ResNet and DenseNet
- Understand and build autoregressive models—autoencoders, VAEs, and GANs
- Discover and implement deep reinforcement learning methods

Leave a review - let other readers know what you think

Please share your thoughts on this book with others by leaving a review on the site that you bought it from. If you purchased the book from Amazon, please leave us an honest review on this book's Amazon page. This is vital so that other potential readers can see and use your unbiased opinion to make purchasing decisions, we can understand what our customers think about our products, and our authors can see your feedback on the title that they have worked with Packt to create. It will only take a few minutes of your time, but is valuable to other potential customers, our authors, and Packt. Thank you!

Index

1

1 × 1 convolutions 226
10-shot learning 308

A

activation function
  about 185
  ELU function 192
  hyperbolic tangent function 186, 187
  leaky ReLU function 189, 190
  PReLU function 190, 191
  ReLU function 188, 189
  sigmoid function 185, 186
  softmax function 188
adaptive gradient (Adagrad) 140
adaptive gradient descent 140, 141
adaptive moment estimation (Adam) 140
adaptive step size 138
addressing mechanism, neural Turing machine
    (NTM)
  content-based 274
  location-based 274
adjacency matrix 149, 150, 151
adversarial training 215
affine sets 126, 127
AlexNet 237
antiderivative 54
approaches, meta learning
  metric-based meta learning 313
  model-based meta learning 310
  optimization-based meta learning 316
artificial neural network (ANN) 218
attention
  global attention 276
  hard attention 276
  local attention 276
  overview 269, 271
  self-attention 275
  soft attention 275
  types 275
autoencoders
  about 284, 285, 287
  denoising autoencoder (DAE) 288, 289
  variational autoencoder (VAE) 290, 291, 292

B

back substitution 17
backpropagation 196, 197
Backpropagation Through Time (BPTT) 261
Bayesian estimation 110, 111
bias-variance trade-off 107
bidirectional RNNs 254, 255
biological neural networks 170, 171
bivariate normal distribution 105
Boston Housing dataset
  features 201
Broyden-Fletcher-Goldfarb-Shanno (BFGS) 133

C

Cholesky decomposition 42, 43, 44
Cholesky factor 43
classical probability
  about 83, 85
  conditional probability 91, 92, 93
  continuous random variables 98, 99, 100, 101
  discrete distributions 90, 91
  independence 89, 90
  multinomial coefficient 86, 87
  multiple random variables 97, 98
  random variables 93, 94, 95
  sampling, with or without replacement 85, 86
  Stirling's formula 87, 88
  variance 95, 96, 97

clockwork RNN (CW-RNN) 263, 264, 265
composite hypothesis 114
conditional probability 91, 92, 93
confidence interval 109, 110
connectedness 156
constrained optimization 123, 124
convex function 127, 128
convex optimization 125
convex sets 125, 126
ConvNet architecture
  exploring 241
  Inception-V1 244
  optimization 239, 241
  training 239, 241
  VGG-16 241
  working with 235, 236, 237, 239
ConvNets
  about 218
  data, types 218, 219, 220
convolutional neural network (CNN) 217, 306
convolutions
  1 × 1 convolutions 226
  about 220
  one-dimensional convolutions 225, 226
  separable convolutions 228, 229, 230
  size 235
  three-dimensional convolutions 227, 228
  transposed convolutions 230, 231, 232, 233
  two-dimensional convolutions 220, 221, 222,
    223, 224, 225
cross entropy 194, 195
cross-entropy loss 139
cumulative distribution function 99

D

data
  implementing 200, 201
dataset augmentation 212, 213
decoder 285
deep neural networks 202, 203, 306
deep RNNs 259, 260
denoising autoencoder (DAE) 288, 289
descent methods
  about 136
  adaptive gradient descent 140, 141

gradient descent 136, 138
gradient descent, with momentum 139
loss functions 139
natural evolution 142
Nesterov's accelerated gradient 140
simulated annealing 141
stochastic gradient descent (SGD) 138
determinant 25, 34, 35, 36, 37
determinator 35
diagonalization 41
differentiation 47
directed acyclic graph (DAG) 145, 153, 154
directed graphs 152
discontinuity 49
discrete distributions 90, 91
discrete manifolds 328, 329
domain 307
dot product 14
dots (pixels) per inch (dpi) 219
downsampling 233
dropout 213, 214, 215

E

early stopping 210, 211
Eigendecomposition 41
eigenvalues 38
eigenvectors 38
elimination
  used, for solving linear equations 17, 18, 20, 21
ELU function 192
encoder 285
estimation
  about 106, 107
  Bayesian estimation 110, 111
  confidence interval 109, 110
  likelihood 109
  mean squared error (MSE) 107
  sufficiency 107, 108
Euclidean data
  versus non-Euclidean data 322, 323
Euclidean space 31
Euler's number 50
event 84
Exponential linear unit (ELU) 192

F

facial recognition
  in 3D 335, 336
features 162
feedforward neural network (FNN) 235
few-shot learning 308
First-Order Model-Agnostic Meta Learning
    (FOMAML) 318
flow-based generative models
  about 298
  advantages 301
flow-based networks 298
flows
  normalizing 298, 299, 300
fuzzy neural networks (FNNs) 248

G

game theory 133, 134, 135
gamma distribution 106
Gated Recurrent Units (GRUs) 253, 258, 259
generative adversarial network (GAN) 292, 294,
    295, 296
generative models
  need for 283, 284
genetic algorithms 143
global attention
  versus local attention 276
global average pooling 234
GoogLeNet 244
gradient descent
  about 136, 138
  with momentum 139
graph Laplacian 157
graph neural networks 330, 331, 332
graph theory
  about 145
  concepts 146, 147, 148, 149
  terminology 146, 147, 148, 149
graphs, types
  about 151
  directed acyclic graph (DAG) 153, 154
  directed graphs 152
  dynamic graphs 154, 155, 156
  multilayer graphs 154, 155, 156

tree graphs 156
weighted graphs 151, 152

H

hard attention
  versus soft attention 276
hinge loss 139
homomorphism of vector spaces 30
Hopfield network 248
Huber loss 139, 194
hyperbolic tangent function 186, 187
hypothesis
  composite hypothesis 114
  multivariate normal theory 114, 115, 116
  simple hypothesis 112, 113
  testing 112, 118

I

identically distributed (iid) 96
inception 244
Inception-V1 244, 246
inner product space 33, 34
integration 47
inverse matrices 25
isomorphism 30

J

Jensen–Shannon (JS) divergence 295
joint distributions 102

K

k-shot learning 308
Kullback-Leibler (KL) divergence 195, 291
Königsberg bridge problem 146

L

L1 regularization 209, 210
L2 regularization 208, 209
Lagrange multiplier 129, 130
Lagrangian sufficiency 130
latent space 289
layers 178, 179, 180, 184
leaky ReLU function 189, 190
learning to learn 308

learning to learn by gradient descent 316
least absolute shrinkage and selection operator
   (lasso) regression 209
Least Recently Used (LRU) 311
Least Recently Used Access (LRUA) 311
least squares 129
linear equations
  about 12, 13
  solving 15
  solving, in n-dimensions 16
  solving, with elimination 17, 18, 20, 21
linear maps
  about 30
  image 31
  kernel 31
linear models
  about 116, 117, 118
  hypothesis, testing 118
linear regression 161, 162, 163, 164
local attention
  versus global attention 276
logistic regression 166, 167
Long Short-Term Memory (LSTM) 316
Long Short-Term Memory meta learner 316, 317
Long Short-Term Models (LSTMs) 253, 256, 257,
  258
loss function
  about 192
  cross entropy 194, 195
  Huber loss 194
  Jensen-Shannon (JS) divergence 196
  KL divergence 195
  mean absolute error (MAE) 193
  mean squared error (MSE) 193
  Root mean squared error (RMSE) 194
loss functions 139
lower-upper (LU) decomposition 20

M

manifolds 323, 324, 325, 326, 327
matrices
  adding 22
  inverse matrices 25
  multiplying 22, 23, 24
matrix decompositions

about 34
Cholesky decomposition 42
determinant 34, 35, 36, 37
diagonalization 41
eigenvalues 38
eigenvectors 38
orthogonal matrices 40
singular value decomposition (SVD) 42
symmetric matrices 41
trace 39
matrix operations
  associativity 24
  commutativity 24
  distributivity 24
matrix transpose 26
matrix
  operations 22
maximum likelihood estimator (MLE) 109
McCulloch-Pitts (MP) neuron
  about 171, 172
  versus perceptron 171
mean absolute error (MAE) 139, 193
mean squared error (MSE) 107, 139, 193
median 101
meta learning
  about 305, 308
  approaches 308, 309
Meta Networks (MetaNet) 312, 313
metric spaces 31
metric-based meta learning
  about 313
  prototypical networks 314
  Siamese neural network 314, 315, 316
Metropolis criterion 141
mixture model network 334, 335
mode 101
Model-Agnostic Meta Learning (MAML) 318, 319
model-based meta learning
  about 310
  Memory-Augmented Neural Networks (MANNs)
  310, 311
  Meta Networks (MetaNet) 312, 313
Most Frequently Used (MRU) 311
MP neuron
  pros and cons 174, 175

multiclass cross entropy 195
multilayer perceptron (MLP)
    about 175, 176, 177, 178, 214, 260, 315
    activation function 185
    backpropagation 196, 197
    layers 178, 179, 180, 184
    loss function 192
multiple regression 162
multivariable calculus
    about 66
    integrals 69, 70, 71, 73, 74, 75
    partial derivatives 67, 68
multivariate normal distribution 104, 105

N

n-dimensions
    linear equations, solving in 16
n-way k-shot learning 309
natural evolution 142
natural isomorphism 30
Nesterov's accelerated gradient 140
neural networks
    data, implementing 200, 201
    parameter initialization 198
    training 198
neural Turing machine (NTM)
    about 271
    adapting 310
    addressing mechanisms 273
    reading operation 272
    writing operation 273
Newton's method 131, 132
nodes 175
non-convex optimization 128
non-Euclidean data
    versus Euclidean data 322, 323
norm penalties
    about 207
    L1 regularization 209, 210
    L2 regularization 208, 209
normal distribution 103, 104
normed space 33

O

objective functions 122
one-dimensional convolutions 225, 226
optimization methods
    descent methods 136
    exploring 129
    game theory 133, 134, 135
    Lagrange multiplier 129, 130
    least squares 129
    Newton's method 131, 132
    quasi-Newton method 133
    secant method 132, 133
optimization-based meta learning
    about 316
    Long Short-Term Memory meta learner 316, 317
    Model-Agnostic Meta Learning (MAML) 318, 319
optimization
    about 122, 123
    affine sets 126, 127
    constrained optimization 123, 124
    convex function 127
    convex optimization 125
    convex sets 125, 126
    issues 128
    methods 129
    non-convex optimization 128
    types 122
    unconstrained optimization 124
orthogonal matrices 40
orthonormal 34

P

parameter initialization
    about 198
    random initialization 199
    weights and biases, initializing 199
    Xavier initialization 200
parameter sharing 211, 212
parameter tying 211
Parametric ReLU (PReLU) 190
partial derivative
    about 67
    chain rule 68

particle swarm optimization 144
perceptron model 172, 173, 174
perceptron
  pros and cons 174, 175
  versus McCulloch-Pitts (MP) neuron 171
permutation 27
permutation matrices 27, 28
polyhedra 148
polynomial regression 164, 165, 166
pooling
  about 233, 234
  size 235
population methods
  exploring 142
  genetic algorithms 143
  particle swarm optimization 144
PReLU function 191
prisoner's dilemma 135
probability density function (PDF) 99
probability distributions
  about 83, 103
  bivariate normal distribution 105
  gamma distribution 106
  multivariate normal distribution 104, 105
  normal distribution 103, 104
probability mass function (PMF) 106
probability space 85
probability
  classical probability 83, 85
  concepts 83
  joint distributions 102
  probability distributions 103
prototypical networks 314

Q

quasi-Newton method 133

R

random variables 93, 94, 95
Rank-Nullity theorem 31
real-valued non-volume preserving (real NVP)
  301, 302
rectified linear unit (ReLU) 188
Recurrent Neural Networks (RNNs)
  about 249

data types 248
exploring 263
need for 248
optimization 261, 262
training 261, 262
vanilla RNN 249, 250, 251, 252, 253, 254
regularization
  need for 206, 207
ReLU function 188, 189
ridge regression 208
Riemannian manifold 326
Root mean squared error (RMSE) 194

S

scalars
  about 10
  versus vectors 10, 11
secant method 132, 133
self-attention 275
separable convolutions 228, 229, 230
Siamese neural network 314, 315, 316
sigmoid function 185, 186
simple hypothesis 112, 113
simulated annealing 141
single variable calculus, derivatives
  about 46, 47, 48
  chain rule 54
  first derivative 51
  power rule 49
  product rule 52, 53
  quotient rule 53
  second derivative 51
  sum rule 49
  trigonometric functions 50
single variable calculus, integrals
  about 56, 57, 58, 60
  area between curves 64
  fundamental theorem of calculus 61, 62
  integration, by parts 65, 66
  substitution rule 62, 63
single variable calculus
  about 45
  antiderivative 54, 55
singular value decomposition (SVD) 42
soft attention

versus hard attention 275
softmax function 188
span 29
spectral decomposition 41, 329, 330
spectral graph CNNs 333, 334
square loss 139
statistics
  concepts 106
  estimation 106
  hypothesis, testing 112
  linear models 116, 117, 118
step size 123
Stirling's formula 87, 88
stochastic gradient descent (SGD) 138
subsampling 233
subspaces 29
symmetric matrices 41
system of equations 12

T

task 307
three-dimensional convolutions 227, 228
three-symbol Turing machine 271
trace 39
transfer learning
  about 305, 306
  conditional probabilities 307
  domain adaptation 307
  feature space 307
  label space 307
  limitations 307
transformers 276, 277, 279, 280
transposed convolutions 230, 231, 232, 233
tree graphs 156
triangle inequality 32
triangular factorization 17

Turing machine (TM) 271
two-dimensional convolutions 220, 221, 222, 223, 224, 225

U

unconstrained optimization 124
undercomplete autoencoder 286

V

vanilla RNN 249, 250, 251, 252, 253, 254
variational autoencoder (VAE) 290, 291, 292
vector calculus
  about 75
  derivatives 76, 77, 78, 80
  inverse functions 81
  vector fields 80
vector spaces 28, 29
vectors
  about 10
  versus scalars 10, 11
VGG blocks 242
VGG network 241
VGG-16
  about 241
  operations 242, 243
Visual Geometry Group (VGG) 241

W

Wasserstein GAN (WGAN) 296, 297
weight decay 208
weighted graphs 151, 152

Z

zero vector 11
zero-shot learning 308